MILK STREET

cookish

MILK STREET

COOKish

Throw It Together

CHRISTOPHER KIMBALL

WITH WRITING AND EDITING BY
J. M. Hirsch and Michelle Locke

RECIPES BY
Matthew Card, Diane Unger and the Cooks at Milk Street

ART DIRECTION BY
Jennifer Baldino Cox and Brianna Coleman

PHOTOGRAPHY BY
Connie Miller of CB Creatives

FOOD STYLING BY
Christine Tobin

VORACIOUS
LITTLE, BROWN AND COMPANY
NEW YORK   BOSTON   LONDON

Voracious

Little, Brown and Company
Hachette Book Group
1290 Avenue of the Americas,
New York, NY 10104
littlebrown.com

First edition: October 2020

Voracious is an imprint of Little, Brown and Company, a division of Hachette Book Group, Inc. The Voracious name and logo are trademarks of Hachette Book Group, Inc.

The publisher is not responsible for websites (or their content) that are not owned by the publisher.

The Hachette Speakers Bureau provides a wide range of authors for speaking events. To find out more, go to hachettespeakersbureau.com or call (866) 376-6591.

Prop Styling by Brianna Coleman
Photography © CB Creatives, Inc.
Author photograph by Channing Johnson

ISBN 978-0-316-54030-8

LCCN 2020935607

10 9 8 7 6 5 4 3 2

IM

Print book interior design by
Gary Tooth / Empire Design Studio

Printed in China

It's Not Cooking. It's COOKISH.

Historically, I've had little love for cookbooks that promise meals in minutes or sport titles along the lines of "5-Ingredient Cookbook!" They too often deliver recipes that taste like they didn't get much love and attention – somebody smeared mustard on chicken parts and threw them into the oven. My rule of thumb was you get what you deserve with speed cooking.

That was before I founded Milk Street, which completely changed how I cook. The classic American recipe handbook is based on a Northern European tradition that depends on time and heat to build flavor from mostly dull ingredients – big hunks of meat, root vegetables, etc. The rest of the world, however, takes a different tack. Time is no longer the key ingredient – it's the ingredients themselves that make the difference. An approach which, it turns out, can be surprisingly speedy.

A bottle of fish sauce, a bit of miso, a good sherry vinegar, some smoked paprika, a tablespoon of Aleppo pepper, and a few of the many cooking techniques found in Sichuan cooking, for example, are transformative. Start there and you are almost at the finish line. And while you are at it, mix and match. Put sweet with sour. Mix creamy with crunchy. Add a touch of bitter when least expected. All of a sudden, that 30-minute supper looks a whole lot better. This is the heart of *Cookish*.

Cookish does have a few rules. It is a lot more than quick cooking. We depend on a powerhouse supermarket pantry, ingredients that do the work for us, like orange marmalade, miso, garam masala, black bean garlic sauce, harissa, Thai red curry paste, pickled ginger, ground turmeric. We offer alternatives for hard-to-find ingredients, though pretty much anything is now a click away.

We have limited ingredients to six, other than salt, pepper, oil, and water. Most recipes call for no more than one piece of cookware. And cooking techniques are dead simple, many of them borrowed from what we have learned on our travels. For those of us who grew up in New England, it is a world of cooking that offers myriad solutions to getting dinner on the table quickly.

Underlying all of our work on *Cookish* is the notion that a recipe has to be informed by an idea, a concept that makes it special. Whether that is a contrast in flavors or textures, applying a cooking technique typically used for one ingredient to another, or mixing different cultural traditions in one dish, a recipe has to sing for its supper. It needs to come alive and justify its existence on the plate. It's not enough to be "good" – it has to be special.

Most of all, *Cookish* is about having fun in the kitchen. As we like to say, "Throw it together." These recipes are a great foundation for learning how to cook *without* recipes. We all are looking forward to the day when we walk into the kitchen and simply throw dinner together.

That's the promise of *Cookish*.

Cordially,
Christopher Kimball

Vegetables

Recipes

Vegetables are a great fit for the no-fuss philosophy of Cookish.

Most of the problems associated with vegetable dishes stem from doing too much—they're cooked too long or smothered in a muddle of flavors. So, we look for easy ways to highlight the fresh flavor of vegetables and add interest to the plate with pops of contrasting ingredients and textures.

Take carrots, often served up as watery boiled coins or swamped in gloopy mayonnaise slaws. Instead, we grate them to break down cell walls and release more flavor. We balance that intense, earthy sweetness with warm spices in our curried carrot salad, one of a clutch of dishes that show off the bright freshness of grated root vegetables. And we don't stop there. Shaved and wilted briefly in the microwave, sweet and smooth carrot strips are combined with the mild brininess of olives in our carrot salad inspired by a Moroccan classic. Softened and pureed, carrots make a simple, and colorful soup—we add the unusual pairing of rosemary and ginger for a spicy-herbal kick. And when roasted, the sugars in carrots caramelize. We find a scattering of honey, turmeric and cumin or coriander seeds with a splash of lime complements the carrots' mellow sweetness.

We avoid over-boiling and instead use a low-liquid technique that preserves the color, flavor and texture of vegetables. We begin by simmering them in a small amount of water, then remove the lid so the moisture evaporates, leaving plenty of flavor behind. The whole process is done in about 20 minutes and we do this with dishes as varied as broccoli paired with nutty browned butter and almonds and a crisp dish of radishes, mint and snap peas. Meanwhile, we turn up the heat to tackle the challenge of much-maligned Brussels sprouts, and conquer the bitterness of the brassicas by charring them in a hot skillet; they turn out crisp, sweet and earthy.

Steamed green beans are another side that can easily turn humdrum. So we blister and char them in a hot skillet to develop flavor before adding liquid. Adding just a bit of water to the hot pan creates a burst of steam that quickly cooks the beans with no chance of sogginess. We came up with four variations, including one inspired by Indian sabzi that uses unsweetened shredded coconut, poppy seeds and ground cardamom.

Some of our vegetable dishes can easily be turned into mains, like our turmeric potatoes inspired by South Asia's aloo chaat street food and our pan-seared broccolini with pork. And our whole roasted cauliflower presented with a few flavor variations makes a simple—and fabulous-looking—supper. You put in 10 minutes effort, the oven does the rest.

Celery and Greens Salad with Lemony Vinaigrette

Start to finish: 25 minutes
Servings: 4

This refreshing salad with plenty of texture was inspired by a recipe in "Catalan Food" by Daniel Olivella. We soften and flavor the celery with a brief soak in a lemony vinaigrette, then toss it with parsley, frisée and toasted walnuts, which add richness and a little umami. The salad is good with grilled meats and seafood, hearty braises or even a platter of cured meats and cheeses.

Grated zest and juice of 1 lemon **OR** 1 lime

3 tablespoons extra-virgin olive oil

Kosher salt and ground black pepper

10 medium celery stalks, peeled and thinly sliced on the diagonal (about 4 cups)

2 cups lightly packed fresh flat-leaf parsley leaves, torn if large

1 medium head frisée **OR** chicory **OR** escarole, cored and torn into bite-sized pieces (about 4 cups)

½ cup walnuts **OR** hazelnuts, toasted and finely chopped

In a large bowl, whisk together the zest and juice, and oil, then season with salt and pepper. Add the celery and toss, then let stand for 10 minutes. Add the parsley, frisée and nuts, then toss again. Season with salt and pepper.

Sweet-Sour Swiss Chard with Apricots and Almonds

Start to finish: 20 minutes
Servings: 4 to 6

This sweet-tart side combines crisp-tender chard stems and silky, succulent leaves. Chewy dried apricots and crunchy toasted nuts add contrasting flavor and texture. Use rainbow chard if available—the multihued stems make the dish colorful. If you like, to make the chard even heartier or turn it into a vegetarian main, simply stir in a can of white beans or chickpeas, rinsed and drained, at the very end.

3 tablespoons extra-virgin olive oil

2 bunches Swiss chard (1½ pounds total), stems cut into 1-inch pieces, leaves torn into rough 2-inch pieces, reserved separately

2 medium shallots, halved and thinly sliced

¾ cup dried apricots, chopped OR golden raisins

¼ cup balsamic vinegar OR red wine vinegar OR white wine vinegar, plus more to serve

2 tablespoons honey, plus more to serve

¼ cup slivered almonds, chopped OR pine nuts, toasted

Kosher salt and ground black pepper

In a large Dutch oven, heat the oil until shimmering. Add the chard stems and shallots, then cook, stirring, until beginning to brown. Add ½ cup water and the apricots. Cook, stirring, until the water has evaporated. Add the chard leaves, then toss until wilted and tender. Off heat, stir in the vinegar, honey and almonds. Season with salt and pepper. Serve with additional vinegar and honey for drizzling.

Red Cabbage and Parsley Salad with Toasted Walnuts

Start to finish: 15 minutes
Servings: 4

This colorful chopped salad, full of contrasting flavors and textures, comes together quickly thanks to the food processor. If you prefer, the cabbage and parsley can be chopped with a chef's knife. Either way, the nuts or seeds are best chopped by hand, as they become a little dusty when pulsed in a food processor. The salad pairs well with roasted or grilled meats, poultry or salmon, or stuff it into flatbread with hummus or falafel. It can also be made into a heartier dish by folding in cooked bulgur, brown rice, farro or lentils.

1 pound red cabbage (1 small head), cored and cut into 2-inch pieces

3 tablespoons lemon juice OR ¼ cup sherry vinegar

Kosher salt and ground black pepper

1 bunch flat-leaf parsley, leaves and tender stems (about 4 cups)

1½ cups walnuts, toasted and chopped OR 1 cup pumpkin seeds, toasted and roughly chopped

3 scallions, thinly sliced OR ½ cup golden raisins, roughly chopped OR both

3 tablespoons extra-virgin olive oil

½ teaspoon ground allspice

In a food processor, pulse the cabbage until finely chopped. Transfer to a large bowl, then add the lemon juice and ½ teaspoon salt. Toss until the cabbage wilts. In the processor, pulse the parsley until roughly chopped, then add to the cabbage along with the walnuts, scallions, oil, allspice, ¾ teaspoon salt and ¼ teaspoon pepper. Toss, then season with additional salt and pepper.

Shredded

When root vegetables such as carrots are shredded, cell walls break down and release sugars and other compounds, resulting in sweeter, more intense flavor. This technique also boosts the flavor of salads by creating more surface area to which dressings can cling.

Left to right: Fennel and Celery Root Salad with Pecans and Grainy Mustard, Curried Carrot Salad with Golden Raisins, Jicama and Mango Salad with Chili-Lime Vinaigrette, Beet and Carrot Salad with Horseradish and Dill.

Curried Carrot Salad with Golden Raisins

Start to finish: 35 minutes (15 minutes active)
Servings: 4 to 6

Let shredded carrots stand for 20 minutes in the dressing to slightly soften them and give the flavors time to meld. Serve this salad as part of an Indian-inspired meal or alongside roasted chicken, pork or lamb.

¼ cup extra-virgin olive oil

¼ cup cider vinegar

1 tablespoon curry powder

1 tablespoon finely grated fresh ginger

Kosher salt and ground black pepper

4 medium carrots (about 1 pound total), peeled

¾ cup golden raisins OR dried cranberries

½ cup lightly packed fresh cilantro, chopped

In a large bowl, whisk together the oil, vinegar, curry powder, ginger and 1¼ teaspoons salt. Using the large holes of a box grater, shred the carrots. Add the carrots, raisins and cilantro, then toss to combine. Let stand for 20 minutes. Season with salt and pepper, then toss again.

Optional garnish: Toasted sesame seeds OR chopped roasted cashews

Fennel and Celery Root Salad with Pecans and Grainy Mustard

Start to finish: 20 minutes
Servings: 4 to 6

Sweet, fresh fennel and crunchy celery root complement each others' flavors and textures. Once cut, celery root oxidizes, so shred it after the fennel, then immediately toss the vegetables with the dressing to prevent discoloration. This salad is excellent with roasted pork, chicken or beef.

¼ cup extra-virgin olive oil

2 tablespoons whole-grain mustard

2 tablespoons white wine vinegar

Kosher salt and ground black pepper

1 medium fennel bulb (about 8 ounces), trimmed

8 ounces celery root, peeled and halved

1 cup lightly packed fresh flat-leaf parsley

½ cup pecans, toasted and chopped

In a large bowl, whisk together the oil, mustard, vinegar, 1 teaspoon salt and ½ teaspoon pepper. Using the large holes of a box grater, shred the fennel and celery root. Add the shredded vegetables and parsley to the dressing, then toss. Season with salt and pepper. Transfer to a serving dish and sprinkle with the pecans.

Jicama and Mango Salad with Chili-Lime Vinaigrette

Start to finish: 30 minutes
Servings: 4 to 6

Jicama is a root vegetable with a mild, refreshing flavor and a light, crisp texture that shreds nicely. To peel the jicama, use a paring knife, cut into chunks and peel each piece, as the skin can be difficult to remove with a standard vegetable peeler. For this salad, choose a firm, slightly underripe mango, as a ripe one will be too soft to shred.

¼ cup extra-virgin olive oil

3 tablespoons lime juice

½ teaspoon ground allspice

Kosher salt

1 or 2 Fresno or jalapeño chilies, stemmed, halved and thinly sliced

12 ounces jicama, peeled and halved

1 firm mango (about 12 ounces; see note), peeled

½ cup lightly packed fresh cilantro, roughly chopped

In a large bowl, whisk together the oil, lime juice, allspice and 1 teaspoon salt, then stir in the chili(es). Using the large holes of a box grater, shred the jicama, then the mango, rotating the mango when you reach the pit; discard the pit. Add the jicama, mango and cilantro to the bowl, then toss. Let stand for 20 minutes. Season with salt and pepper, then toss again.

Beet and Carrot Salad with Horseradish and Dill

Start to finish: 30 minutes
Servings: 4 to 6

Shredded red beets and carrots tossed with lemon juice, horseradish and good measure of fresh dill make a salad that's vibrant in both flavor and color. The beets do not need to be peeled before shredding, but do scrub them well, then pat them completely dry. Shred the carrots before the beets so the carrots aren't stained by the beets. That said, after tossing, the entire salad eventually will turn deep red.

¼ cup extra-virgin olive oil

3 tablespoons lemon juice

2 tablespoons prepared horseradish

Kosher salt and ground black pepper

2 medium carrots (about 8 ounces total), peeled

2 medium red beets (about 8 ounces total), trimmed, scrubbed and patted dry

⅓ cup lightly packed fresh dill, roughly chopped, plus more to serve

1 tablespoon caraway seeds, crushed

In a large bowl, whisk together the oil, lemon juice, horseradish, 1 teaspoon salt and ½ teaspoon pepper, then let stand for about 10 minutes. Using the large holes of a box grater, shred the carrots, followed by the beets; reserve separately. Add the shredded vegetables, dill and caraway to the bowl, then toss. Season with salt and pepper. Transfer to a serving bowl and sprinkle with additional chopped dill.

Optional garnish: Sour cream

VEGETABLES

Arugula and Avocado Salad with Jalapeño Vinaigrette

Start to finish: 15 minutes
Servings: 4

Using pickling liquid in a salad dressing is an easy way to boost flavor while also adding acidity. In this vinaigrette, pickled jalapeños bring heat while their liquid lends an extra dose of green-chili earthiness. The pumpkin seeds and avocado offer enough richness to make the salad a light main course, or pair it with sliced grilled skirt steak or hearty grains, such as barley, farro or quinoa.

3 to 4 tablespoons pickled jalapeño slices, chopped, plus ¼ cup pickling liquid

2 tablespoons extra-virgin olive oil

Kosher salt and ground black pepper

4 cups lightly packed baby arugula

3 radishes, halved and thinly sliced
OR ½ English cucumber, halved lengthwise and thinly sliced

1 cup lightly packed fresh cilantro
OR 4 scallions, thinly sliced on the diagonal

¼ cup pumpkin seeds, toasted

2 ripe but firm avocados, halved, pitted, peeled and sliced

In a large bowl, whisk together the jalapeños and their liquid, the oil and ¼ teaspoon pepper. Add the arugula, radishes, cilantro and half of the pumpkin seeds, then toss. Season with salt and pepper. Fold in the avocado. Transfer to a serving bowl, then sprinkle with the remaining pumpkin seeds.

Shaved Carrot Salad with Olives and Parsley

Start to finish: 30 minutes (15 minutes active)
Servings: 4

This is a play on the classic Moroccan carrot salad. Instead of shredding, we shave the carrots into thin ribbons, then wilt them in the microwave before dressing them with olive oil, lemon and honey. When shopping, look for large carrots, as they're easier to shave than small and slender ones. The sweet-savory flavor of the salad works especially well with roasted or grilled chicken or lamb.

1½ pounds carrots (4 or 5 large), peeled

½ teaspoon ground cumin
OR ¼ teaspoon ground cinnamon

Kosher salt and ground black pepper

1 cup pitted green olives OR black olives
OR a mix, chopped

2 tablespoons lemon juice

1 tablespoon extra-virgin olive oil

2 teaspoons honey

⅔ cup lightly packed fresh flat-leaf parsley OR fresh mint, chopped

Using a Y-style peeler or a mandoline, shave the carrots lengthwise into long ribbons, rotating as you go; discard the cores. In a large, microwave-safe bowl, toss the carrots with the cumin, 1 teaspoon salt and ½ teaspoon pepper. Cover and microwave on high until wilted but still crisp-tender, 3 to 5 minutes. Toss with the olives, lemon juice, oil and honey. Let stand 15 minutes. Stir in the parsley; season with salt and pepper.

Low-Liquid Boil

Boiled vegetables get a bad rap. But done right, they can be delicious. We simmer vegetables in a small amount of water in a covered pot, then the lid comes off so the moisture fully evaporates. This cooks the vegetables quickly while producing clean, concentrated flavors and avoiding sogginess.

Upper left: Minty Radishes and Snap Peas; Bottom left: Broccoli with Browned Butter and Almonds; Upper right: Sweet Potatoes with Cumin and Cilantro; Bottom right: Honey-Caraway Parsnips with Cider Vinegar

Honey-Caraway Parsnips with Cider Vinegar

Start to finish: 20 minutes
Servings: 4

In this autumnal side dish, we pair the earthiness and subdued sweetness of parsnips with floral honey, spicy caraway and fruity cider vinegar. It's an excellent accompaniment to roasted turkey or lamb.

3 tablespoons extra-virgin olive oil
OR salted butter

2 sprigs fresh rosemary

2 tablespoons honey

1 teaspoon caraway seeds

Kosher salt and ground black pepper

2 pounds parsnips, peeled, thick portions halved lengthwise, sliced ½ inch thick on the diagonal

3 tablespoons cider vinegar

In a large Dutch oven, combine the oil, rosemary, honey and caraway seeds. Cook, stirring, until the mixture is fragrant and lightly browned. Add 1¼ cups water and a pinch each of salt and pepper, then bring to a boil. Stir in the parsnips, cover and cook, stirring only once or twice, until just tender. Uncover and cook until the moisture has evaporated and the parsnips begin to sizzle. Off heat, stir in the vinegar. Discard the rosemary, then season with salt and pepper.

Broccoli with Browned Butter and Almonds

Start to finish: 25 minutes
Servings: 4

Paired with butter and toasted almonds, broccoli gets the classic "amandine" treatment in this recipe. When sautéing the shallots and almonds in the butter, be sure to cook the mixture long enough so the milk solids that separate out from the butter turn golden brown, as this infuses the dish with rich, nutty flavor. Lemon zest and juice added at the end balance with citrusy brightness.

3 tablespoons salted butter, cut into 3 pieces

2 shallots, sliced into thin rings

¼ cup slivered almonds

Kosher salt and ground black pepper

2 pounds broccoli, florets cut into 1-inch pieces, stems sliced ½ inch thick

Grated zest and juice of 1 lemon

In a large Dutch oven, melt the butter. Add the shallots and almonds. Cook, stirring, until the shallots, almonds and milk solids from the butter are fragrant and lightly browned. Add 1¼ cups water and a pinch each of salt and pepper, then bring to a boil. Stir in the broccoli, cover and cook, stirring only once or twice, until crisp-tender. Uncover and cook until the moisture has evaporated and the broccoli begins to sizzle. Off heat, stir in the lemon zest and juice, then season with salt and pepper.

Minty Radishes and Snap Peas

Start to finish: 25 minutes
Servings: 4

Snap peas (or snow peas, if you prefer) and red and white radishes make this a colorful dish that's full of crisp-tender texture. Radishes vary greatly in size, so cut them into evenly sized wedges to help them cook evenly. Smaller radishes may only require quartering, while larger ones may need to be cut into eighths.

3 tablespoons extra-virgin olive oil
OR salted butter

1 tablespoon yellow mustard seeds

1 sprig fresh mint, plus ½ cup chopped mint leaves

Kosher salt and ground black pepper

1 pound radishes, cut into ½-inch wedges

1 pound sugar snap peas OR snow peas, trimmed

In a large Dutch oven, combine the oil, mustard seeds and mint sprig. Cook, stirring, until fragrant. Add 1¼ cups water and a pinch each of salt and pepper, then bring to a boil. Stir in the radishes and peas, cover and cook, stirring just once or twice, until crisp-tender. Uncover and cook until the moisture evaporates and the vegetables begin to sizzle. Off heat, discard the mint sprig, then stir in the chopped mint. Season with salt and pepper.

Optional garnish: Crumbled blue cheese

Sweet Potatoes with Cumin and Cilantro

Start to finish: 20 minutes
Servings: 4

Orange-fleshed sweet potatoes are ideal here because of their vibrant color. We offset their natural sweetness with the savoriness of cumin seeds, the subtle smoky notes of ancho chili powder and chopped fresh cilantro. Serve this as a side to chicken or pork, or make into a meal by offering black beans and rice alongside.

3 tablespoons extra-virgin olive oil
OR salted butter

1 teaspoon cumin seeds

1 teaspoon ancho chili powder

1 tablespoon packed brown sugar

Kosher salt and ground black pepper

2 pounds sweet potatoes, peeled, halved lengthwise and sliced ½ inch thick

1 cup chopped fresh cilantro

In a large Dutch oven, combine the oil, cumin seeds, ancho powder and sugar. Cook, stirring, until fragrant. Add 1¼ cups water and a pinch each of salt and pepper, then bring to a boil. Stir in the sweet potatoes, cover and cook, stirring only once or twice, until just tender. Uncover and cook until the moisture evaporates and the potatoes begin to sizzle. Off heat, stir in the cilantro, then season with salt and pepper.

VEGETABLES

Tomato and Watermelon Salad with Basil and Goat Cheese

Start to finish: 30 minutes
Servings: 4

This is a salad for the height of summer, when tomatoes and melons are at their peak. The sweet fruit mingles with savory shallot, which has had its pungency tempered by a short soak in white balsamic vinegar. Fresh basil (or mint) adds color and herbal notes, and creamy, tangy cheese balances with its saltiness.

2 cups (about 8 ounces) 1-inch cubes watermelon OR honeydew

2 pounds ripe tomatoes, cored and cut into rough 1-inch chunks

Kosher salt and ground black pepper

¼ cup white balsamic vinegar

1 medium shallot, sliced into thin rings

1 cup lightly packed fresh basil OR mint, torn if large

Extra-virgin olive oil, to serve

2 ounces fresh goat cheese OR feta cheese, crumbled (½ cup)

In a colander, toss the melon and tomatoes with ½ teaspoon salt; set aside. In a large, bowl combine the vinegar and shallot, then let stand for 10 minutes. Pour off and discard the vinegar, then add the melon-tomato mixture and basil to the bowl. Drizzle with oil and toss, then season with salt and pepper. Transfer to a serving bowl and top with the cheese.

VEGETABLES

19

Tomato-Zucchini Tart

Start to finish: 45 minutes
Servings: 6

Frozen puff pastry sheets make this elegant and impressive vegetable tart easy to pull together. We use za'atar, a Middle Eastern herb blend, to add a perfect flavor accent for the vegetables. Poking holes in the center of the rolled-out pastry moderates the puffiness, but leave a 1-inch border around the edges so the pastry forms a light, crisp outer crust.

¼ cup extra-virgin olive oil

1 tablespoon za'atar

1 cup grape tomatoes OR cherry tomatoes, halved

6 ounces zucchini, thinly sliced OR 6 ounces asparagus, trimmed and cut in 1-inch pieces

½ small red onion, thinly sliced

Kosher salt and ground black pepper

1 sheet frozen puff pastry, thawed

2 ounces feta cheese, crumbled (½ cup) OR 1 ounce Parmesan cheese, finely grated (½ cup), divided

Heat the oven to 450°F. Line a rimmed baking sheet with kitchen parchment. Toss the oil, za'atar, tomatoes, zucchini, onion, 1 teaspoon salt and ½ teaspoon pepper. With a rolling pin, roll the pastry into a 10-by-14-inch rectangle, then place on the prepared baking sheet. Using a fork, poke holes all over the pastry, leaving a 1-inch border at the edges. Top evenly with half the feta and all of the vegetable mixture, avoiding the edges. Bake at 450°F until the pastry is golden brown, 15 to 20 minutes. Top with remaining feta and drizzle with oil.

Optional garnish: Chopped fresh mint OR fresh basil

Beet and Pumpkin Seed Salad

Start to finish: 25 minutes
Servings: 4

Canned or refrigerated prepared beets make quick work of this robust salad. The sweet-and-sour dressing gets texture and richness from pumpkin seeds mixed with honey and vinegar. To keep the salad tasting bright and fresh, be generous with the honey and vinegar. Letting the shallots rest for a few minutes after dressing mellows their bite.

1 pound cooked, peeled beets (canned or refrigerated), sliced ¼-inch thick

1 medium shallot, sliced into thin rings

Kosher salt and ground black pepper

¼ cup extra-virgin olive oil

¼ cup pumpkin seeds, roughly chopped

¼ cup cider vinegar, plus more as needed

1 tablespoon honey, plus more as needed

2 cups baby arugula OR lightly packed watercress

Arrange the beets on a serving plate; scatter the shallot over them, then season with salt and pepper. In a small saucepan, heat the oil and pumpkin seeds, stirring, until sizzling. Reduce to low and whisk in the vinegar and honey, tasting and adding more of either ingredient until you get a strongly sweet-and-sour dressing. Pour over the beets and shallots, then let stand for about 15 minutes. Top with the greens and serve.

Harissa-Spiced Cauliflower-Almond Soup

Start to finish: 45 minutes
Servings: 4 to 6

Almonds toasted in olive oil with harissa (use the spice blend, not the paste) serve double duty here, first as a base for the flavor-packed vegetarian soup and then as a garnish that adds contrasting texture. Simmered and pureed with tender cauliflower, the nuts add a unique richness and body. If you own an immersion blender, the soup can be pureed directly in the pot.

½ cup extra-virgin olive oil

1½ cups sliced almonds

2 tablespoons harissa spice blend

1 medium yellow onion, chopped

2½-pound head cauliflower, trimmed and cut into 1-inch chunks

Kosher salt

¼ cup lemon juice

1 cup lightly packed fresh cilantro, chopped

In a large pot, cook the oil, almonds and harissa, stirring, until the oil bubbles. Set aside ½ cup of the mixture. Add the onion and cauliflower to the pot. Cook, stirring, until the cauliflower begins to soften. Add 7 cups water and 1 tablespoon salt, then boil. Cover and cook until fully tender. Using a blender, puree in batches until smooth, then return to the pot. Add the lemon juice and reheat. Season with salt. Serve topped with the cilantro and the reserved almond mixture.

Asparagus with Pickled Ginger and Scallions

Start to finish: 20 minutes
Servings: 4 to 6

Japanese pickled ginger, the type offered alongside sushi, is a tangy-sweet, fiery accent for grassy asparagus. We first cook the ginger with a little sugar in a good dose of butter so the sugars caramelize lightly as the butter browns, developing a solid flavor base for the sauté. Pickled ginger may be yellowish-white or pink; we prefer the former because no colorings are added, but both types work. Look for it in the Asian aisle of the supermarket or in the refrigerator case near the tofu.

3 tablespoons salted butter, cut into 3 pieces

½ cup drained sliced pickled ginger (see note), roughly chopped

¼ teaspoon white sugar

2 pounds asparagus, trimmed and cut into 2-inch lengths

Kosher salt and ground black pepper

4 scallions, cut into 1-inch lengths on the diagonal

In a 12-inch nonstick skillet over medium-high, melt the butter. Add the ginger and sugar, then cook, stirring, until the ginger is golden brown. Stir in the asparagus, ¾ teaspoon salt and 1 tablespoon water. Cover, reduce to medium and cook, stirring once or twice, until the asparagus is crisp-tender. Uncover, increase to medium-high and cook, stirring, until almost dry. Off heat, toss in the scallions, then season with salt and pepper.

Charred Broccoli with Miso Vinaigrette

Start to finish: 25 minutes
Servings: 4

Miso and oil–rubbed broccoli florets and stems char under the broiler, bringing out a natural sweetness and nutty flavor. The pieces also retain an appealing crisp-tender texture. The just-cooked broccoli is tossed with a tangy, umami-packed miso dressing that complements the bittersweet char. Make sure to line the baking sheet with foil, as the miso-coated broccoli is prone to sticking.

1½ pounds broccoli, florets cut into 1½-inch pieces, stems peeled and sliced ¼ inch thick

5 tablespoons white miso, divided

5 tablespoons neutral oil, divided

2 tablespoons unseasoned rice vinegar OR lemon juice

2 teaspoons mirin OR honey

2 teaspoons finely grated fresh ginger

4 scallions, thinly sliced on the diagonal

Heat the broiler with a rack 4 inches from the element. In a bowl, rub the broccoli with 3 tablespoons of miso, then toss with 1 tablespoon of oil. Spread in an even layer on a foil-lined rimmed baking sheet. Broil the broccoli until charred and crisp-tender, 6 to 8 minutes. In the bowl, whisk together the remaining 2 tablespoons miso, the remaining 4 tablespoons oil, the vinegar, mirin and ginger. Add the broccoli and toss. Transfer to a platter and sprinkle with scallions.

Charred Corn with Coconut, Chilies and Lime

Start to finish: 15 minutes
Servings: 4

Sweet corn pairs with coconut to make a delicious savory-sweet side that's perfect for cookouts or potlucks. The natural sugars and fat in the coconut milk speed the charring of the corn kernels (be sure to use a broiler-safe baking sheet for this recipe). Lime and coconut are a natural pairing, and whisked together they make an excellent finishing drizzle that's bright, yet creamy. If corn is in season, cut the kernels from freshly shucked ears; you'll need 3 large or 4 medium ears.

1 pound frozen corn kernels, thawed, drained and patted dry (about 3 cups)

2 Fresno chilies OR 3 serrano chilies, stemmed, quartered lengthwise, seeded and thinly sliced

⅔ cup coconut milk, divided

Kosher salt

½ cup unsweetened shredded coconut

Grated zest of 1 lime, plus 1 tablespoon lime juice

Heat the broiler with a rack in the uppermost position. In a large bowl, stir together the corn, chilies, ⅓ cup coconut milk and 1¼ teaspoons salt. Spread evenly on a rimmed baking sheet; reserve the bowl. Broil until charred, 5 to 7 minutes. Sprinkle evenly with the coconut, then broil until deeply toasted, 10 to 20 seconds. Transfer to a serving dish. In the same bowl, whisk the remaining coconut milk, lime juice and ¼ teaspoon salt, then drizzle over the corn. Sprinkle with the lime zest.

Carrot Soup with Rosemary and Ginger

Start to finish: 30 minutes
Servings: 4

The unusual combination of rosemary and ginger is delicious with the natural sweetness of carrots. We shred both the carrots and the onion so the vegetables soften quickly and puree easily. Use the large holes on a box grater or, for speed, the shredding disk of a food processor. If you own an immersion blender, use it to puree the soup directly in the pan.

1 tablespoon neutral oil

1½ pounds carrots (5 or 6 medium), peeled and shredded

1 medium yellow onion, shredded

Kosher salt

2 cups carrot juice, plus more if needed

2 rosemary sprigs

1-inch piece fresh ginger, peeled, cut into 2 pieces and smashed

Greek yogurt OR sour cream, to serve

In a large saucepan, heat the oil until shimmering. Add the carrots, onion and ½ teaspoon salt, then cook, stirring, until lightly browned. Add the juice, rosemary and ginger, then simmer, covered, until tender. Off heat, discard the rosemary and ginger. Using a blender, puree until smooth, then return to the pan. If desired, thin with additional carrot juice. Reheat, then season with salt. Serve topped with yogurt.

Skillet-Charred

High heat neutralizes the bitterness of Brussels sprouts, bringing out sweetness, nuttiness and tons of complex flavors. Using a scorching-hot skillet—a cast-iron pan works best—speeds up the process and results in a delicious char, further boosting flavor.

Upper Left: Skillet-Charred Brussels Sprouts with Dates and Pickled Peppers

Skillet-Charred Brussels Sprouts with Coriander and Cashews

Start to finish: 30 minutes
Servings: 4

Skillet-charring works best with sprouts that are small to medium; large ones won't cook through in time. We use a cast-iron pan because it retains heat well and its dark finish is not easily marred by high-heat searing. In this version, a rice vinegar and coriander dressing brightens the charred sprouts, while cashews add texture and cilantro brings fresh herbal notes.

1 pound small to medium Brussels sprouts, trimmed and halved

1 tablespoon neutral oil

2 teaspoons honey, plus more to serve

Kosher salt and ground black pepper

2 tablespoons unseasoned rice vinegar

1 tablespoon ground coriander

½ cup lightly packed fresh cilantro, roughly chopped

⅓ cup roasted cashews, finely chopped

In a medium bowl, toss the sprouts with the oil, honey, 1 teaspoon salt and ½ teaspoon pepper. Heat a 12-inch cast-iron skillet over medium-high until droplets of water evaporate in 1 to 2 seconds. Place the sprouts cut side down in the pan, then reduce to medium; reserve the bowl. Cook until deeply browned, then flip and cook until tender. In the bowl, mix the vinegar and coriander. When the sprouts are done, add them to the bowl along with the cilantro and cashews, then toss. Season with salt, pepper and honey.

Skillet-Charred Brussels Sprouts with Sesame and Scallions

Start to finish: 30 minutes
Servings: 4

These Brussels sprouts are salty-sweet, with umami from fish sauce and subtle spiciness from Sriracha. Loads of toasted sesame seeds add a nuttiness that accentuates the sprouts' deep char. This is an excellent side to any Asian-inspired meal or even alongside simple grilled steak, chicken or fish.

1 pound small to medium Brussels sprouts, trimmed and halved

1 tablespoon neutral oil

2 teaspoons honey, plus more to serve

Kosher salt and ground black pepper

3 tablespoons sesame seeds, toasted

5 teaspoons fish sauce

2 teaspoons Sriracha

3 scallions, cut into 1-inch lengths

In a medium bowl, toss the sprouts with the oil, honey, 1 teaspoon salt and ½ teaspoon pepper. Heat a 12-inch cast-iron skillet over medium-high until droplets of water evaporate in 1 to 2 seconds. Place the sprouts cut side down in the pan, then reduce to medium; reserve the bowl. Cook until deeply browned, then flip and cook until tender. Return the sprouts to the bowl. Add the sesame seeds, fish sauce, Sriracha and scallions, then toss. Season with salt, pepper and honey.

Skillet-Charred Brussels Sprouts with Apple, Pecans and Pecorino

Start to finish: 30 minutes
Servings: 4

The classic combination of apples, nuts and salty cheese provides lots of textural contrast as well as flavor complexity to charred sprouts. A touch of sherry vinegar adds both woodsy notes and an acidity that brings all the elements together. This dish can be served as either a salad or a side.

1 pound small to medium Brussels sprouts, trimmed and halved

1 tablespoon neutral oil

2 teaspoons honey, plus more to serve

Kosher salt and ground black pepper

1 medium Granny Smith apple, quartered, cored and thinly sliced

⅓ cup pecans, toasted and roughly chopped

1 tablespoon sherry vinegar

1 ounce pecorino Romano cheese, shaved with a vegetable peeler

In a medium bowl, toss the sprouts with the oil, honey, 1 teaspoon salt and ½ teaspoon pepper. Heat a 12-inch cast-iron skillet over medium-high until droplets of water evaporate in 1 to 2 seconds. Place the sprouts cut side down in the pan, then reduce to medium; reserve the bowl. Cook until deeply browned, then flip and cook until tender. Return the sprouts to the bowl. Add the apple, pecans and vinegar, then toss. Season with salt, pepper and honey. Serve topped with the cheese.

Skillet-Charred Brussels Sprouts with Dates and Pickled Peppers

Start to finish: 30 minutes
Servings: 4

Bitterness from the Brussels sprouts' char meets sweetness from chopped dates and mild spiciness and tanginess from pickled peppers. Chopped parsley adds fresh, grassy notes that keep things in balance. This is a particularly good match for pork or lamb.

1 pound small to medium Brussels sprouts, trimmed and halved

1 tablespoon neutral oil

2 teaspoons honey, plus more to serve

Kosher salt and ground black pepper

½ cup lightly packed fresh flat-leaf parsley

¼ cup pitted dates, chopped

¼ cup pickled cherry peppers
OR Peppadew peppers, chopped, plus 2 tablespoons pickling liquid

In a medium bowl, toss the sprouts with the oil, honey, 1 teaspoon salt and ½ teaspoon pepper. Heat a 12-inch cast-iron skillet over medium-high until droplets of water evaporate in 1 to 2 seconds. Place the sprouts cut side down in the pan, then reduce to medium; reserve the bowl. Cook until deeply browned, then flip and cook until tender. Return the sprouts to the bowl. Add the parsley, dates and pickled peppers plus liquid, then toss. Season with salt, pepper and honey.

VEGETABLES

31

Mustard-Roasted Cauliflower

Start to finish: 30 minutes
Servings: 4

This recipe balances the sweet, nutty flavor of cauliflower roasted on a searing-hot baking sheet with the tanginess of whole-grain and Dijon mustards spiked with honey and lemon.

⅓ cup whole-grain mustard

2 tablespoons Dijon mustard

3 tablespoons extra-virgin olive oil

Grated zest and juice of 1 lemon

Honey OR brown sugar

Kosher salt

2-pound head cauliflower, trimmed and cut into 1½-inch florets

Chopped fresh dill OR flat-leaf parsley

Heat the oven to 500°F with a rimmed baking sheet inside. In a large bowl, whisk both mustards, the oil and lemon zest and juice, then season with honey and salt. Add the cauliflower and toss. Quickly remove the hot baking sheet from the oven and distribute the cauliflower in an even layer on it, scraping the bowl. Roast until well browned and tender, about 20 minutes, stirring once halfway through. Serve sprinkled with dill.

Roasted Butternut Squash with Hoisin and Chives

Start to finish: 35 minutes
Servings: 4

Hoisin mixed with rice vinegar and sesame oil makes a salty-sweet-tangy-nutty dressing for tender chunks of roasted butternut squash. You can purchase already peeled and cut squash from the grocery store, but keep in mind that if the pieces are smaller or larger than specified here, you may need to adjust the cooking time. Use a broiler-safe rimmed baking sheet, as the squash chars for about 10 minutes under the broiler.

3 pounds peeled and seeded butternut squash, cut into 1½- to 2-inch cubes (about 6 cups)

2 tablespoons neutral oil

2 teaspoons packed brown sugar

Kosher salt and ground black pepper

¼ cup hoisin sauce

2 tablespoons unseasoned rice vinegar

1 teaspoon toasted sesame oil

3 tablespoons chopped fresh chives
OR 3 scallions, thinly sliced on the diagonal

Heat the oven to 475°F with a rack 6 inches from the element. In a large bowl, toss the squash with the neutral oil, sugar, 1 tablespoon salt and ¼ teaspoon pepper. Spread in an even layer on a rimmed baking sheet and roast until just shy of tender, 10 to 12 minutes. Turn the oven to broil and broil until charred and fully tender, about 10 minutes. In a large bowl, whisk together the hoisin, vinegar and sesame oil. When the squash is done, immediately add it and the chives to the bowl, then toss to combine.

Chutney-Roasted Eggplant with Scallions

Start to finish: 30 minutes
Servings: 4 to 6

Tamarind or mango chutney mixed with honey and cumin seeds gives charred, silky-textured roasted eggplant an irresistible sweet-savory flavor. Scallion greens and chopped cashews are mixed in just before serving to give the dish color, freshness and texture. Serve with lime wedges for squeezing—the acidity is a nice flavor balance. Make sure to use a broiler-safe baking sheet and, if you like, line it with foil for easy cleanup.

Two 1-pound eggplants, cut into 1-inch cubes

1 bunch scallions, whites thinly sliced, greens cut into 1-inch pieces, reserved separately

½ cup tamarind chutney OR mango chutney

3 tablespoons extra-virgin olive oil

2 tablespoons honey

1 tablespoon cumin seeds

Kosher salt and ground black pepper

¼ cup roasted cashews, chopped

Heat the oven to 500°F. In a large bowl, combine the eggplant and scallion whites. In a small bowl, whisk the chutney, oil, honey, cumin, 1 teaspoon salt and ½ teaspoon pepper. Add half the mixture to the eggplant mixture and toss to coat, then spread evenly on a rimmed baking sheet. Roast until the eggplant starts to soften, 10 to 12 minutes. Switch to broil and cook until charred in spots, 6 to 10 minutes. In a large bowl, toss the hot eggplant mixture, the remaining chutney mixture, the scallion greens and cashews.

Mashed Sweet Potatoes with Harissa and Pistachios

Start to finish: 25 minutes
Servings: 4

Sweet potatoes are enriched with browned butter, then are roughly mashed. We add spice with harissa, but balance it with cooling yogurt. A sprinkle of chopped pistachios adds contrasting color and texture. Serve as a side to roasted or grilled chicken, pork or lamb.

4 tablespoons salted butter, cut into 4 pieces

2 pounds sweet potatoes, peeled and cut into 2- to 3-inch chunks

Kosher salt and ground black pepper

2 tablespoons lemon juice

Whole-milk plain yogurt, to serve

Harissa paste, to serve

2 to 3 tablespoons roasted, salted pistachios, roughly chopped

In a large Dutch oven, melt the butter, then cook, stirring, until browned and fragrant. Add the sweet potatoes, ½ teaspoon salt, ¼ teaspoon pepper and 1¼ cups water. Boil, then cover and cook until just shy of tender. Uncover and cook until fully tender and beginning to sizzle. Off heat, stir in the lemon juice, gently smashing the chunks, then season with salt and pepper. Transfer to a serving dish. Drizzle with yogurt and harissa, then sprinkle with pistachios.

Seared Radicchio with Sherry Vinegar, Blue Cheese and Walnuts

Start to finish: 15 minutes
Servings: 4

Radicchio and Belgian endive, members of the chicory family, both have a natural bitterness, but also a subtle sweetness. Charring brings out the sweetness and develops rich, complex flavors. A buttery sweet-sour pan sauce, toasted nuts and salty blue cheese finish the dish.

14-ounce head radicchio, cut into 4 wedges **OR** 2 heads Belgian endive (each about 6 ounces), quartered lengthwise

4 tablespoons salted butter, cut into 4 pieces

⅓ cup sherry vinegar **OR** white balsamic **OR** cider vinegar

2 teaspoons honey, plus more as needed

Kosher salt and ground black pepper

¼ cup chopped toasted walnuts **OR** hazelnuts **OR** pumpkin seeds

2 ounces blue cheese, crumbled (¾ cup)

Heat a 12-inch skillet until droplets of water flicked on the surface evaporate in 1 to 2 seconds. Place the radicchio wedges cut side down in the skillet and cook until lightly charred. Flip and cook until the cores are tender. Transfer to a platter and let the skillet cool slightly. Add the butter and melt over medium-low, then add the vinegar and honey. Cook, stirring, until emulsified and thickened. Season with salt and pepper, then pour the mixture over the radicchio. Sprinkle with the nuts and cheese.

Roasted Fennel with Capers and Olives

Start to finish: 45 minutes
Servings: 4

Roasting brings out the sweetness of fresh fennel and red onion and renders them supple and tender. We add capers and pitted olives to the baking sheet partway through roasting—the capers offer crisp pops of briny flavor and the olives become meaty and concentrated. Citrus zest and juice at the end brighten the dish. If your fennel bulbs have fronds attached, save them for garnish; otherwise use fresh dill.

2 fennel bulbs, trimmed, each cut lengthwise into 8 wedges

1 small red onion, halved and sliced ¼ inch thick

Extra-virgin olive oil, for drizzling

Honey OR maple syrup, for drizzling

Kosher salt and ground black pepper

¼ cup drained capers

¼ cup pitted black OR green olives OR a combination

Grated zest and juice of 1 lemon OR 1 orange

On a rimmed baking sheet, evenly arrange the fennel and onion. Drizzle with oil and honey, then sprinkle with salt and pepper. Cover with foil and roast at 475°F for 10 minutes. Add the capers and olives, then roast, uncovered, until the fennel is tender and browned, about 20 minutes, rotating the baking sheet halfway through. Sprinkle with the lemon zest and juice, then toss, scraping up the browned bits.

Optional garnish: Roughly chopped fennel fronds OR roughly chopped fresh dill

Seared and Steamed Green Beans

Green beans turn both tender and flavorful when we use the sear-steam method. The vegetables blister and char in a hot skillet before a scant amount of water is added and the lid goes on. The liquid produces a burst of steam that cooks the beans in just a few minutes; the moisture evaporates by the time the beans are done so the flavors are bold and concentrated.

Left to right: Seared and Steamed Green Beans with Ginger and Coconut, Seared and Steamed Green Beans and Tomatoes with Feta, Seared and Steamed Green Beans with Anchovies, Garlic and Capers, Indian-Spiced Seared and Steamed Green Beans

Indian-Spiced Seared and Steamed Green Beans

Start to finish: 20 minutes
Servings: 4

These green beans are a type of Indian sabzi, or cooked spiced vegetable dish. Shredded coconut and poppy seeds are used like spices, adding both flavor and texture. A squeeze of lemon juice at the end makes all the flavors pop. If your coconut shreds are coarse and wiry, finely chop them before use.

2 tablespoons neutral oil OR coconut oil

1 pound green beans, trimmed and halved

Kosher salt and ground black pepper

¼ cup unsweetened shredded coconut, finely chopped (see note)

1 tablespoon poppy seeds

½ teaspoon ground cardamom

1 Fresno chili OR serrano chili, stemmed, halved and thinly sliced

Juice of ½ lemon

In a 12-inch skillet, heat the oil until barely smoking. Add the beans and a pinch each of salt and pepper. Cook, stirring only a few times, until charred. Stir in the coconut, poppy seeds and cardamom. Add 3 tablespoons water, then immediately cover. Reduce to low and cook, stirring just once or twice, until crisp-tender. Off heat, stir in the chili and lemon juice, then season with salt and pepper.

Seared and Steamed Green Beans with Anchovies, Garlic and Capers

Start to finish: 25 minutes
Servings: 4

A trio of savory, high-impact ingredients—anchovies, garlic and capers, plus some of their brine—pack this dish with loads of flavor and umami. Fresh parsley stirred in at the end adds grassy notes and lemon zest and juice brighten the dish and balance the saltiness.

2 tablespoons neutral oil

1 pound green beans, trimmed and halved

Kosher salt and ground black pepper

3 oil-packed anchovy fillets, chopped

3 medium garlic cloves, chopped

¼ cup drained capers, plus 1 tablespoon caper brine

1½ cups lightly packed fresh flat-leaf parsley, roughly chopped

Grated zest and juice of 1 lemon

In a 12-inch skillet, heat the oil until barely smoking. Add the beans and a pinch each of salt and pepper. Cook, stirring only a few times, until charred. Stir in the anchovies, garlic and capers. Add the caper brine and 2 tablespoons water, then immediately cover. Reduce to low and cook, stirring just once or twice, until crisp-tender. Off heat, stir in the parsley and lemon zest and juice, then season with salt and pepper.

Seared and Steamed Green Beans with Ginger and Coconut

Start to finish: 20 minutes
Servings: 4

Sweet, savory and spicy Southeast Asian flavors give this green bean side plenty of character. Chili-garlic sauce adds both garlic pungency and spicy heat. Use however much you'd like to achieve the kick you're looking for (and you can always stir in more at the end).

2 tablespoons neutral oil OR coconut oil

1 pound green beans, trimmed and halved

Kosher salt and ground black pepper

⅓ cup coconut milk

1 tablespoon finely grated fresh ginger

2 teaspoons packed brown sugar

1 to 1½ teaspoons chili-garlic sauce

3 scallions, thinly sliced on the diagonal

In a 12-inch skillet, heat the oil until barely smoking. Add the beans and a pinch each of salt and pepper, then cook, stirring only a few times, until charred. Stir in the coconut milk, ginger, sugar and chili-garlic sauce. Add 3 tablespoons water, then immediately cover. Reduce to low and cook, stirring just once or twice, until crisp-tender. Off heat, stir in the scallions, then season with salt and pepper.

Seared and Steamed Green Beans and Tomatoes with Feta

Start to finish: 20 minutes
Servings: 4

Sweet cherry (or grape) tomatoes go into the skillet with green beans to blister and char. Feta cheese sprinkled on at the end adds salty, chewy texture.

2 tablespoons neutral oil

1 pound green beans, trimmed and halved

1 pint cherry tomatoes OR grape tomatoes, halved

Kosher salt and ground black pepper

2 teaspoons Aleppo pepper OR smoked paprika

1 jalapeño chili, stemmed, seeded and chopped

2 ounces feta cheese, crumbled (½ cup)

In a 12-inch skillet, heat the oil until barely smoking. Add the beans, tomatoes and a pinch each of salt and pepper. Cook, stirring only a few times, until charred. Stir in the Aleppo pepper and jalapeño. Add 3 tablespoons water, then immediately cover. Reduce to low and cook, stirring just once or twice, until the beans are crisp-tender and the tomatoes have broken down. Off heat, season with salt and pepper. Transfer to a serving dish and sprinkle with the feta.

VEGETABLES

Turmeric Potatoes with Red Onion and Chutney

Start to finish: 25 minutes
Servings: 4

South Asian aloo chaat inspired this recipe. The dish, a type of street food, is defined by a lively combination of contrasting tastes and textures. With the potatoes cooked mostly in the microwave, store-bought fried noodles adding crunch and jarred chutney supplying spice along with savoriness or sweetness (depending on the variety of chutney you use), our version is as quick and easy to make as it is flavor-packed. Mango chutney is available at most supermarkets; coriander chutney can often be found in well-stocked grocery stores or may require a trip to the Indian grocer. Serve as a side or make it into a main by serving with basmati rice and dal.

1½ pounds Yukon Gold potatoes, cut into ¾- to 1-inch chunks

Kosher salt and ground black pepper

½ teaspoon ground turmeric

2 tablespoons salted butter

½ medium red onion, thinly sliced

½ cup fried chow mein noodles OR fried wonton strips

⅓ cup coriander chutney OR mango chutney

In a large microwave-safe bowl, toss the potatoes with 1 teaspoon salt. Cover and microwave on high until tender, 8 to 10 minutes, stirring halfway. Drain, then toss with the turmeric, ½ teaspoon salt and ¼ teaspoon pepper. In a 12-inch nonstick skillet, melt the butter. Add the potatoes and cook without stirring until well-browned. Stir and continue to cook, now stirring occasionally, until browned all over. Add the onion and cook, stirring, until slightly softened. Transfer to a bowl and fold in the fried noodles. Dollop with chutney.

Optional garnish: Whole-milk yogurt OR roughly chopped fresh cilantro OR diced tomatoes OR a combination

Roasted Pepper and Walnut Salad with Mint and Feta

Start to finish: 20 minutes
Servings: 4

For this salad, we borrowed flavors from muhammara, a Syrian roasted pepper and walnut spread. The vibrant colors and complex flavors and textures belie how simple it is to put together. If you can find jarred roasted peppers packed in olive oil, use them. We've found that they're sweeter and fresher tasting than roasted peppers packed in water.

2 tablespoons extra-virgin olive oil

1 tablespoon pomegranate molasses

Kosher salt

Two 12-ounce jars roasted red peppers, drained, patted dry and cut into ¼-inch-wide strips

½ cup walnuts, toasted and roughly chopped

⅓ cup lightly packed fresh mint, chopped

½ teaspoon hot paprika OR ½ teaspoon sweet paprika plus ¼ teaspoon cayenne pepper

2½ ounces feta cheese, crumbled (⅔ cup)

Whisk together the oil, pomegranate molasses and ¾ teaspoon salt. Stir in the peppers and let stand for 10 minutes. Add half the walnuts, half the mint, the paprika, and two-thirds of the feta, then toss. Season with salt, then transfer to a serving plate. Sprinkle with the remaining walnuts, mint and feta.

Broiled Asparagus with Cardamom and Orange

Start to finish: 15 minutes
Servings: 4 to 6

Cardamom and orange bring floral and citrus notes to grassy asparagus, while butter lends richness and makes the flavors linger on the palate. We double up the orange in this dish—marmalade sweetens as it adds a touch of bitterness, and the zest and juice of a fresh orange lightens and brightens. Flaky finishing salt provides spikes of salinity and a nice crunch.

2 pounds asparagus, trimmed

4 tablespoons salted butter, melted, divided

1¼ teaspoons ground cardamom

Kosher salt and ground white pepper

2 tablespoons orange marmalade

1 teaspoon grated orange zest, plus orange juice, to serve

Flaky salt (optional)

Heat the broiler with a rack 4 inches from the element. On a broiler-safe rimmed baking sheet, toss the asparagus with 1 tablespoon of butter, the cardamom, salt and pepper. Spread evenly, then broil until crisp-tender and browned, about 8 minutes, rotating the sheet halfway through. Transfer to a serving plate. In a small bowl, stir the remaining butter, marmalade, orange zest and ¼ teaspoon pepper. Drizzle onto the asparagus, then squeeze on some orange juice and sprinkle with flaky salt (if using).

Sweet-and-Savory Skillet-Steamed Eggplant

Start to finish: 20 minutes
Servings: 4

For this salty-sweet vegetable dish, we sear chunks of eggplant before steaming them in an umami-packed sauce until silky and tender. You will need a large skillet with a lid that fits securely and traps steam in for proper cooking. Long, slender Chinese eggplant will be done after only a couple minutes of steaming; large globe eggplant may take up to 5 minutes.

3 tablespoons oyster sauce OR soy sauce

1 tablespoon white sugar

1 Fresno or jalapeño chili, stemmed and sliced into thin rings OR 1 large garlic clove, thinly sliced OR both

Ground black pepper

3 tablespoon neutral oil

1½ pounds Chinese OR globe eggplants, cut into 1-inch chunks

2 scallions, thinly sliced on the diagonal OR ¼ cup chopped fresh cilantro

Sesame seeds, toasted OR toasted sesame oil, to serve

Stir together the oyster sauce, sugar, chili, 2 tablespoons water and a pinch of pepper. In a 12-inch skillet, heat the oil until barely smoking. Add the eggplant and cook, stirring once or twice, until well charred. Add the sauce mixture, quickly cover and reduce to low. Cook, occasionally shaking the skillet (do not uncover the pan), until the eggplant is tender and translucent and the skillet is dry, 2 to 5 minutes. Off heat, stir in the scallions. Sprinkle with sesame seeds or drizzle with sesame oil.

Roasted Green Beans and Shiitake Mushrooms with Pecans

Start to finish: 25 minutes
Servings: 4

Tossed with soy sauce then roasted in a hot oven, green beans and mushrooms caramelize and take on deep, meaty flavors. A final toss with more soy and balsamic vinegar lends additional salty, savory depth and a balancing hit of sweet-tart acidity. For easy cleanup, line the baking sheet with foil before spreading the vegetables on it.

12 ounces green beans, trimmed

8 ounces fresh shiitake mushrooms, stemmed and sliced OR mixed mushrooms, sliced

¼ cup neutral oil

2 tablespoons soy sauce, divided

Kosher salt and ground black pepper

2 tablespoons balsamic vinegar

⅓ cup pecans OR walnuts, toasted and chopped

Heat the oven to 475°F. On a rimmed baking sheet, toss the green beans and mushrooms with the oil, 1 tablespoon of the soy sauce and ¼ teaspoon each salt and pepper. Distribute in an even layer, then roast until tender and lightly browned, about 15 minutes. In a small bowl, mix the remaining 1 tablespoon soy sauce and the vinegar. When the vegetables are done, immediately drizzle with the soy-vinegar mixture and toss. Season with salt and pepper. Transfer to a serving dish and sprinkle with the pecans.

Roasted Carrots with Turmeric-Honey

Start to finish: 35 minutes
Servings: 4

For this dish, try to use carrots that are similarly sized so they cook at the same rate. However, if the top halves of some are very thick, simply cut those sections in half lengthwise. To crush the cumin or coriander seeds, use a mortar and pestle or grind them against a cutting board with the back of a small skillet.

3 pounds medium carrots, peeled and halved on the diagonal

Neutral oil

Kosher salt and ground black pepper

¼ cup honey

1 teaspoon cumin seeds OR coriander seeds, lightly crushed

½ teaspoon ground turmeric

Grated zest and juice of 1 lime

Heat the oven to 500°F with a rimmed baking sheet on an oven rack. In a bowl, drizzle the carrots with oil, then season with salt and pepper; toss well. Transfer to the hot baking sheet and roast until browned in spots and just tender, about 20 minutes. In a small saucepan, bring the honey, cumin and turmeric to a simmer, stirring. Remove from the heat and cover to keep warm. Serve the carrots drizzled with the honey and sprinkled with the lime zest and juice.

Pan-Seared Broccolini with Pork and Oyster Sauce

Start to finish: 20 minutes
Servings: 4

Broccolini is a hybrid of conventional broccoli and Chinese broccoli (gai lan). We sear, then steam it with a mixture of umami-rich oyster sauce and fragrant five-spice powder. (You will need a large skillet with a tight-fitting lid.) Deeply browned ground pork and fresh scallions complete the dish. If you like, top with a fried egg or two and serve with steamed rice.

3 tablespoons oyster sauce

¼ teaspoon Chinese five-spice powder

Ground black pepper

2 tablespoons neutral oil

8 ounces ground pork

1 pound broccolini, cut into 2-inch lengths

4 scallions, thinly sliced on the diagonal

Stir together the oyster sauce, five-spice, ¼ teaspoon pepper and ⅓ cup water. In a 12-inch skillet, heat the oil until shimmering. Add the pork and cook, breaking it into small pieces, until browned and crisp. Transfer to a plate, leaving the fat in the skillet. Heat the fat until barely smoking, then add the broccolini. Cook, stirring once or twice, until well charred. Add the oyster sauce mixture, cover and reduce to low. Cook until tender. Off heat, stir in the pork and scallions.

Whole Roasted Cauliflower

A simple, delicious way to cook cauliflower is to put a whole head into the oven to roast. After about an hour, the cauliflower emerges tender and caramelized and needs only to be cut into wedges for serving. We brush on spice and herb blends that permeate the cauliflower as it cooks, adding both flavor and color.

Top Left: Roasted Whole Cauliflower with Cumin and Turmeric; Bottom Left: Chermoula-Roasted Whole Cauliflower; Top right: Ginger-Hoisin Roasted Whole Cauliflower; Bottom right: Chili-Garlic Roasted Whole Cauliflower.

Chermoula-Roasted Whole Cauliflower

Start to finish: 1 hour 10 minutes (10 minutes active)
Servings: 4

These flavors are drawn from North African chermoula, an aromatic spice and herb relish that's used as a condiment as well as a marinade.

2-pound head cauliflower, trimmed

¼ cup neutral oil

1½ tablespoons coriander seeds

1½ tablespoons cumin seeds

1 tablespoon sweet paprika

2 teaspoons granulated garlic

Kosher salt and ground black pepper

⅓ cup lightly packed fresh mint
OR fresh flat-leaf parsley, chopped

Heat the oven to 425°F. Place the cauliflower on a rimmed baking sheet. Mix the oil, coriander, cumin, paprika, garlic and 2 teaspoons each salt and pepper. Brush the mixture onto the cauliflower, then roast until deeply browned and a skewer inserted into the center meets no resistance, 55 to 70 minutes. Cut into wedges and sprinkle with mint.

Optional garnish: Lemon wedges

Chili-Garlic Roasted Whole Cauliflower

Start to finish: 1 hour 10 minutes (10 minutes active)
Servings: 4

Gobi Manchurian, an Indo-Chinese dish of deep-fried and seasoned cauliflower, is widely popular partly for its crisp-saucy quality, but also for its addictive savory-sweet spiciness. We've applied that flavor profile to roasted whole cauliflower.

2-pound head cauliflower, trimmed

¼ cup neutral oil

2 tablespoons chili-garlic sauce

2 tablespoons ketchup

1 tablespoon garam masala

Kosher salt and ground black pepper

2 scallions, thinly sliced

Heat the oven to 425°F. Place the cauliflower on a rimmed baking sheet. Mix the oil, chili-garlic sauce, ketchup, garam masala and 2 teaspoons each salt and pepper. Brush half the mixture onto the cauliflower, then roast until deeply browned and a skewer inserted into the center meets just a little resistance, 40 to 55 minutes. Brush on the remaining mixture and roast for another 10 minutes. Cut into wedges and sprinkle with scallions.

Ginger-Hoisin Roasted Whole Cauliflower

Start to finish: 1 hour 10 minutes (10 minutes active)
Servings: 4

This roasted cauliflower is a non-spicy play on kung pao, the popular Sichuan stir-fry. The optional fresh chili garnish adds some spice as well as bright color. If you're looking for even more burn, sprinkle the cauliflower with red pepper flakes, as well.

2-pound head cauliflower, trimmed

⅓ cup hoisin sauce

¼ cup neutral oil

**2 tablespoons toasted sesame oil
OR roasted peanut oil**

1 tablespoon finely grated fresh ginger

Kosher salt and ground black pepper

⅓ cup roasted peanuts, chopped

Heat the oven to 425°F. Place the cauliflower on a rimmed baking sheet. Mix the hoisin, both oils, ginger and 2 teaspoons each salt and pepper. Brush half the mixture onto the cauliflower, then roast until deeply browned and a skewer inserted into the center meets just a little resistance, 40 to 55 minutes. Brush on the remaining mixture and roast for another 10 minutes. Cut into wedges and sprinkle with peanuts.

Optional garnish: Fresno or serrano chilies, stemmed and sliced into thin rings OR red pepper flakes

Roasted Whole Cauliflower with Cumin and Turmeric

Start to finish: 1 hour 10 minutes (10 minutes active)
Servings: 4

Hawaij is the name for two different Yemeni spice blends. One is sweet and used as a flavoring for coffee; the other is savory, with a curry-like profile. The latter was the inspiration for this roasted cauliflower. A two-stage application of the spice mixture—half at the start, half near the end—creates depth of flavor.

2-pound head cauliflower, trimmed

¼ cup neutral oil

**3 tablespoons plain whole-milk yogurt,
plus more to serve**

1 tablespoon ground cumin

1 tablespoon ground turmeric

¾ teaspoon ground cardamom

½ teaspoon ground cloves

Kosher salt and ground black pepper

Heat the oven to 425°F. Place the cauliflower on a rimmed baking sheet. Mix the oil, yogurt, cumin, turmeric, cardamom, cloves, 1½ teaspoons salt and 2 teaspoons pepper. Brush half the mixture onto the cauliflower, then roast until deeply browned and a skewer inserted into the center meets just a little resistance, 40 to 55 minutes. Brush on the remaining mixture and roast for another 10 minutes. Cut into wedges and serve with additional yogurt.

VEGETABLES

55

Curried Potatoes, Tomatoes and Cabbage

Start to finish: 30 minutes
Servings: 4 to 6

Sautéed onion, cabbage and tomatoes, along with earthy spices, create a flavor-packed base for potato chunks that steam with the vegetables' natural moisture. We stir in a second wave of fresh tomatoes at the end to add brightness and acidity. Serve as a side or make it into a meal by topping it with a fried egg and offering basmati rice alongside.

¼ cup neutral oil

1 tablespoon cumin seeds OR mustard seeds

1 medium yellow onion, roughly chopped

8 ounces green cabbage (½ small head)
cored and cut into rough 1-inch pieces

1½ teaspoons ground turmeric

4 medium tomatoes, cored and chopped

Kosher salt and ground black pepper

1 pound Yukon Gold potatoes,
cut into 1-inch chunks

In a 12-inch nonstick skillet over medium-high, stir the oil and cumin until fragrant. Add the onion, cabbage, turmeric, half the tomatoes, 2½ teaspoons salt and 1½ teaspoons pepper. Cook, stirring, until the tomatoes break down. Stir in the potatoes, cover and reduce to medium. Cook until the potatoes are tender, stirring once or twice. Fold in the remaining tomatoes, scraping up any browned bits. Season with salt and pepper.

Optional garnish: Plain yogurt OR sliced fresh chilies OR chopped fresh cilantro OR a combination

Pozole with Collard Greens

Start to finish: 1¼ hours (20 minutes active)
Servings: 4

Traditional Mexican pozole is a stew of hominy (also called pozole) and pork flavored with fresh or dried chilies. In this simpler, lighter version, hearty collard greens stand in for the meat; cooking the puree of ancho chilies, tomatoes and onion eliminates excess moisture and concentrates the ingredients for a robustly flavored vegetarian soup. Serve with warmed tortillas and a few garnishes (see below).

2 ancho chilies (about 1 ounce), stemmed, seeded and soaked in boiling water for 10 minutes until softened

1 white onion, roughly chopped

1 pound plum tomatoes, cored

2 teaspoons dried oregano OR cumin seeds

2 tablespoons neutral oil

28-ounce can white hominy, drained

1 bunch collard greens, stemmed and chopped

Kosher salt and ground black pepper

In a blender, puree the chilies, onion, tomatoes and oregano. In a large pot, heat the oil until shimmering. Add the puree and cook, stirring, until thick and slightly darkened, about 10 minutes. Add the hominy and collards, then cook, stirring, until the collards are just wilted. Add 6 cups water, 2 teaspoons salt and 1 teaspoon pepper. Boil, then cover and simmer, stirring occasionally, until the collards are tender, about 45 minutes. Season with salt and pepper.

Optional garnish: Lime wedges **OR** sliced radishes **OR** crumbled queso fresco **OR** diced avocado **OR** a combination

VEGETABLES

57

Beans & Grains

Recipes

Versatile beans and grains fit perfectly into casual cooking—with a few tweaks.

Dried beans and their overnight soaks are out, of course. Enter canned beans, which are terrific paired with the right seasonings. For salads, we heat the beans so they better absorb the dressings. Grains typically don't take long to cook, but they can be dull. We fix that by pairing mild white rice with aromatic herbs and warm spices, and by expanding our repertoire to include options like chewy, nutty bulgur and farro.

For both beans and grains, we rethink texture, mashing chickpeas with some mild poblano chili and cilantro to create an excellent side dish or sandwich stuffing. And rice doesn't always have to be fluffy and dry. Our soupy rice with mushrooms and greens is based on Chinese pao fan. It was created as a way to use up leftover cooked rice, but for true throw-it-together ease, we developed a recipe that starts with uncooked rice—it still only takes 30 minutes start-to-finish.

Since beans and grains are a staple of cuisines everywhere, we had plenty of flavor options. Our Indian dal tarka is a lentil stew (dal) seasoned by a mixture of spices and aromatics bloomed in fat (tarka). The warm tarka goes on at the end. And since lentils cook quickly and don't require an overnight soak, we use dried. The Turkish dish known as kissir gave rise to our bulgur salad with scallions and pomegranate molasses; we cook the bulgur with tomato paste and aromatics to infuse the grains with flavor. And from Italy we got the idea of a brothy farro and vegetable soup; we use semi-pearled farro which cooks relatively quickly.

Fried rice makes an ideal thrown-together supper. We came up with four variations, including a savory, spicy kimchi and bacon version and another based on the Anglo-Indian dish kedgeree, a hearty mixture of curry-seasoned rice and smoked fish. Traditionally, smoked haddock first soaked in milk is used; we opt for much easier smoked trout used straight from the package.

Red Lentil Soup

Start to finish: 45 minutes (15 minutes active)
Servings: 4

This simple yet robust soup is rich with butter and earthy paprika. Red lentils cook quickly and become creamy as they break down. The infused butter that's drizzled on at the end gives the soup a moderate heat; adjust it by reducing or increasing the red pepper flakes.

6 tablespoons salted butter, cut into 1-tablespoon pieces, divided

1 medium yellow onion, chopped

1 tablespoon plus 1 teaspoon sweet paprika

2 teaspoons ground cumin

1 cup red lentils

Kosher salt

Big pinch of red pepper flakes

In a large saucepan, melt 3 tablespoons of the butter. Add the onion and cook, stirring, until golden brown. Stir in 1 tablespoon paprika, cumin, lentils, 4½ cups water and 2 teaspoons salt. Bring to a simmer, then cover and cook, stirring occasionally, for 30 minutes. In an 8-inch skillet, melt the remaining 3 tablespoons butter. Swirl in the remaining 1 teaspoon paprika and pepper flakes, then cook until the butter turns red. Serve the soup drizzled with the butter.

Optional garnish: Chopped fresh mint

Coconut-Cilantro Rice

Start to finish: 25 minutes
Servings: 6

To make this colorful, highly aromatic rice, we stir a vibrant puree of cilantro, scallions and jalapeño into the cooked rice after it has had a chance to rest. For the best flavor and texture, make sure to use jasmine rice. If needed, dribble more water into the blender to help the ingredients puree easily, but add only as much as is needed or the rice will end up soggy. This is an excellent side to chicken or fish.

1½ cups jasmine rice, rinsed and drained

14-ounce can coconut milk

Kosher salt

2 cups lightly packed fresh cilantro leaves and tender stems, roughly chopped

3 scallions, roughly chopped

1 jalapeño chili, stemmed, seeded and quartered

2 tablespoons coconut oil

In a medium saucepan, stir together the rice, coconut milk, ½ cup water and 1 teaspoon salt. Bring to a simmer, then cover, reduce to low and cook until the rice has absorbed the liquid, 12 to 14 minutes. Remove the pan from the heat. Uncover, drape a kitchen towel across the top and replace the lid; let stand for 10 minutes. In a blender, puree the cilantro, scallions, jalapeño, coconut oil, ½ teaspoon salt and ¼ cup water. When the rice is done, use a fork to fluff the grains, then fold in the cilantro puree.

Optional garnish: Lime wedges **OR** toasted unsweetened shredded coconut **OR** both

BEANS & GRAINS

Warm Lentil Salad with Charred Grapes and Scallions

Start to finish: 20 minutes
Servings: 4

In this warm salad, charred grapes add pops of fruity sweetness balanced by the earthiness of lentils and pungent sliced scallions. Canned lentils make this a breeze to prepare, but be sure to rinse and drain them first.

1 tablespoon extra-virgin olive oil, plus more to serve

2 cups seedless red grapes

Pinch of red pepper flakes

Kosher salt and ground black pepper

Two 14½-ounce cans lentils, rinsed and drained

1 bunch scallions, thinly sliced on the diagonal

Lime juice

In a large saucepan, heat the oil until shimmering. Add the grapes, pepper flakes and a pinch each of salt and pepper. Cook, occasionally shaking the pan, until the grapes are charred and the skins begin to split. Add the lentils and cook, stirring, until they absorb any liquid. Off heat, stir in the scallions, then season with salt, black pepper, lime juice and additional oil.

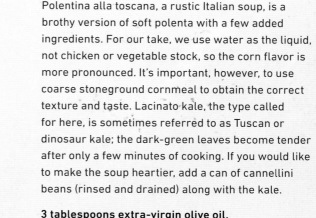

Polenta Soup with Kale and Parmesan

Start to finish: 30 minutes
Servings: 4 to 6

Polentina alla toscana, a rustic Italian soup, is a brothy version of soft polenta with a few added ingredients. For our take, we use water as the liquid, not chicken or vegetable stock, so the corn flavor is more pronounced. It's important, however, to use coarse stoneground cornmeal to obtain the correct texture and taste. Lacinato kale, the type called for here, is sometimes referred to as Tuscan or dinosaur kale; the dark-green leaves become tender after only a few minutes of cooking. If you would like to make the soup heartier, add a can of cannellini beans (rinsed and drained) along with the kale.

3 tablespoons extra-virgin olive oil, plus more to serve

1 large yellow onion, chopped

2 medium garlic cloves, finely chopped

1 tablespoon fresh rosemary, minced

Kosher salt and ground black pepper

¾ cup coarse stoneground yellow cornmeal

1 bunch lacinato kale, stemmed, leaves torn into rough 1-inch pieces

4 ounces Parmesan cheese, finely grated (2 cups), plus more to serve

In a large pot, heat the oil until shimmering. Add the onion, garlic, rosemary, 2 teaspoons salt and 1 teaspoon pepper. Cook, stirring, until the onion is translucent. Add 2 quarts water, then whisk in the cornmeal and bring to a simmer. Reduce to low and cook, uncovered, stirring occasionally and scraping the bottom of the pot to prevent sticking, for 15 minutes. Stir in the kale, then cook, stirring, until both the kale and cornmeal are tender, about 5 minutes. Stir in the Parmesan, then season with salt and pepper. Serve drizzled with oil and sprinkled with cheese.

Afghan-Style Bean Curry

Start to finish: 25 minutes
Servings: 4

The Afghan dish called lubya (sometimes spelled lobia) is a simple curry made with kidney beans. In our version, we use Roman or pinto beans, which have a creamier, more yielding texture than kidneys. The ingredients are few and the cooking time is brief, but the flavors in this vegetarian dish are rich, aromatic and satisfying. Serve with warmed flatbread to scoop up the beans or with basmati rice.

3 tablespoons extra-virgin olive oil

1 medium yellow onion, chopped

4 medium garlic cloves, minced

1 tablespoon ground coriander

1 teaspoon ground cumin

Kosher salt and ground black pepper

15-ounce can tomato puree

Two 15½-ounce cans Roman beans **OR** pinto beans, rinsed and drained

Kosher salt and ground black pepper

In a large pot, heat the oil until shimmering. Add the onion, garlic, coriander, cumin, 2 teaspoons salt and 1 teaspoon pepper, then cook, stirring, until the onion is translucent. Stir in the tomato puree, beans and 1 cup water, then bring to a simmer. Simmer, uncovered and stirring occasionally, for 15 minutes. Season with salt and pepper.

Optional garnish: Chopped fresh mint **OR** cilantro **OR** finely chopped red onion **OR** a combination

66

Arroz con Pollo

Start to finish: 40 minutes (15 minutes active)
Servings: 4

This Spanish-style arroz con pollo (rice with chicken) gets a flavor boost from browning the chicken and cooking the tomato paste until it darkens. The caramelization develops flavor compounds that add complexity to the finished dish. We use Italian Arborio rice—it has a starch content that yields a satisfyingly creamy consistency and is easier to find than similarly high-starch Spanish varieties.

2 tablespoons extra-virgin olive oil

1 pound boneless, skinless chicken thighs, trimmed, patted dry and cut into 1-inch pieces

1 medium yellow onion, chopped

¼ cup tomato paste

1 tablespoon smoked paprika

Kosher salt and ground black pepper

1 cup Arborio rice, rinsed and drained

2 cups frozen green peas

In a Dutch oven, heat the oil until barely smoking. Add the chicken and cook without stirring until browned on the bottom. Add the onion and cook, stirring often, until it has softened, about 5 minutes. Add the tomato paste, paprika, 2 teaspoons salt and 1 teaspoon pepper, then cook, stirring, until the tomato paste is well browned. Stir in the rice and 2 cups water. Bring to a simmer, then cover, reduce to low and cook for 20 minutes. Off heat, scatter the peas over the rice. Cover and let stand for 5 minutes.

Optional garnish: Sliced pitted green olives OR chopped roasted red peppers OR both

Quinoa Cakes with Gruyère and Herbs

Start to finish: 30 minutes
Servings: 4

These pan-fried, crisp-crusted quinoa cakes can be served on their own with a side dish or can be made into sandwiches by tucking them into buns with toppings. To cook just enough quinoa to make the cakes, in a large saucepan bring 1½ cups water and ½ cup quinoa (rinsed and drained) to a boil. Stir in 1 teaspoon kosher salt, then cover, reduce to low and cook until the water has been absorbed, about 15 minutes. Remove from the heat, uncover, drape a towel across the pan, re-cover and let stand for 10 minutes. Fluff with a fork, spread on a parchment-lined baking sheet and cool to room temperature.

2 large eggs

⅓ cup panko breadcrumbs

1½ cups cooked red or yellow quinoa, room temperature

2 scallions, finely chopped

¼ cup chopped fresh tarragon OR dill OR a combination

3 ounces Gruyère cheese OR Gouda cheese OR smoked Gouda cheese, shredded (¾ cup)

Kosher salt and ground black pepper

2 tablespoons neutral oil

In a large bowl, beat the eggs, then add the panko and mix until moistened; set aside for 15 minutes to hydrate. To the panko-egg mixture, add the quinoa, scallions, tarragon, cheese, 1 teaspoon salt and ½ teaspoon pepper. Mix by hand, then form into four 3-inch patties, pressing firmly so they hold together. In a 12-inch nonstick skillet, heat the oil until shimmering. Add the patties and cook until well browned on both sides, flipping once.

Optional garnish: Mayonnaise mixed with chopped fresh herbs

Basmati Rice with Ginger and Turmeric

**Start to finish: 40 minutes
(15 minutes active)
Servings: 4 to 6**

Indian pulihora, also known as tamarind rice, gave us the idea for this basmati rice that's aromatic with spices and ginger, and finished with tangy lime. For simplicity, crush the mustard and cumin seeds together. Use a mortar and pestle or the bottom of a small skillet, or pulse them a couple times in a spice grinder. For some fresh-chili heat, add a minced jalapeño or serrano when adding the spices, ginger and rice to the shimmering oil. This pairs well with garam masala and tamarind roasted chicken (p. 230) or curried shrimp cakes (p. 175).

1 tablespoon neutral oil

2 teaspoons yellow OR brown mustard seeds, lightly crushed

2 teaspoons cumin seeds, lightly crushed

1½ cups basmati rice

1 tablespoon finely grated fresh ginger

½ teaspoon ground turmeric

Kosher salt and ground black pepper

¼ cup lime juice

In a large saucepan, heat the oil until shimmering. Add the mustard and cumin seeds, rice and ginger. Cook, stirring, until fragrant, about 1 minute. Stir in the turmeric, 2 teaspoons salt, ½ teaspoon pepper and 2¼ cups water. Bring to a simmer, then cover, reduce to low and cook until the liquid is absorbed, about 15 minutes. Off heat, stir in the lime juice, cover and let stand for 10 minutes. Fluff with a fork.

Optional garnish: Chopped fresh cilantro OR chopped roasted peanuts or cashews OR chutney OR a combination

Heat Your Beans

To make plain canned beans taste better, we briefly heat them in the microwave, then toss them while hot with aromatics or other high-impact ingredients. As they cool, the beans absorb the seasonings, so each bite is flavor-packed.

Top left: Chickpea and Cucumber Salad with Mango Chutney; Bottom left: White Bean and Avocado Salad with Lemon and Herbs; Top right: Roman Bean and Artichoke Salad with Olive Oil Tuna; Bottom right: Black Bean Salad with Scallion and Charred Tomatoes.

White Bean and Avocado Salad with Lemon and Herbs

Start to finish: 15 minutes, plus cooling
Servings: 4

This colorful salad is based on one we tasted in Athens. Though the flavors are terrific with either parsley or dill, use both if you can, as they each add unique herbal notes. Serve on its own as a light meal, offer it on leafy greens or make it a side to grilled shrimp or fish.

Two 15½-ounce cans cannellini beans, rinsed and drained

Kosher salt and ground black pepper

1 large shallot, halved and thinly sliced

¼ cup extra-virgin olive oil

Grated zest and juice of 2 lemons

⅓ cup chopped fresh flat-leaf parsley OR chopped fresh dill OR a combination

1 ripe avocado, pitted, peeled and chopped

In a large microwave-safe bowl, toss the beans with 1 teaspoon salt. Cover and microwave on high until hot, 1½ to 2 minutes. Immediately add the shallot, oil and lemon zest and juice; toss, then season with salt and pepper. Cool to room temperature, stirring once or twice. Stir in the parsley and avocado.

Black Bean Salad with Scallions and Charred Tomatoes

Start to finish: 15 minutes, plus cooling
Servings: 4

Charring grape or cherry tomatoes in a hot skillet gives them a subtle smokiness and intensifies their sweetness and flavor. This salad is a good companion to grilled pork or beef, or alongside chipotle-lime slashed chicken (p. 204).

1 pint grape tomatoes OR cherry tomatoes

Two 15½-ounce cans black beans, rinsed and drained

Kosher salt and ground black pepper

1 bunch scallions, thinly sliced

¼ cup extra-virgin olive oil

¼ cup lime juice

1 cup lightly packed fresh cilantro OR flat-leaf parsley

2 ounces queso fresco OR feta cheese, crumbled (½ cup)

Heat a 12-inch skillet over high for 2 minutes. Add the tomatoes and cook, occasionally shaking the pan, until the skins split and char; transfer to a small bowl and set aside. In a large microwave-safe bowl, toss the beans with 1 teaspoon salt. Cover and microwave on high until hot, 1½ to 2 minutes. Immediately add the tomatoes, scallions, oil and lime juice; toss, then season with salt and pepper. Cool to room temperature, stirring once or twice. Stir in the cilantro. Serve sprinkled with the queso fresco.

Roman Bean and Artichoke Salad with Olive Oil Tuna

Start to finish: 15 minutes, plus cooling
Servings: 4

For this Italian-inspired bean salad, look for good-quality tuna packed in olive oil. Its texture is silkier than tuna packed in water, and its flavor is richer than varieties packed in vegetable oil. A couple of our favorite brands are Genova and Wild Planet. If you like, serve with thick slices of rustic bread that have been toasted or grilled, then rubbed with garlic.

Two 15½-ounce cans Roman beans
OR cannellini beans, rinsed and drained

Kosher salt and ground black pepper

1 cup drained marinated artichoke hearts, cut into 1-inch chunks

½ cup drained peperoncini, sliced into thin rings OR roasted red peppers, thinly sliced OR both

⅓ cup red wine vinegar

¼ cup extra-virgin olive oil

5-ounce can olive oil–packed tuna, drained and broken into chunks

1 cup lightly packed fresh basil
OR baby arugula OR a combination

In a large microwave-safe bowl, toss the beans with 1 teaspoon salt. Cover and microwave on high until hot, 1½ to 2 minutes. Immediately add the artichokes, peperoncini, vinegar and oil; toss, then season with salt and pepper. Cool to room temperature, stirring once or twice. Stir in the tuna and basil.

Optional garnish: Soft- or hard-cooked eggs, peeled and chopped or cut into wedges

Chickpea and Cucumber Salad with Mango Chutney

Start to finish: 15 minutes, plus cooling
Servings: 4

Chana chaat, a South Asian street snack, was the inspiration for this simple salad with loads of contrasting tastes and textures—sweet, tart and spicy, as well as creamy and crunchy. A combination of cucumber, tomatoes and red onion yields the best color and flavor, but the salad is delicious made with whichever of those vegetables you have on hand.

Two 15½-ounce cans chickpeas, rinsed and drained

2 teaspoons curry powder

Kosher salt and ground black pepper

1 English cucumber, halved lengthwise, seeded and cut into ½-inch cubes OR 1 pint cherry tomatoes, halved OR 1 small red onion, chopped OR a combination

⅓ cup mango chutney OR tamarind chutney OR hot pepper jelly

2 cups fried wonton strips

½ cup roughly chopped fresh cilantro

In a large microwave-safe bowl, toss the chickpeas with the curry powder and 1 teaspoon salt. Cover and microwave on high until hot, 1½ to 2 minutes. Immediately add the cucumber and chutney; toss, then season with salt and pepper. Cool to room temperature, stirring once or twice. Stir in the wonton strips and cilantro.

Cannellini Beans and Cabbage with Pancetta and Parmesan

Start to finish: 30 minutes
Servings: 4

The combination of creamy white beans, silky cabbage, crisp pancetta and salty Parmesan cheese is a winning one. If you wish to make this vegetarian, omit the pancetta and increase the olive oil to 2 tablespoons. Serve alongside roasted pork, chicken or sausages.

4 ounces pancetta, chopped

1 tablespoon extra-virgin olive oil, plus more to serve

1 medium yellow onion, halved and sliced

One 15½-ounce can cannellini beans, rinsed and drained

½ cup dry white wine

Kosher salt and ground black pepper

1½ pounds green cabbage (½ large head), cored and thinly sliced

2 ounces Parmesan cheese, finely grated (1 cup)

In a large pot, cook the pancetta and oil, stirring, until crisp. Using a slotted spoon, transfer the pancetta to a small plate. To the fat in the pot, add the onion and beans. Cook, stirring, until the onion is translucent. Add the wine and 1 teaspoon pepper, then cook, stirring, until the pot is almost dry. Stir in the cabbage and ¼ teaspoon salt. Cover and cook, stirring, until the cabbage is tender. Off heat, stir in half the Parmesan, then season with salt and pepper. Transfer to a serving bowl. Top with remaining cheese, the pancetta and additional oil.

Optional garnish: Chopped fresh flat-leaf parsley

Brown Rice Pilaf with Chickpeas and Herbs

Start to finish: 1¼ hours (20 minutes active)
Servings: 4

This hearty vegetarian pilaf combines nutty brown rice and chickpeas and gets lots of savory sweetness from a generous amount of sautéed onions. Cooking garam masala with the onions blooms the spices in the blend, creating a fragrant flavor base. We scatter shredded carrots or baby spinach—or both—over the rice immediately after simmering and allow the vegetables to steam for a few minutes before mixing them in. This gentle cooking helps preserve their freshness. A salad of tomatoes, onion and cucumber is a good accompaniment.

2 tablespoons extra-virgin olive oil

2 medium yellow onions, halved and thinly sliced

1 tablespoon garam masala

Kosher salt and ground black pepper

1 cup long-grain brown rice, rinsed and drained

15½-ounce can chickpeas, rinsed and drained

2 medium carrots, peeled and shredded on the large holes of a box grater OR 5-ounce container baby spinach OR both

1 cup lightly packed fresh dill OR fresh flat-leaf parsley OR both, chopped

In a large pot, heat the oil until shimmering. Add the onions, garam masala, 2 teaspoons salt and ½ teaspoon pepper. Cook, stirring, until the onions are golden brown. Stir in the rice and chickpeas, followed by 1¾ cups water. Bring to a simmer, then cover, reduce to medium-low and cook until the rice has absorbed the liquid, 45 to 55 minutes. Off heat, scatter the carrots over the top. Re-cover and let stand for 5 minutes. Using a fork, fluff the mixture, incorporating the carrots into the rice, then stir in the dill. Season with salt and pepper.

Optional garnish: Sliced or slivered almonds, toasted OR soft- or hard-cooked eggs, cut into wedges or chopped OR plain yogurt OR pomegranate seeds OR a combination

75

Lebanese-Style Chicken and Rice with Toasted Vermicelli

Start to finish: 40 minutes
Servings: 4 to 5

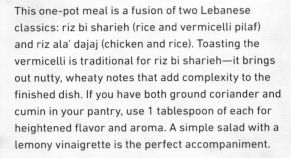

This one-pot meal is a fusion of two Lebanese classics: riz bi sharieh (rice and vermicelli pilaf) and riz ala' dajaj (chicken and rice). Toasting the vermicelli is traditional for riz bi sharieh—it brings out nutty, wheaty notes that add complexity to the finished dish. If you have both ground coriander and cumin in your pantry, use 1 tablespoon of each for heightened flavor and aroma. A simple salad with a lemony vinaigrette is the perfect accompaniment.

4 ounces vermicelli pasta, broken into rough 1-inch pieces (about 1 cup)

2 tablespoons extra-virgin olive oil

1 medium yellow onion, chopped

1 pound boneless, skinless chicken thighs, trimmed and cut into 1-inch pieces

1 tablespoon ground coriander OR 1 tablespoon ground cumin OR both

1 cup long-grain white rice

2½ cups low-sodium chicken broth

Kosher salt and ground black pepper

In a large saucepan over medium-high, toast the vermicelli, stirring, until golden, 3 to 4 minutes. Add the oil, onion and chicken. Cook, stirring, until the onion has softened and the pasta is slightly darker. Stir in the coriander, rice, broth, 1 teaspoon salt and ½ teaspoon pepper. Boil, then cover, reduce to low and cook until the liquid has been absorbed, 12 to 14 minutes. Uncover, drape a towel across the top and replace the lid; let stand for 10 minutes. Using a fork, fluff the mixture, then season with salt and pepper.

Optional garnish: Toasted pine nuts OR chopped fresh flat-leaf parsley OR lemon wedges OR a combination

Bacon and Red Wine–Braised Kidney Beans

Start to finish: 45 minutes (15 minutes active)
Servings: 4

The rustic French dish called haricots rouges à la vigneronne, or winemaker's red beans, boasts rich, bold, beef bourguignon-like flavors. Our version, made with canned kidney beans, is quick and easy. Carrots and onion add sweetness to balance the tannins of the red wine, while bacon contributes a smoky, long-cooked flavor. This is the perfect accompaniment to roasted pork or chicken. Or make it the center of a meal with a bright arugula salad and crusty bread alongside.

4 ounces bacon, chopped

2 medium carrots, peeled, halved lengthwise and thinly sliced

1 medium yellow onion, finely chopped

Two 15½-ounce cans red kidney beans, rinsed and drained

1 cup dry red wine

1 cup lightly packed fresh flat-leaf parsley, chopped

Kosher salt and ground black pepper

In a large saucepan, cook the bacon, stirring, until browned and crisp. Using a slotted spoon, transfer to a plate; set aside. To the fat in the pot, add the carrots and onion. Cook, stirring, until lightly browned. Add the beans, wine and 1 cup water, scraping up any browned bits. Simmer and cook, uncovered and stirring occasionally, until only a little liquid remains. Stir in the parsley and half the bacon, then season with salt and pepper. Top with remaining bacon.

Black Bean Stew with Chorizo and Roasted Tomatoes

Start to finish: 25 minutes
Servings: 4 to 6

Made with canned black beans, this chili-like stew can be on the table in about 30 minutes. Poblano chilies add earthy, green-chili flavor but they don't pack much heat; if you're seeking spiciness, include a chopped jalapeño or two when sautéing the poblano and onion. Serve with warm cornbread or tortillas.

3 tablespoons extra-virgin olive oil

2 poblano chilies, stemmed, seeded and chopped

1 medium yellow onion, chopped

Kosher salt and ground black pepper

12 ounces fresh Mexican chorizo sausage, casing removed

28-ounce can diced fire-roasted tomatoes

Two 15½-ounce cans black beans, rinsed and drained

1 bunch cilantro, chopped (leaves and tender stems)

In a large pot, heat the oil until shimmering. Add the chilies, onion and 1 teaspoon salt, then cook, stirring, until the onion is translucent. Add the chorizo and cook, breaking it into small pieces, until lightly browned. Add the tomatoes with juices, beans and most of the cilantro, reserving some for garnish; bring to a simmer. Cook, uncovered and stirring occasionally, for 15 minutes. Season with salt and pepper. Serve sprinkled with the reserved cilantro.

Optional garnish: Shredded Monterey jack cheese OR pickled jalapeños OR chopped red onion OR a combination

Barley Risotto with Leeks and Mushrooms

Start to finish: 50 minutes
(10 minutes active)
Servings: 4 to 6

Traditional risotto transforms simple grains of starchy rice into a luxuriously creamy dish. We do something similar with barley. Pearled barley, the type used here, has had its husk and bran removed so the grains cook more quickly than whole-grain. To bring out a rich, nutty flavor in the barley, we toast it in olive oil before simmering.

2 tablespoons extra-virgin olive oil, plus more to serve

1 cup pearled barley

8 ounces cremini mushrooms, thinly sliced

3 medium leeks, white and light green parts thinly sliced, rinsed and drained

½ cup dry white wine

Kosher salt and ground black pepper

2 ounces Parmesan cheese, finely grated (1 cup), plus more to serve

1 cup lightly packed fresh flat-leaf parsley, roughly chopped

In a large saucepan, heat the oil until shimmering. Add the barley and cook, stirring, until lightly browned. Add the mushrooms, leeks, wine, 1 teaspoon salt and ½ teaspoon pepper. Cook, stirring, until the pan is almost dry. Add 2¾ cups water and bring to a simmer. Reduce to low, cover and cook until the barley is tender and most of the water has been absorbed, about 35 minutes. Let stand off heat and covered for 5 minutes. Stir in the Parmesan and parsley, then season with salt and pepper. Serve drizzled with oil and sprinkled with cheese.

Optional garnish: Grated lemon zest

Quinoa Chaufa

Start to finish: 25 minutes
Servings: 4

The influx of Chinese immigrants into Peru in the 19th and 20th centuries gave rise to chifa cuisine, a fusion of Peruvian and Cantonese cooking. Chaufa, a popular chifa dish, is fried rice, but it's not uncommon to see versions made with quinoa, the grain (seeds, actually) native to the Andes. For our version of quinoa chaufa, you can use store-bought ready-to-eat quinoa; you will need two 8.8-ounce packages (make sure the sodium content doesn't exceed about 250 mg per serving). Or to cook your own, in a large saucepan, bring 3 cups water and 1 cup quinoa (rinsed and drained) to a boil. Stir in 1 teaspoon kosher salt, then cover, reduce to low and cook until the water has been absorbed, about 15 minutes. Remove from the heat, uncover, drape a towel across the pan, re-cover and let stand for 10 minutes. Fluff with a fork, spread on a parchment-lined baking sheet and cool to room temperature.

3 tablespoons neutral oil

1 bunch scallions, thinly sliced, whites and greens reserved separately

2 tablespoons finely grated fresh ginger

2 medium garlic cloves, finely grated

1 medium red bell pepper, stemmed, seeded and chopped **OR** 1 cup shelled frozen edamame **OR** a combination

4 cups cooked yellow or red quinoa, room temperature (see note)

¼ cup soy sauce

Kosher salt and ground black pepper

In a 12-inch nonstick skillet, heat the oil until shimmering. Add the scallion whites, ginger and garlic, then cook, stirring, until fragrant. Add the bell pepper and cook, stirring occasionally, until the pepper begins to soften. Add the quinoa and soy sauce, then cook, stirring, until the quinoa absorbs the soy sauce and is heated through. Season with salt and pepper. Serve sprinkled with scallion greens.

Optional garnish: Chopped scrambled eggs **OR** toasted sesame oil **OR** both

Toasted Bulgur and Lentil Soup with Garlic, Lemon and Parsley

Start to finish: 45 minutes
Servings: 4 to 6

Traditional Lebanese kibbet raheb, often translated as "monk's soup," is hearty with both bulgur dumplings and lentils (or beans). The dish inspired this soup, which builds rich, nutty flavor and aroma by toasting coarse bulgur in olive oil before simmering. We use both the parsley stems and leaves, so make sure to reserve them separately. A Y-style vegetable peeler is the best tool for removing the zest in strips from the lemons.

1 tablespoon extra-virgin olive oil, plus more to serve

1 cup coarse bulgur

1 bunch flat-leaf parsley, stems and leaves chopped, reserved separately

6 medium garlic cloves, chopped

2 quarts low-sodium chicken broth

1 cup dried brown lentils, rinsed and drained

Four 3-inch-long strips of lemon zest (see note), plus ⅓ cup lemon juice

Kosher salt and ground black pepper

In a large pot, heat the oil until shimmering. Add the bulgur and cook, stirring, until deep golden brown. Add the parsley stems and garlic, then cook, stirring, until fragrant. Add the broth, lentils, lemon zest, 1 tablespoon salt and 1 teaspoon pepper. Simmer, then reduce to low, cover and cook, stirring occasionally, until the lentils are tender, 20 to 25 minutes. Remove and discard the zest. Stir in most of the parsley leaves and the lemon juice. Serve drizzled with oil and sprinkled with the remaining parsley.

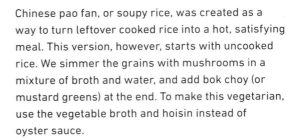

Soupy Rice with Mushrooms and Greens

Start to finish: 30 minutes
Servings: 4

Chinese pao fan, or soupy rice, was created as a way to turn leftover cooked rice into a hot, satisfying meal. This version, however, starts with uncooked rice. We simmer the grains with mushrooms in a mixture of broth and water, and add bok choy (or mustard greens) at the end. To make this vegetarian, use the vegetable broth and hoisin instead of oyster sauce.

3 tablespoons neutral oil

12 ounces shiitake mushrooms, stemmed and thinly sliced OR cremini mushrooms, thinly sliced

Kosher salt and ground black pepper

1 quart low-sodium chicken OR vegetable broth

1 cup jasmine OR long-grain rice, rinsed and drained

2 tablespoons oyster sauce OR hoisin sauce, plus more as needed

12 ounces baby bok choy OR 1 bunch mustard greens, trimmed and thinly sliced

1 tablespoon finely grated fresh ginger

In a large Dutch oven, heat the oil until shimmering. Add the mushrooms and a pinch of salt, then cook, stirring, until the released moisture evaporates and the mushrooms begin to brown. Add 1 quart water, the broth, rice, oyster sauce and 1 teaspoon pepper. Boil, then reduce to low, cover and cook, stirring once or twice, until the rice is tender, 8 to 12 minutes. Stir in the bok choy and ginger. Cover and cook just until the bok choy stems are tender. Season with additional oyster sauce and pepper.

Optional garnish: Toasted sesame oil OR chili oil OR thinly sliced scallions OR chopped fresh cilantro OR a combination

Chickpea and Tomato Curry

Start to finish: 30 minutes
Servings: 4 to 6

Open a few cans, measure some spices, prep a couple aromatics, stir for a few minutes at the stovetop and dinner is on the table. Our starting point was chana masala, a popular Indian curry of chickpeas and tomatoes. To simplify the seasoning, we reach for two spice blends that offer big, complex flavor in a single jar: garam masala and curry powder. Serve with basmati rice or warmed naan.

3 tablespoons neutral oil

4 medium garlic cloves, chopped

2 tablespoons grated fresh ginger

2 teaspoons garam masala

2 teaspoons curry powder

Kosher salt and ground black pepper

Four 15½-ounce cans chickpeas, rinsed and drained

14½-ounce can crushed tomatoes

In a large saucepan, heat the oil until shimmering. Add the garlic and ginger, then cook, stirring, until lightly browned. Stir in the garam masala, curry powder, 1 teaspoon salt and ½ teaspoon pepper. Cook, stirring, just until fragrant. Stir in the chickpeas, tomatoes and 1 cup water. Simmer, uncovered and stirring occasionally, until the sauce thickens and clings to the chickpeas. Season with salt and pepper.

Optional garnish: Chopped fresh cilantro **OR** finely chopped white onion **OR** thinly sliced jalapeño chilies **OR** plain yogurt **OR** a combination

Fried Rice

Cooked rice that's been chilled until firm makes the best fried rice. When rewarmed, the grains separate easily, yielding fried rice that's light and fluffy, not soggy and wet. Make sure to break up clumps as you add the rice to the pan. Your hands are the best tool for this task.

To make the amount of cooked rice needed for each of the fried rice recipes, in a medium saucepan, combine 1½ cups long-grain white rice (rinsed and drained) and 2¼ cups water. Bring to a boil, then cover, reduce to low and cook until the water is absorbed, 13 to 15 minutes. Remove from the heat and let stand, covered, for 10 minutes. Fluff with a fork, then transfer to a storage container, cool and refrigerate, covered, until cold and firm.

Top left: Kimchi and Bacon Fried Rice; Bottom Left: Thai-Style Fried Rice with Shrimp and Eggs; Top right: Kedgeree; Bottom right: Fried Rice with Ham and Vegetables

Fried Rice with Ham and Vegetables

Start to finish: 25 minutes
Servings: 4

This basic fried rice is seasoned only with soy sauce, so the flavor is simple and clean, and each ingredient contributes taste and texture. Be sure to use a nonstick skillet; it allows the rice to develop some browning without risk of sticking. There's no need to thaw the peas (or edamame) before use; they'll thaw in the pan.

3 tablespoons neutral oil

4 ounces thinly sliced deli ham, chopped

1 small yellow onion, chopped

1 small carrot, peeled, quartered and thinly sliced

½ cup frozen peas OR shelled edamame

4 cups cooked and chilled long-grain white rice

3 tablespoons soy sauce

Kosher salt and ground black pepper

In a 12-inch nonstick skillet, cook the oil and ham, stirring occasionally, until the ham is crisp. Add the onion and carrot and cook, stirring, until the carrot is tender. Add the rice, breaking up any clumps, followed by the peas. Stir, then cook without stirring until heated through and beginning to brown on the bottom. Stir in the soy sauce, then season with salt and pepper.

Optional garnish: Sliced scallions OR toasted sesame seeds OR chili-garlic sauce OR a combination

Kimchi and Bacon Fried Rice

Start to finish: 25 minutes
Servings: 4

Smoky bacon and spicy, tangy, garlicky kimchi are a delicious pairing. This is a good way to use up the jar of kimchi that has been languishing in the refrigerator; we use kimchi juice in addition to soy sauce to amp up the flavor. This is especially delicious topped with runny-yolked fried eggs.

8 ounces thick-cut bacon, chopped

1 bunch scallions, thinly sliced, whites and greens reserved separately

3 medium garlic cloves, minced

1 cup cabbage kimchi, chopped, plus 3 tablespoons kimchi juice

4 cups cooked and chilled long-grain white rice

3 tablespoons soy sauce

Kosher salt and ground black pepper

In a 12-inch nonstick skillet, cook the bacon, stirring occasionally, until crisp. Add the scallion whites and cook, stirring, until softened. Add the garlic and kimchi, then cook until the garlic is fragrant. Add the rice, breaking up any clumps; stir to combine, then cook without stirring until heated through and beginning to brown on the bottom. Add the soy sauce and kimchi juice; cook, stirring, until the rice has absorbed the liquid. Stir in the scallion greens, then season with salt and pepper.

Optional garnish: Toasted sesame oil OR toasted sesame seeds OR both

Thai-Style Fried Rice with Shrimp and Eggs

Start to finish: 25 minutes
Servings: 4

For a Thai flavor profile, we season this fried rice with fish sauce and sugar, and we recommend offering lime wedges on the side to brighten the flavors with a hit of acidity. You can use cooked shrimp from the grocery-store seafood counter, or cook your own by dropping peeled and deveined raw shrimp into a saucepan of boiling water, then allowing them to stand off heat until just opaque throughout (timing depends on the size of the shrimp).

2 teaspoons plus 3 tablespoons neutral oil

2 large eggs, lightly beaten

2 medium shallots, chopped

4 cups cooked and chilled long-grain white rice

8 ounces cooked shelled shrimp, roughly chopped

1 tablespoon fish sauce

1 teaspoon white sugar

Kosher salt and ground black pepper

In a 12-inch nonstick skillet, heat 2 teaspoons oil until barely smoking. Add the eggs and cook, stirring, until just set; transfer to a plate. Add the remaining 3 tablespoons oil and the shallots, then cook, stirring, until softened. Add the rice, breaking up any clumps, followed by the shrimp and the eggs. Stir, then cook without stirring until heated through and beginning to brown on the bottom. Stir in the fish sauce and sugar, then season with salt and pepper.

Optional garnish: Chopped fresh cilantro OR red pepper flakes OR lime wedges OR sliced cucumbers OR a combination

Kedgeree

Start to finish: 25 minutes
Servings: 4

Kedgeree is an Anglo-Indian dish of curry-seasoned rice studded with smoked fish. Smoked haddock is classic, but we use easier-to-find smoked trout, which also offers the advantage of being ready to use straight from the package (smoked haddock requires poaching in milk). We recommend offering at least a couple of the optional garnishes listed below.

3 tablespoons salted butter, cut into 3 pieces

1 small yellow onion, chopped

2 tablespoons minced fresh ginger

4 cups cooked and chilled long-grain white rice

4 ounces smoked trout, skin removed, broken into flakes

2 tablespoons curry powder

Kosher salt and ground black pepper

In a 12-inch nonstick skillet, melt the butter until foamy. Add the onion and cook until soft and translucent. Add the ginger and cook until aromatic. Using your hands, break apart any clumps in the rice and add to the skillet along with the trout, curry powder, ½ teaspoon salt and ¼ teaspoon pepper. Stir, then cook without stirring until heated through and beginning to brown on the bottom. Season with salt and pepper.

Optional garnish: Chopped soft- or hard-cooked eggs OR chopped fresh cilantro OR chopped roasted cashews OR lemon wedges OR chutney OR a combination

BEANS & GRAINS

89

French Lentils with Sun-Dried Tomatoes and Blue Cheese

Start to finish: 35 minutes
Servings: 4

This riff on a recipe in "Plenty" by Yotam Ottolenghi pairs sun-dried tomatoes and creamy blue cheese (or goat cheese) with hearty lentils. Sliced shallots tempered by a brief soak in red wine vinegar add balancing sharp notes, while chopped chives or dill (or a mixture) offer freshness. Use French lentils du Puy for this dish, as they retain their shape when cooked. Serve warm or at room temperature as an accompaniment to beef or lamb, or turn it into a light dinner with crusty bread and a leafy salad.

1 cup dried lentils du Puy, rinsed and drained

½ cup drained oil-packed sun-dried tomatoes, patted dry

Kosher salt and ground black pepper

2 tablespoons red wine vinegar

2 medium shallots, thinly sliced and separated into rings

3 ounces blue cheese OR fresh goat cheese (chèvre), crumbled (about ¾ cup)

½ cup chopped fresh chives OR fresh dill OR a combination

Extra-virgin olive oil, to serve

In a large saucepan, combine the lentils, tomatoes, 4 cups water and a pinch of salt. Bring to a simmer and cook, uncovered and stirring occasionally, until the lentils are tender, 20 to 25 minutes. Meanwhile, in a large bowl, combine the vinegar and shallots. When the lentils are done, drain, then immediately add to the shallots and toss. Stir in the cheese and chives, then season with salt and pepper. Serve drizzled with oil.

Mashed Chickpeas with Poblano Chili and Cilantro

Start to finish: 25 minutes
Servings: 4 to 6

These mashed chickpeas are a savory, hearty match for grilled steak or chicken, but they're also excellent stuffed into pita bread along with fresh tomatoes, cucumbers and leafy greens. Or make them into vegetarian tacos with warm tortillas and a tangy slaw or pico de gallo for spooning on top. When mashing the chickpeas, we like to leave them with some chunks for texture, but feel free to mash until smooth if that's your preference.

Three 15½-ounce cans chickpeas, rinsed and drained

2 teaspoons ground cumin

1 teaspoon ancho chili powder OR smoked paprika

Kosher salt and ground black pepper

3 tablespoons neutral oil

1 medium yellow onion, chopped

1 medium poblano chili, stemmed, seeded and chopped

½ cup lightly packed fresh cilantro, chopped, plus more to serve

In a large bowl, mash the chickpeas with the cumin, chili powder, 1 teaspoon salt and ½ teaspoon pepper. In a 12-inch nonstick skillet, heat the oil until shimmering. Add the onion and poblano, then cook, stirring occasionally, until the chili has softened and the onion is golden. Add the chickpea mixture and cook, stirring, just until heated through. Off heat, stir in the cilantro and ½ cup water, then season with salt. Serve sprinkle with additional cilantro.

Optional garnish: Lime wedges

Turkish-Style Bulgur with Scallions and Pomegranate Molasses

Start to finish: 30 minutes, plus cooling
Servings: 4 to 6

The Turkish bulgur salad called kisir inspired this recipe. To develop depth of flavor, we lightly cook the bulgur with tomato paste and aromatics before adding the liquid. Both pomegranate molasses and lemon juice add tartness to perk up the nutty, wheat grains, and scallions add oniony pungency. Be sure to use coarse bulgur; fine or medium bulgur will wind up mushy. Serve the dish as is or finish it with some or all of the optional garnishes; either way, it's an excellent accompaniment to kebabs and grilled meats or fish.

3 tablespoons extra-virgin olive oil, divided

1 cup coarse bulgur

1 tablespoon tomato paste

1 teaspoon sweet paprika

Three 3-inch strips lemon zest, plus 1 tablespoon lemon juice

1 bunch scallions, thinly sliced, whites and greens reserved separately

Kosher salt and ground black pepper

1 tablespoon pomegranate molasses, plus more to serve

In a medium saucepan, cook 1 tablespoon of oil, the bulgur, tomato paste, paprika, lemon zest and scallion whites, stirring constantly, for 1 minute. Stir in 2 cups water and 1 teaspoon each salt and pepper. Bring to a simmer, then reduce to low, cover and cook until the liquid is absorbed, about 15 minutes. Off heat, remove and discard the zest; cool to room temperature. In a medium bowl, whisk the remaining 2 tablespoons oil, molasses, lemon juice and ¼ teaspoon each salt and pepper. Stir in the bulgur mixture and scallion greens. Serve drizzled with additional molasses.

Optional garnish: Diced cucumber **OR** chopped tomato **OR** chopped fresh mint **OR** chopped fresh flat-leaf parsley **OR** a combination

Italian Farro and Vegetable Soup

Start to finish: 35 minutes
Servings: 4

Farro, a type of wheat, cooks up with a chewy texture and a nutty, subtly sweet flavor. It's an ideal grain for adding substance to brothy soups like this one. When shopping, look for semi-pearled farro—the grains have had some of the germ and bran removed and therefore cook relatively quickly. Pearled farro will also work, but the cooking time will be slightly shorter.

3 tablespoons extra-virgin olive oil, plus more to serve

1 large yellow onion, halved and thinly sliced

1 teaspoon dried thyme

Kosher salt and ground black pepper

1 cup semi-pearled farro (see note)

28-ounce can whole tomatoes, crushed by hand

2 quarts low-sodium chicken broth

2 medium zucchini, cut into ½-inch cubes OR 3 small carrots, peeled and thinly sliced OR 4 cups lightly packed torn kale leaves OR a combination

In a large pot, heat the oil until shimmering. Add the onion, thyme, 1½ teaspoons salt and ½ teaspoon pepper. Cook, stirring, until the onion is translucent. Stir in the farro, then add the tomatoes with juices and the broth. Simmer and cook, uncovered and stirring occasionally, for 20 minutes. Stir in the zucchini and cook until both the farro and zucchini are tender, about 5 minutes. Season with salt and pepper. Serve drizzled with oil.

Optional garnish: Pesto OR chopped fresh flat-leaf parsley OR finely grated Parmesan cheese

Dal Tarka

Start to finish: 30 minutes
Servings: 4

Dal tarka combines two classic Indian preparations: dal, or lentil stew, and tarka, a mixture of spices and aromatics and the fat used to bloom them. The warm tarka is poured onto the dal as a finishing touch, adding color, complex flavor and aroma to the creamy lentils. For this version, we use dried red lentils that cook quickly and readily break down to a coarse but velvety puree.

1 cup dried red lentils

1 teaspoon turmeric OR garam masala

Kosher salt and ground black pepper

3 tablespoons neutral oil OR salted butter
OR ghee

1 tablespoon cumin seeds
OR mustard seeds OR a combination

1 large shallot, halved and thinly sliced
OR 1 bunch scallions, thinly sliced
OR ½ medium red onion, thinly sliced

1 Fresno OR serrano chili, stemmed,
seeded and thinly sliced

1 small tomato, finely chopped OR 1 tablespoon
finely grated fresh ginger OR a combination

In a medium saucepan, combine the lentils, turmeric, a big pinch of salt and water to cover by 1½ inches. Bring to a boil, then cook uncovered, stirring often and adjusting the heat to maintain a vigorous simmer, until the lentils are creamy and broken down. Season with salt and pepper, then cover and set aside. In a small saucepan over medium-high, cook the oil and cumin, swirling, until beginning to sizzle. Add the shallot and cook, stirring, until lightly browned, then stir in the chili. Off heat, stir in the tomato. Transfer the lentils to a serving dish, then top with the tarka.

Optional garnish: Chopped fresh cilantro OR plain yogurt OR lemon wedges OR a combination

Refried Beans with Chipotle Chilies

Start to finish: 15 minutes
Servings: 4

Chipotle chilies in adobo sauce give these quick and easy refried beans smoky notes and moderate spiciness. Pinto beans are slightly sweeter and creamier than black beans, but either works well. If you prefer a perfectly smooth texture, puree the beans in a food processor instead of mashing them by hand. Serve as part of a Mexican or Tex-Mex meal or use to make simple, delicious bean and cheese tacos.

4 tablespoons neutral oil, divided

1 medium yellow onion, chopped

3 medium cloves garlic, finely chopped

1 teaspoon ground cumin

1 teaspoon ground coriander

Kosher salt and ground black pepper

Two 15½-ounce cans pinto beans OR black beans, rinsed and drained

2 chipotle chilies in adobo sauce, plus 1 tablespoon adobo sauce

In a 12-inch nonstick skillet, heat 2 tablespoons oil until shimmering. Add the onion, garlic, cumin, coriander, 1 teaspoon salt and ½ teaspoon pepper. Cook, stirring occasionally, until the onion begins to brown. Add the beans and chipotle chilies with adobo sauce. Cook, stirring, just until heated through. Off heat, add ⅓ cup water and mash to a coarse puree. Add the remaining 2 tablespoons oil and cook, stirring, until heated through and browning on the bottom, thinning with water as needed. Season with salt and pepper.

Optional garnish: Crumbled cotija cheese OR chopped fresh cilantro OR both

Pasta

Recipes

Soba or spaghetti, couscous or cavatappi, we love pasta for casual cooking.

Pasta of any shape creates a warm and soothing foundation that needs only the right counterpoint (think vibrantly flavored sauces) and embellishment (a snap of herbal crunch goes well here) to make a satisfying, casual supper.

For high-flavor, but low-labor, we look for one-stroke seasoning solutions, like the jarred black bean garlic sauce in our noodles with zucchini. And harissa, the chili and spice paste from North Africa, contrasts beautifully with cool, tangy yogurt in the no-cook sauce for our pasta with lemon and yogurt.

Italian pastas particularly lend them-selves to the wonder of one-pot cooking, which means less cleanup and—equally important—full-bodied sauces that cling to the noodles. We use just enough water to cook the noodles, skip the draining, then use the starchy cooking liquid to pull the sauce together. We came up with four different treatments, including one based on pasta all'arrabbiata, from the Lazio region of Italy. Arrabbiata translates as "angry" and refers to the heat level of the sauce of tomatoes, garlic and pepper flakes; we let you decide whether you want the sauce mildly annoyed or full-on raging.

We also present a quartet of takes on pesto. Though they feature non-traditional pesto ingredients such as aged Gouda and briny capers, all four employ the techniques we learned when making classic basil pesto in Italy: Grind the cheese, chop the herbs, then process ingredients individually to keep textures and flavors distinct.

Building flavor into dishes requires more than dumping a spoonful of this or that into the pot. We use cured chorizo, the savory sausage from Spain, to add depth to our paella-inspired fideos and amplify the flavor by toasting the noodles in the paprika-infused fat rendered by cooking the meat. The starchy udon noodles we use in our Korean seafood and noodle soup are cooked directly in the broth— the noodles soak up flavor; the broth gets extra body with no extra effort.

And cooking with noodles doesn't stop at sauces and soups. We make a vermicelli omelet inspired by Maltese froga tat-tarja and treat couscous like rice to create a kind of risotto that was inspired by a dish we had in Tel Aviv. We simplify the cooking method— the pasta simmers to tenderness—and add sweet, fresh asparagus at the end, a perfect pairing to the creamy, chewy couscous.

Fusilli with Fresh Herbs and Artichokes

Start to finish: 20 minutes
Servings: 4 to 6

The inspiration for this recipe comes from "Autentico" by Rolando Beramendi. The sauce is a cheese-free pesto of mixed herbs and artichokes with a backdrop of pepperiness from arugula (or watercress), tempered by grassy parsley. We preferred neutral oil blended into the sauce because its flavor doesn't compete with the other ingredients, but we drizzle on extra-virgin olive just before serving. Either canned or marinated artichoke hearts work well.

3 cups lightly packed baby arugula OR baby watercress

1½ cups lightly packed fresh flat-leaf parsley

4 scallions, roughly chopped

2 tablespoons fresh marjoram OR fresh oregano

2 marinated artichoke hearts, quartered, plus chopped marinated artichoke hearts to serve

6 tablespoons neutral oil

Kosher salt and ground black pepper

1 pound fusilli OR cavatappi OR gemelli pasta

Extra-virgin olive oil, to serve

In a blender or food processor, combine the arugula, parsley, scallions, marjoram, artichokes, neutral oil, ¼ cup water, 1 teaspoon salt and ¾ teaspoon pepper. Puree until smooth; transfer to a large bowl. Cook the pasta in a large pot of boiling salted water until al dente. Reserve ½ cup cooking water, then drain. Add the pasta and ¼ cup cooking water to the pesto; toss, adding more cooking water to thin. Season with salt and pepper. Serve topped with chopped artichokes and drizzled with olive oil.

Optional garnish: Toasted sliced almonds OR shaved pecorino Romano cheese OR lemon wedges OR toasted bread crumbs

Garlic Noodles with Shiitake Mushrooms

Start to finish: 30 minutes
Servings: 4

The An family, which owns and operates two
well-regarded Vietnamese restaurants in California,
often is credited with the creation of the dish known
simply as "garlic noodles." Buttery, umami-rich and
intensely garlicky, the noodles are not traditional
Vietnamese fare, but were such a hit many other
Vietnamese restaurants now offer them. This recipe
is our version of those noodles, but we've added
mushrooms and scallions to round out the dish.
Use dried Asian noodles with a hearty chew, such
as lo mein or udon; in a pinch, linguine works, too.

**10 ounces dried Asian wheat noodles
(see note)**

**8 tablespoons salted butter, cut into
1-tablespoon pieces, divided**

6 medium garlic cloves, minced

**8 ounces shiitake mushrooms,
stemmed, caps thinly sliced**

3 tablespoons oyster sauce

**4 scallions, thinly sliced OR ½ cup
finely chopped fresh flat-leaf parsley**

Cook the noodles in a large pot of boiling water
until tender. Reserve 1 cup cooking water, then
drain, rinse and drain again. In a 12-inch skillet,
melt 6 tablespoons of butter. Add the garlic and
mushrooms, then cook, stirring occasionally, until
the mushrooms are tender. Stir in the oyster sauce
and reserved cooking water. Simmer, stirring, until
slightly thickened. Add the noodles, the remaining
2 tablespoons butter and most of the scallions.
Off heat, toss until the butter has melted. Serve
sprinkled with the remaining scallions.

Bucatini with Sweet Corn and Scallions

Start to finish: 20 minutes
Servings: 4 to 6

This creamy yet light pasta dish is delicious made with frozen corn kernels, but it's even better with peak-season fresh corn. If using fresh corn, you'll need to cut the kernels from 3 large or 4 medium ears to get the amount called for in the recipe. Fresh chilies, a generous amount of scallions and grated pecorino Romano cheese add a spiciness and savoriness that balance the corn's natural sweetness.

1 pound frozen corn kernels, thawed, drained and patted dry (about 3 cups)

1 bunch scallions, thinly sliced, whites and greens reserved separately

Kosher salt and ground black pepper

1 pound bucatini pasta OR spaghetti

4 tablespoons salted butter, cut into 4 pieces

2 ounces pecorino Romano cheese, finely grated (1 cup)

1 or 2 Fresno OR jalapeño chilies, stemmed, seeded and thinly sliced

In a blender, puree 2 cups of corn, the scallion whites, ½ cup water, 1 teaspoon salt and ½ teaspoon pepper. Cook the pasta in a large pot of salted boiling water until al dente. Reserve 1 cup cooking water, then drain. In a 12-inch skillet, melt the butter. Add the corn puree and remaining kernels, then cook, stirring, until darkened slightly. Off heat, add the pasta, cheese and chilies, then toss, adding cooking water to thin. Season with salt and pepper. Serve sprinkled with scallion greens.

Couscous "Risotto" with Asparagus

Start to finish: 30 minutes
Servings: 4

Traditional risotto is made with starchy medium-grain Italian rice. This "risotto" uses pearl couscous (which actually is a pasta) and a simplified risotto cooking method to produce "grains" with a rich, creamy consistency. The wheaty flavor of pearl couscous (sometimes called Israeli couscous) is a perfect match for grassy, subtly sweet asparagus. When shopping, choose pencil-sized asparagus; larger spears won't cook through in time and smaller ones will end up too soft.

¼ cup extra-virgin olive oil

1 medium yellow onion, chopped

Kosher salt and ground black pepper

3 medium garlic cloves, thinly sliced

⅓ cup dry white wine

1 cup pearl couscous

1 pound asparagus (see note), trimmed and sliced about ⅛ inch thick **OR** 2 cups frozen peas

1 ounce Parmesan cheese, finely grated (½ cup), plus more to serve

In a 12-inch skillet, heat the oil until shimmering. Add the onion, 1 teaspoon salt and ½ teaspoon pepper. Cook, stirring, until softened. Add the garlic and cook, stirring, until fragrant. Add the wine and cook, stirring, until evaporated. Stir in 4 cups water and the couscous, then simmer uncovered until just shy of tender. Add the asparagus and cook, stirring, until both it and the couscous are tender. Off heat, stir in the Parmesan. Season with salt and pepper. Serve sprinkled with additional cheese.

Penne with Potatoes, Prosciutto and Blue Cheese

Start to finish: 25 minutes
Servings: 4 to 6

Made with several high-impact ingredients, this satisfying one-pot pasta and potato dish is loaded with bold flavor. We add a generous amount of black pepper and cook it with the garlic to draw out its flavor. Cooking the potatoes and pasta in a modest amount of water creates a starchy liquid that becomes the base for a creamy sauce that brings together all the elements. Don't prep the potatoes in advance and soak them in water to prevent oxidation; the added moisture will cause them to stick to the pot.

3 tablespoons extra-virgin olive oil

4 ounces thinly sliced prosciutto, chopped

12 ounces fingerling potatoes OR small potatoes (about 1 inch in diameter), sliced into ½-inch-thick rounds

4 medium garlic cloves, thinly sliced

Kosher salt and ground black pepper

12 ounces penne pasta

4 cups lightly packed baby arugula, chopped

4 ounces blue cheese, crumbled (1 cup)

In a large pot, heat the oil until shimmering. Add the prosciutto and potatoes and cook, stirring and breaking up the prosciutto, until the potatoes are golden brown and the prosciutto is crisp. Add the garlic and 1 tablespoon pepper. Cook, stirring, until fragrant. Add the pasta and 4 cups water and bring to a boil. Cover and cook, stirring and adjusting the heat as needed to maintain a gentle simmer, until al dente and the potatoes are tender. Off heat, stir in the arugula and cheese. Season with salt.

Farfalle with Kale, Garlic and Lemon

Start to finish: 30 minutes
Servings: 4 to 6

The kale for this pasta dish is quickly blanched, then whirred in a food processor to make a vibrant puree for coating al dente noodles. The kale's green, mineral notes are balanced by lightly browned garlic, bright lemon juice and zest, and savory grated cheese. To make prep a breeze, we use bagged kale that doesn't require stemming or washing; curly, baby and lacinato (also called Tuscan or dinosaur) kale all worked well.

Kosher salt and ground black pepper

1-pound bag kale (see note)

1 pound farfalle OR cavatappi pasta

¼ cup extra-virgin olive oil, plus
more to serve

6 medium garlic cloves, thinly sliced

Grated zest and juice of 1 lemon

1 teaspoon red pepper flakes

1 ounce pecorino Romano OR
Parmesan cheese, finely grated (½ cup)

In a large pot of salted boiling water, cook the kale until wilted. Using a slotted spoon, transfer to a food processor; puree until smooth. Add the pasta to the boiling water; cook until al dente. Reserve 2 cups cooking water, then drain. In the same pot, cook the oil and garlic, stirring, until starting to brown. Add the pureed kale, lemon juice, pasta and ½ teaspoon each salt and black pepper. Toss, adding pasta water to thin. Off heat, stir in the zest, pepper flakes and cheese; season with salt and pepper. Drizzle with additional oil.

Optional garnish: Ricotta cheese

Pesto Pasta

In Italy, we learned the steps to a better pesto. Grind the cheese, don't grate it. Roughly chop the herbs before processing. Add the ingredients to the processor in stages rather than dump them all in at once. Process only until grainy, not pureed. And use the pasta-cooking water to marry the pesto and noodles. The result is pesto with layers of texture and flavor.

———

Left to right: Pasta with Pistachio–Aged Gouda Pesto, Pasta with Roasted Pepper–Manchego Pesto, Pasta with Parsley, Caper and Hazelnut Pesto, Pasta with Sage, Walnut and Parmesan Pesto.

Pasta with Sage, Walnut and Parmesan Pesto

Start to finish: 30 minutes
Servings: 4 to 6

Parmesan and walnuts add rich, meaty flavor; sage brings woodsy, earthy notes; parsley brightens with its fresh flavor; and a small amount of creamy ricotta ties everything together.

2¾ ounces Parmesan cheese (without rind), chopped into rough 1-inch pieces

⅓ cup walnuts

⅓ cup lightly packed fresh sage, roughly chopped

Kosher salt and ground black pepper

⅓ cup whole-milk ricotta cheese

⅓ cup extra-virgin olive oil

Leaves from 1 bunch flat-leaf parsley, roughly chopped

1 pound rigatoni OR paccheri pasta

In a food processor, pulse the Parmesan to the texture of coarse sand; transfer to a bowl. Process the walnuts, sage, ¾ teaspoon salt and ½ teaspoon pepper until finely chopped. Add the Parmesan, ricotta and half the oil, then process until smooth. Add the parsley and remaining oil; pulse until creamy. Cook the pasta in a large pot of boiling salted water until al dente. Reserve 1 cup cooking water, then drain. Toss the pasta with the pesto, adding cooking water as needed to help the sauce cling. Season with salt and pepper.

Pasta with Roasted Pepper-Manchego Pesto

Start to finish: 30 minutes
Servings: 4 to 6

The idea for this pesto came from Spanish romesco, a heady sauce that counts nuts, olive oil, smoked paprika and dried ñora chilies among its ingredients. In keeping with the Spanish theme, we use manchego cheese, a semi-hard aged sheep's-milk cheese with grassy notes, a subtle piquancy and a salty-savory finish. A generous dose of oregano adds bold herbal flavor and freshness.

2¾ ounces manchego cheese (without rind), chopped into rough 1-inch pieces

⅓ cup whole almonds

2 tablespoons fresh oregano

1½ teaspoons smoked paprika

Kosher salt and ground black pepper

⅓ cup extra-virgin olive oil

¾ cup drained roasted red peppers, patted dry

1 pound fusilli OR gemelli pasta

In a food processor, pulse the manchego to the texture of coarse sand; transfer to a bowl. Process the almonds, oregano, paprika, ¾ teaspoon salt and ½ teaspoon pepper until finely chopped, scraping the bowl. Add the manchego and half the oil, then process until smooth. Add the peppers and remaining oil; pulse until creamy. Cook the pasta in a large pot of boiling salted water until al dente. Reserve 1 cup cooking water, then drain. Toss the pasta with the pesto, adding cooking water as needed to help the sauce cling. Season with salt and pepper.

Optional garnish: Chopped fresh flat-leaf parsley

Pasta with Pistachio-Aged Gouda Pesto

Start to finish: 30 minutes
Servings: 4 to 6

Aged Gouda is a different cheese than the mild, semi-firm variety. With a firm, dry texture similar to Parmesan and a nutty flavor that hints at caramel and chocolate, aged Gouda is an excellent choice for making pesto. In this recipe, we pair the cheese with pistachios, as well as with rosemary and tarragon for a rich, complexly flavored pasta dish.

2¾ ounces aged Gouda cheese (without rind), chopped into rough 1-inch pieces

⅓ cup pistachios

1 tablespoon chopped fresh rosemary

Kosher salt

⅓ cup extra-virgin olive oil

1 cup lightly packed fresh tarragon, roughly chopped

1 teaspoon honey

1 pound campanelle OR strozzapreti pasta

In a food processor, pulse the Gouda to the texture of coarse sand; transfer to a bowl. Process the pistachios, rosemary and ¾ teaspoon salt until finely chopped, scraping the bowl. Add the Gouda and half the oil, then process until smooth. Add the tarragon, honey and remaining oil; pulse until creamy. Cook the pasta in a large pot of boiling salted water until al dente. Reserve 1 cup cooking water, then drain. Toss the pasta with the pesto, adding cooking water as needed to help the sauce cling. Season with salt and pepper.

Pasta with Parsley, Caper and Hazelnut Pesto

Start to finish: 30 minutes
Servings: 4 to 6

With salty, tangy pecorino Romano as the cheese, this pesto is chock-full of bold ingredients, but the leaves from a full bunch of grassy, verdant parsley keeps the flavors in check. Be sure to use flat-leaf parsley, as it's more flavorful than curly. We liked this with long, skinny pasta shapes.

2¾ ounces pecorino Romano cheese (without rind), chopped into rough 1-inch pieces

⅓ cup hazelnuts

¼ cup drained capers

1 medium garlic clove, smashed and peeled

Kosher salt and ground black pepper

⅓ cup extra-virgin olive oil

Leaves from 1 bunch flat-leaf parsley, roughly chopped

1 pound fettuccini OR linguine

In a food processor, pulse the pecorino to the texture of coarse sand; transfer to a bowl. Process the hazelnuts, capers, garlic and ½ teaspoon pepper until finely chopped, scraping the bowl. Add the pecorino and half the oil, then process until smooth. Add the parsley and remaining oil; pulse until creamy. Cook the pasta in a large pot of boiling salted water until al dente. Reserve 1 cup cooking water, then drain. Toss the pasta with the pesto, adding cooking water as needed to help the sauce cling. Season with salt and pepper.

Optional garnish: Red pepper flakes OR lemon wedges OR both

PASTA

113

Couscous with Chickpeas, Dates and Scallions

Start to finish: 20 minutes
Servings: 4

This simple dish inspired by North African savory-sweet-spicy flavors requires no cooking beyond boiling water. Canned chickpeas add substance to fine-textured couscous and a good measure of fruity, peppery olive oil lends richness and carries all the flavors. Serve as a side to just about any type of poultry, meat or seafood, or offer it as a light vegetarian main.

1 cup couscous

15½-ounce can chickpeas, rinsed and drained

2 tablespoons harissa paste

½ cup pitted dates, chopped **OR** ½ cup dried apricots, chopped

Kosher salt and ground black pepper

1 cup boiling water

¼ cup extra-virgin olive oil

1 tablespoon grated lemon zest, plus 3 tablespoons lemon juice

1 bunch scallions, thinly sliced

In a large bowl, combine the couscous, chickpeas, harissa, dates, 1 teaspoon salt and ½ teaspoon pepper. Stir in the boiling water, cover and let stand until absorbed, about 10 minutes. In a small bowl, whisk together the oil and lemon zest and juice. Using a fork, fluff the couscous mixture. Add the oil mixture and scallions, then toss. Season with salt and pepper.

Optional garnish: Chopped pimento-stuffed green olives **OR** chopped toasted pistachios **OR** toasted sliced almonds **OR** a combination

Toasted Pearl Couscous with Butternut Squash and Apricots

Start to finish: 40 minutes
Servings: 4

Toasting pearl couscous before cooking it with liquid brings out the pasta's wheaty, nutty notes and an enticing aroma. In this recipe, we pair the couscous with butternut squash for creamy texture and subtle sweetness, then add pops of flavor with caraway seeds, dried fruits (including sun-dried tomatoes) and toasted nuts. Serve as a vegetarian main or as a side to roasts or kebabs.

¼ cup extra-virgin olive oil

1 cup pearl couscous

1 tablespoon caraway seeds

1 pound butternut squash, peeled, seeded and cut into 1-inch cubes (about 3 cups)

½ cup dried cranberries **OR** dried cherries

¼ cup drained oil-packed sun-dried tomatoes, patted dry and chopped

Kosher salt and ground black pepper

⅓ cup pistachios **OR** pumpkin seeds, toasted and chopped

In a large Dutch oven over medium, combine the oil, couscous and caraway. Cook, stirring, until the couscous is golden brown. Add the squash, cranberries, tomatoes, 1 teaspoon salt and ½ teaspoon pepper, then add 3 cups water. Simmer, then cover and cook, stirring only once or twice, until the couscous and squash are tender but not mushy, 10 to 14 minutes. Off heat, stir in the pistachios, then season with salt and pepper.

Optional garnish: Chopped fresh dill **OR** chopped fresh mint

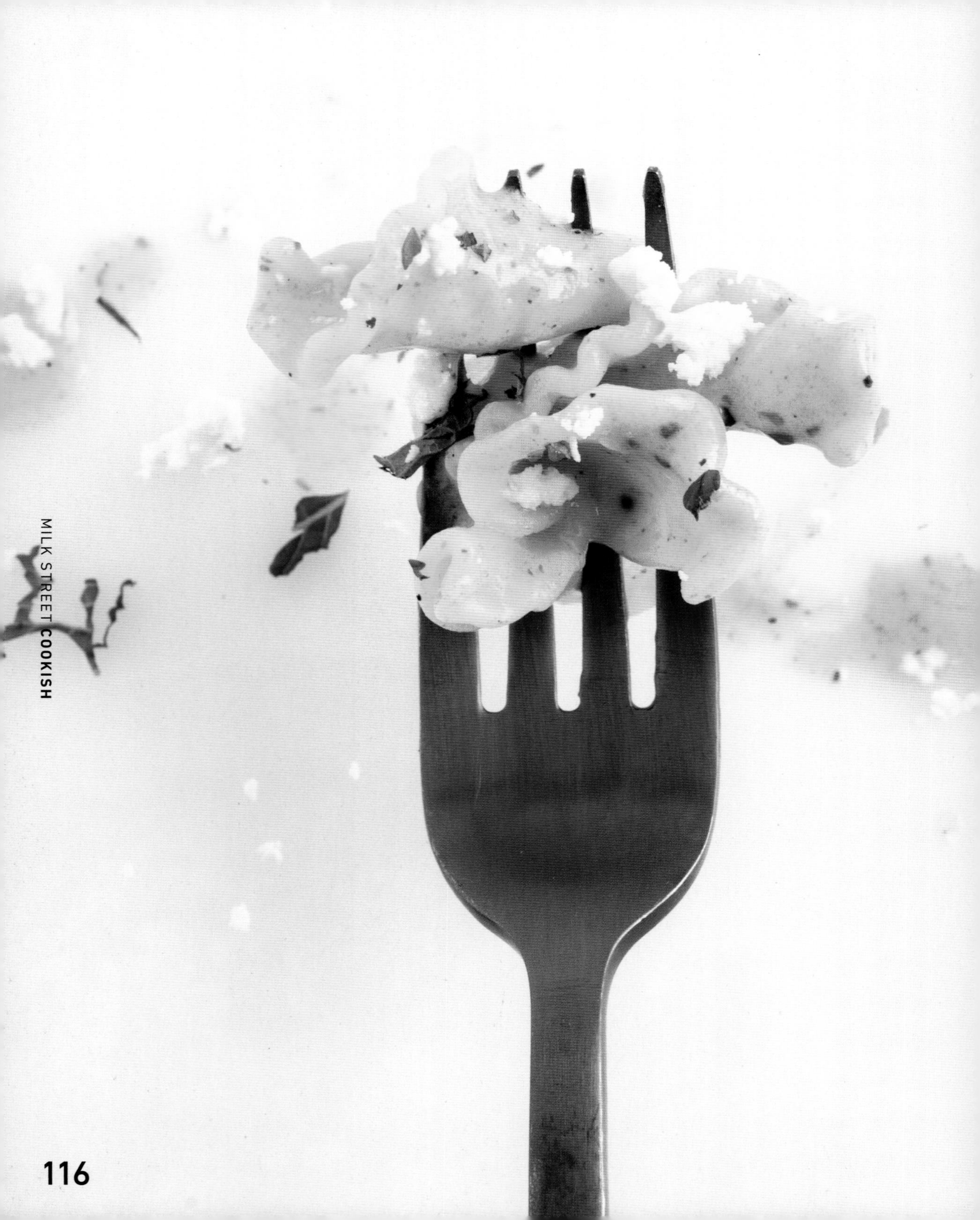

Pasta with Harissa, Lemon and Yogurt

Start to finish: 20 minutes
Servings: 4 to 6

This easy pasta dish has a citrusy, spicy no-cook sauce that comes together with almost no effort. Yogurt may be a surprising pairing with pasta, but it makes for a silky-smooth sauce that's lightly creamy and subtly tangy. Butter adds richness while rounding out and carrying the flavors. You can increase or decrease the spiciness by adjusting the amount of harissa.

Kosher salt and ground black pepper

1 pound campanelle OR gemelli OR fusilli pasta

¾ cup plain whole-milk yogurt

2 tablespoons harissa paste

2 tablespoons honey

2 teaspoons grated lemon zest, plus 2 tablespoons lemon juice

4 tablespoons salted butter, cut into 4 pieces

Cook the pasta in a large pot of boiling salted water until al dente. Reserve ½ cup cooking water, then drain. In a large bowl, whisk together the yogurt, reserved cooking water, harissa, honey, lemon zest and juice, 1 teaspoon salt and ½ teaspoon pepper. Add the hot drained pasta and butter, then toss until the butter has melted. Season with salt and pepper.

Optional garnish: Chopped fresh mint OR crumbled feta cheese OR both

Lemon-Caper Spaghetti with Pancetta and Toasted Breadcrumbs

Start to finish: 25 minutes
Servings: 4 to 6

In this dish, bright, bracing lemon zest and juice perk up the savoriness of garlic, pancetta and capers, and a dusting of golden crisp breadcrumbs adds texture. This is a one-pot wonder: We cook the pasta in a minimal amount of water, and the starchy liquid that results forms a lightly thickened sauce that coats the noodles.

½ cup panko breadcrumbs

2 tablespoons extra-virgin olive oil

Kosher salt and ground black pepper

4 ounces pancetta, chopped

4 medium garlic cloves, minced

⅓ cup drained capers, chopped

1 pound spaghetti

Grated zest and juice of 1 lemon

In a large pot, cook the panko and oil, stirring, until golden brown. Transfer to a small bowl and stir in a pinch of salt. In the same pot, cook the pancetta, stirring, until crisp. Add the garlic and most of the capers; cook, stirring, until fragrant. Add 4 cups water, 1 teaspoon salt and ½ teaspoon pepper, then boil. Stir in the pasta, cover and cook, stirring, until al dente. Off heat, stir in the remaining capers and lemon zest and juice; season with salt and pepper. Sprinkle with the breadcrumbs.

Optional garnish: Chopped fresh flat-leaf parsley **OR** finely grated pecorino Romano cheese **OR** both

Egg Noodles with Beef, Cabbage and Caraway

Start to finish: 30 minutes
Servings: 4 to 6

The Hungarian dish called káposztás tészta inspired this recipe. We added beef to what usually is a simple mix of cabbage and onions to create a hearty, satisfying meal in a bowl. For fresh color and flavor, we recommend finishing the noodles with at least one of the optional herb garnishes. And a dollop of sour cream to add a little creaminess doesn't hurt, either.

Kosher salt and ground black pepper

12 ounces egg noodles

1 tablespoon neutral oil

1 pound green cabbage, (1 small head) cored and thinly sliced

1 medium yellow or red onion, halved and thinly sliced

1 tablespoon caraway seeds

1 pound 80 percent lean ground beef

1 tablespoon salted butter

Cook the noodles in a large pot of boiling salted water. Reserve ½ cup cooking water, then drain and return to the pot. In a 12-inch skillet, heat the oil until barely smoking. Add the cabbage and cook, stirring, until browned. Stir in the onion, caraway and 2 teaspoons salt. Cook, stirring, until the onion has softened. Add the beef and cook, breaking it up, until no longer pink. Add it, the butter and ¼ cup noodle cooking water to the noodles, then toss, adding water if needed. Season with salt and pepper.

Optional garnish: Chopped fresh dill **or** chopped fresh chives **or** sour cream **or** a combination

Pasta with Sausage, Onion and Grainy Mustard

Start to finish: 30 minutes
Servings: 4 to 6

For this quick and easy dinner, we dress al dente pasta with Italian sausage, sautéed onion and tangy mustard. Fresh rosemary and chives perk up the flavors with fragrant herbal notes. We like this topped with spoonfuls of ricotta cheese; it adds a creaminess that brings all the elements together.

2 tablespoons extra-virgin olive oil

1 pound sweet OR hot Italian sausage, casings removed

1 medium red onion, halved and thinly sliced

1 tablespoon chopped fresh rosemary

¼ cup whole-grain mustard

Kosher salt and ground black pepper

1 pound orecchiette OR cavatelli pasta

½ cup chopped fresh chives

In a 12-inch skillet, cook the sausage in the oil, breaking it into small pieces, until browned. Add the onion and rosemary and cook, stirring, until translucent, then stir in the mustard; set aside. Cook the pasta in a large pot of boiling salted water until al dente. Reserve 1 cup cooking water, then drain and return it to the pot. Add the sausage mixture, chives and cooking water. Toss, then season with salt and pepper.

Optional garnish: Ricotta cheese

Ramen Salad with Shrimp and Scallions

Start to finish: 25 minutes
Servings: 4

This is a delicious pared-down version of Japanese hiyashi chuka, or cold ramen noodles with various toppings. This recipe calls for seasoned rice vinegar, which is flavored with sugar and salt; it's a three-in-one ingredient and a simple way to make a well-seasoned dressing. When shopping, look for non-instant dried ramen, sometimes called chukamen or chuka soba; the noodles may be either straight or curly. Additional options for topping the salad include shredded carrots, slivers of tomato and shredded lettuce.

10 ounces non-instant dried ramen noodles (see note)

⅓ cup low-sodium soy sauce

2 tablespoons seasoned rice vinegar

2 teaspoons toasted sesame oil, plus more to serve

1 pound cooked, peeled shrimp, cut into ½-inch pieces OR 2 cups cooked shredded chicken

1 bunch scallions, thinly sliced OR 1 small cucumber, halved lengthwise and thinly sliced OR both

Cook the noodles in a large pot of boiling water until tender, then drain, rinse with cold water and drain again. In a large bowl, mix the soy sauce, vinegar and sesame oil. Add the noodles and toss. Divide among 4 serving bowls, then top with shrimp and scallions. Drizzle each portion with additional sesame oil.

Optional garnish: Toasted sesame seeds OR pickled ginger OR both

PASTA

121

Miso-Walnut Soba with Bok Choy

Start to finish: 20 minutes
Servings: 4

Nutty, wholesome Japanese buckwheat noodles and bok choy are sauced with a puree of toasted walnuts and miso that delivers a double hit of umami. The starchy water that results from cooking soba is called soba yu; we use a little of it to help the sauce blend smoothly and also cling to the noodles. You can use either sweeter, milder white miso, or saltier, earthier red miso—or even a blend if you happen to have both types.

10 ounces dried soba noodles

1 pound baby bok choy, trimmed and thinly sliced crosswise

⅓ cup walnuts, toasted, plus chopped toasted walnuts, to serve

3 tablespoons white miso OR red miso

2 tablespoons neutral oil

2 medium garlic cloves, smashed and peeled

Kosher salt and ground black pepper

Cook the soba in a large pot of boiling water until al dente. Reserve ¾ cup cooking water, then add the bok choy to the pot and cook until the soba is tender and the bok choy is crisp-tender, about 1 minute. Drain, rinse and drain well; return to the pot. In a blender, combine 3 tablespoons of cooking water, the walnuts, miso, oil and garlic; puree until smooth. Add to the soba mixture, then toss, adding more cooking water to thin. Season with salt and pepper. Serve sprinkled with chopped toasted walnuts.

Optional garnish: Shichimi togarashi OR lemon wedges OR both

Spaghetti with Lemon, Parmesan and Herbs

Start to finish: 30 minutes
Servings: 4 to 6

A recipe from "The River Café London" inspired this light, fresh pasta dish. We boil the spaghetti in a scant amount of water, then use some of the starchy liquid to help form a sauce that clings lightly. Lemon zest and juice and a generous amount of fresh herbs add brightness, and a combination of extra-virgin olive oil and butter lends the pasta just the right richness.

3 tablespoons extra-virgin olive oil, plus more to serve

1 tablespoon grated lemon zest, plus ¼ cup lemon juice

3 ounces grated Parmesan OR pecorino Romano cheese (1½ cups)

Kosher salt and ground black pepper

1 pound spaghetti

4 tablespoons salted butter, cut into 4 pieces

½ cup finely chopped fresh flat-leaf parsley

½ cup finely chopped fresh chives OR fresh dill OR fresh oregano OR a combination

Whisk together the oil, lemon zest and juice, ⅓ of the cheese and 1 teaspoon pepper; set aside. In a large pot, boil 2 quarts water. Add 1 tablespoon salt and the pasta; cook until al dente. Reserve 1 cup cooking water, drain and return the pasta to the pot. Set over medium and add the lemon-cheese mixture, the butter and cooking water. Cook, tossing constantly, until the pasta is glossy and coated. Off heat, toss in the herbs and half the remaining cheese. Serve drizzled with additional oil and sprinkled with the remaining cheese.

Optional garnish: Red pepper flakes

Noodles with Zucchini and Black Bean Sauce

Start to finish: 25 minutes
Servings: 4

Variations of chewy wheat noodles tossed with a savory pork and fermented black bean sauce can be found throughout China and Korea. In the former, it is called zhajiangmian; in the latter, it is jjajangmyeon. Our recipe is a simplified, meat-free spin on the dish and uses widely available prepared Chinese black bean garlic sauce as the flavor base. Look for it in jars in the Asian aisle of the supermarket.

10 ounces dried udon noodles

3 tablespoons neutral oil

1 medium yellow onion, chopped

2-inch piece fresh ginger, peeled and minced

4 medium garlic cloves, minced

2 medium zucchini (about 14 ounces total), halved lengthwise and sliced ½ inch thick

6 tablespoons black bean garlic sauce (see note)

Ground black pepper

Cook the noodles in a large pot of boiling water until tender. Drain, rinse and drain again, then return them to the pot. In a 12-inch skillet, heat the oil until shimmering. Add the onion and cook, stirring, until softened. Stir in the ginger and garlic; cook until fragrant. Add the zucchini, black bean sauce and ½ teaspoon pepper; cook, stirring constantly, for 1 minute. Add ¾ cup water, cover and cook until the zucchini is tender. Add the mixture to the noodles, then toss, adding water as needed to thin.

Optional garnish: Cucumber, halved and thinly sliced on the diagonal **OR** thinly sliced scallions **OR** both

Chili-Soy Noodles with Bok Choy and Peanuts

Start to finish: 20 minutes
Servings: 4

These noodles are an addictive combination of salty, spicy and sweet. For best results, use thick Asian wheat noodles, such as udon or lo mein, that cook up with chewy resilience. Chili crisp, a Chinese condiment sold in jars, is chili oil amped up with red pepper flakes and additional spices. If you can find it, it's a more flavorful alternative to standard chili oil.

10 ounces dried Asian wheat noodles

1 tablespoon neutral oil

1 pound baby bok choy, trimmed and sliced crosswise into ½-inch pieces

⅓ cup low-sodium soy sauce

2 tablespoons packed brown sugar

1 to 2 tablespoons chili oil OR chili crisp (see note), plus more to serve

¾ cup unsalted roasted peanuts, finely chopped

Cook the noodles in a large pot of boiling water until tender. Drain, rinse and drain again. In a 12-inch skillet, heat the neutral oil until shimmering. Add the bok choy and cook, stirring, until the stems are tender; transfer to a plate. In the same skillet, mix the soy, sugar, chili oil and half the peanuts. Simmer, stirring occasionally, until slightly thickened. Add the bok choy and noodles, then toss until warmed. Serve sprinkled with the remaining peanuts and drizzled with additional chili oil.

Fideos with Chorizo and Arugula

Start to finish: 30 minutes
Servings: 4

Spanish fideos are thin, vermicelli-like noodles that typically are used to make a paella-like dish also called fideos. The noodles are toasted until golden before cooking to bring out a nutty flavor and aroma. In this recipe, we match vermicelli or angel hair pasta, broken into small pieces, with rich and meaty Spanish chorizo, fire-roasted tomatoes that accentuate the smoky notes of the sausage, and peppery arugula or grassy parsley for fresh color and flavor. A simple salad and/or crusty bread are perfect accompaniments.

3 tablespoons neutral oil

4 ounces Spanish chorizo, halved lengthwise and thinly sliced

8 ounces vermicelli or angel hair pasta, broken into rough 1-inch lengths

3 medium garlic cloves, minced

14½-ounce can diced fire-roasted tomatoes

4 cups lightly packed baby arugula, chopped OR 1 bunch flat-leaf parsley, chopped OR a combination

Kosher salt and ground black pepper

In a 12-inch skillet, cook the oil and chorizo, stirring, until the oil turns red and the chorizo begins to sizzle. Using a slotted spoon, transfer to a small bowl. Add the pasta to the oil in the skillet and cook, stirring, until evenly browned. Add the garlic and cook, stirring, until fragrant. Add the tomatoes with juices and 2 cups water. Simmer, uncovered and stirring occasionally and adjusting the heat to maintain a simmer, until the pasta is tender. Stir in the arugula and chorizo, then season with salt and pepper.

Orecchiette with Saffron, Ricotta and Mint

Start to finish: 20 minutes
Servings: 4 to 6

This unusual dish with a no-cook sauce comes from Sardinia, Italy, where saffron often is used to infuse flavor—and color—into pasta and pasta sauces. The cup-like shape of orecchiette is perfect for catching the lightly creamy sauce, but penne works well, too. Use whole milk and whole-milk ricotta; lower-fat milk and cheese will leave the dish tasting too lean.

½ cup whole milk

½ teaspoon saffron threads

1 cup whole-milk ricotta cheese

Kosher salt and ground black pepper

1 pound orecchiette OR penne pasta

½ cup chopped fresh mint

1 ounce pecorino Romano cheese, finely grated (½ cup), plus more to serve

In a liquid measuring cup, microwave the milk and saffron until warm, about 1 minute; stir, then cool. In a large bowl, whisk the ricotta, saffron milk and ½ teaspoon each salt and pepper. Cook the pasta in a large pot of boiling salted water until al dente, then drain. Add the pasta to the ricotta mixture and toss. Stir in the mint and cheese, then season with salt and pepper. Serve sprinkled with additional cheese.

Scallion Noodles

Start to finish: 20 minutes
Servings: 4

These noodles come together in minutes using a combination of high-flavor pantry items. After draining the noodles, make sure to rinse them to remove excess starch and to cool them to room temperature. Allowing the noodles to stand for 10 minutes after tossing with the sauce gives them time to absorb flavor.

1 bunch scallions, thinly sliced, whites and greens reserved separately

¼ cup low-sodium soy sauce

2 tablespoons rice vinegar

1 tablespoon packed brown sugar

1 tablespoon toasted sesame oil

Kosher salt and ground black pepper

10 ounces udon OR soba noodles

In a large bowl, mix the scallion whites, soy sauce, vinegar, sugar, sesame oil and a pinch of salt. Cook the noodles in a large pot of boiling water until tender. Drain, rinse with cool water and drain again. Toss with the scallion-soy mixture, then let stand for 10 minutes. Toss in the scallion greens and season with salt and pepper.

Optional garnish: Fried eggs OR chili oil OR hot sauce

PASTA

129

Pearl Couscous with Chickpeas, Cumin and Tomatoes

Start to finish: 30 minutes
Servings: 4

Pearl couscous, sometimes called Israeli couscous, cooks up with a satisfying chew. In this recipe, we bulk it up with chickpeas and add canned fire-roasted tomatoes for tangy-sweet flavors and cumin for earthy notes. Crushing whole cumin seeds brings out more of their flavor; use a mortar and pestle or the bottom of a small skillet to break them up, or give them a few pulses in an electric spice grinder.

1 tablespoon extra-virgin olive oil, plus more to serve

14½-ounce can diced fire-roasted tomatoes, drained, juices reserved

2 medium shallots, halved and thinly sliced

1 tablespoon cumin seeds, lightly crushed

Kosher salt and ground black pepper

15½-ounce can chickpeas, rinsed and drained

1 cup pearl couscous

1 ounce feta cheese, crumbled (¼ cup)

In a 12-inch nonstick skillet, heat the oil until shimmering. Add the drained tomatoes, shallots, cumin, 1 teaspoon salt and ½ teaspoon pepper. Stir, then cook without stirring until well browned on the bottom. Stir in the tomato juices, chickpeas, couscous and 3 cups water. Cook, uncovered and stirring occasionally, until the couscous is tender and most of the liquid has evaporated. Off heat, season with salt and pepper. Top with the feta and drizzle with additional oil.

Optional garnish: Chopped fresh flat-leaf parsley OR lemon wedges OR both

Greek-Style Beef and Orzo Stew

**Start to finish: 1 hour 10 minutes
(20 minutes active)
Servings: 4**

In the Greek comfort-food dish called youvetsi, the meat (usually beef or lamb) and orzo pasta share equal status. In our version, the cinnamon-spiced tomato sauce is rich with the juices released by the beef chuck during simmering. We cook the orzo directly in the sauce once the beef is tender so it absorbs plenty of flavor and its starch thickens the stew. Chopped herbs at the end add freshness; we prefer a mix of parsley, dill and mint, but just one or two does nicely.

1 tablespoon extra-virgin olive oil, plus more to serve

4 medium garlic cloves, smashed and peeled

1½ pounds boneless beef chuck roast **OR** boneless beef short ribs, trimmed and cut into ¾-inch chunks

28-ounce can diced fire-roasted tomatoes

½ teaspoon ground cinnamon

Kosher salt and ground black pepper

1 cup orzo pasta

½ cup chopped fresh flat-leaf parsley **OR** fresh dill **OR** fresh mint **OR** a combination, plus more to serve

In a large pot, cook the oil and garlic until golden. Stir in the beef, tomatoes with juices, cinnamon, 2 teaspoons salt and ¾ teaspoon pepper. Boil, then lower the heat, cover and simmer, stirring occasionally, until the beef is tender, about 45 minutes. Stir in the orzo and 3½ cups water. Boil and cook, stirring often, until the orzo is tender. Season with salt and pepper, then stir in the parsley. Serve drizzled with additional oil and sprinkled with parsley.

Optional garnish: Crumbled feta cheese

PASTA

133

One-Pot Pasta

Our single-pot pasta technique eases cleanup and enhances the sauce; the starch released by the noodles gives it body. The pasta also absorbs more of the sauce flavors so each bite is seasoned through.

Left to right: Linguine with tomatoes, Olive-Oil Tuna and Toasted Breadcrumbs, (top) Gemelli with Tomatoes, Salami and Fontina, Penne all'Arrabbiata, Spaghetti with Anchovies, Raisins and Cherry Tomatoes

Penne all'Arrabbiata

Start to finish: 20 minutes
Servings: 4 to 6

Pasta all'arrabbiata, from the Lazio region of Italy, features a spicy marriage of tomatoes, garlic and pepper flakes (arrabbiata translates as "angry"). We like this dish made with enough pepper flakes for moderate but not overly assertive heat; adjust the amount to suit your taste.

3 tablespoons extra-virgin olive oil, plus more to serve

4 medium garlic cloves, thinly sliced

½ teaspoon red pepper flakes

28-ounce can diced tomatoes

Kosher salt and ground black pepper

1 pound penne pasta

1 cup lightly packed fresh basil, torn, plus more to serve

2 ounces pecorino Romano cheese, finely grated (1 cup)

In a large pot, heat the oil until shimmering. Add the garlic and pepper flakes, then cook, stirring, until fragrant. Add the tomatoes with juices, 1 teaspoon salt and ½ teaspoon pepper. Add 3 cups water and the pasta, then stir to coat. Boil, cover and cook, stirring occasionally and maintaining a vigorous simmer, until the pasta is al dente. Off heat, stir in the basil, then season with salt and black pepper. Sprinkle with the cheese and additional basil, then drizzle with additional oil.

Gemelli with Tomatoes, Salami and Fontina

Start to finish: 25 minutes
Servings: 4 to 6

In this single-pot pasta dish, sweet-tangy cherry or grape tomatoes are balanced by the savory meatiness of Italian dry salami (pepperoni and sopressata were our favorites). Purchase whole, not pre-sliced, salami so it can be cut into small cubes. Small chunks of fontina cheese stirred in at the end melt with the residual heat of the pasta and sauce, making the dish rich and creamy.

1 tablespoon extra-virgin olive oil

4 ounces pepperoni OR sopressata, cut into ¼-inch cubes

2 pints cherry OR grape tomatoes

1 medium yellow onion, chopped

2 teaspoons fennel seeds

Kosher salt and ground black pepper

1 pound gemelli pasta OR fusilli

4 ounces fontina cheese, cut into ½-inch cubes

In a large pot, heat the oil until shimmering. Add the pepperoni and cook, stirring, until it crisps. Add the tomatoes, onion, fennel seeds and ½ teaspoon pepper. Cover and cook, stirring, until most of the tomatoes have burst; crush any that are still whole. Add 4 cups water and ½ teaspoon salt, then boil. Stir in the pasta. Cover and cook, stirring occasionally and maintaining a vigorous simmer, until the pasta is al dente. Off heat, stir in the fontina, then season with salt and pepper.

Optional garnish: Chopped fresh flat-leaf parsley

Spaghetti with Anchovies, Raisins and Cherry Tomatoes

Start to finish: 25 minutes
Servings: 4 to 6

This one-pot pasta dish features a Sicilian salty-sweet flavor profile, and it requires no knifework. Cherry and grape tomatoes tend to be sweet and of good quality year-round (more so than regular round tomatoes), so they're almost always our first choice for sauces made with fresh tomatoes. To prevent the noodles from sticking together during cooking, be sure to give the pasta a good stir after adding it to the tomato mixture.

3 tablespoons extra-virgin olive oil, plus more to serve

¼ teaspoon red pepper flakes

2-ounce can oil-packed anchovy fillets, drained (10 to 12 fillets)

2 pints cherry OR grape tomatoes

Kosher salt and ground black pepper

1 pound spaghetti

½ cup golden raisins OR dried currants

2 cups lightly packed fresh basil, torn, plus more to serve

In a large pot, cook the oil, pepper flakes and anchovies, stirring, until sizzling. Add the tomatoes, then cover and cook, stirring occasionally, until most have burst; crush any that are still whole. Add 4 cups water, 2 teaspoons salt and ½ teaspoon black pepper, then boil. Stir in the pasta and raisins. Cover and cook, stirring and maintaining a vigorous simmer, until al dente. Off heat, stir in the basil, then season with salt and black pepper. Sprinkle with additional basil and drizzle with oil.

Optional garnish: Shaved pecorino Romano cheese

Linguine with Tomatoes, Olive-Oil Tuna and Toasted Breadcrumbs

Start to finish: 20 minutes
Servings: 4 to 6

Panko breadcrumbs cooked with olive oil until browned and crisp add texture and toasty flavor to this satisfying one-pot pasta dish. After adding the linguine, be sure to stir to fully coat the pasta with sauce; this prevents the noodles from clumping as they cook. For best results, use tuna packed in olive oil, as its flavor is richer and its texture is silkier than the water-packed variety.

½ cup panko breadcrumbs

4 tablespoons extra-virgin olive oil, divided

2 teaspoons dried oregano

28-ounce can diced tomatoes

Kosher salt and ground black pepper

1 pound linguine

Two 5-ounce cans olive oil–packed tuna, drained and flaked

1 cup pitted green olives, chopped

In a large pot, toast the panko in 2 tablespoons of oil, stirring, until golden; transfer to a small bowl. In the same pot, cook the remaining 2 tablespoons oil and oregano, stirring, until fragrant. Stir in the tomatoes with juices. Add 3 cups water and the pasta, then stir well. Boil, cover and cook, stirring occasionally and maintaining a vigorous simmer, until the pasta is al dente. Off heat, stir in the tuna and olives, then season with salt and pepper. Serve sprinkled with the breadcrumbs.

Optional garnish: Chopped fresh flat-leaf parsley OR lemon wedges OR both

PASTA

137

Vermicelli Omelet with Spinach and Pecorino

Start to finish: 45 minutes
Servings: 4

For this dish, our version of the Maltese vermicelli omelet called froga tat-tarja, the pasta does not need to be cooked before it is added to the skillet, making this a tidy one-pan recipe. In addition to pancetta for deeper flavor, we've added wilted spinach to give the omelet color and make it a more complete meal. You will need an oven-safe nonstick 12-inch skillet for this recipe, and keep in mind that when removing the pan from the oven, the handle will be hot.

5 large eggs

2½ ounces pecorino Romano cheese, finely grated (1¼ cups), plus more to serve

Kosher salt and ground black pepper

2 tablespoons extra-virgin olive oil

3 ounces thinly sliced pancetta, chopped

2 medium shallots, chopped

6 ounces vermicelli or angel hair pasta, broken in half

5-ounce container baby spinach

Heat the oven to 400°F. Whisk together the eggs, cheese and 1½ teaspoons each salt and pepper. In an oven-safe 12-inch nonstick skillet, cook the oil, pancetta and shallots, stirring, until golden brown. Add the vermicelli and 3 cups water. Simmer, stirring, until most of the liquid is absorbed. Add the spinach and stir until wilted. Stir in the egg mixture, then cook without stirring until browned at the edges. Bake until set, about 4 minutes. Slide onto a platter and let stand for 10 minutes. Serve with additional cheese.

Whole-Wheat Fettuccine with Leeks, Cabbage and Gruyère

Start to finish: 35 minutes
Servings: 4

Pizzoccheri, a northern Italian buckwheat pasta dish with cabbage, potatoes and cheese, inspired this wintry, stick-to-your-ribs meal. Whole-wheat pasta has a nuttiness similar to buckwheat pasta, and it's the perfect backdrop for the subtle sweetness of gently sautéed leeks and cabbage, as well as the savoriness of Gruyère. Toasted walnuts tangled into the pasta and sprinkled as a garnish add crisp texture and rich umami notes.

Kosher salt and ground black pepper

8 ounces whole-wheat fettuccine
OR linguine, broken into rough 2-inch pieces

2 tablespoons extra-virgin olive oil

1 pound leeks, white and light green parts halved lengthwise, thinly sliced, rinsed and drained

12 ounces savoy cabbage, cored and thinly sliced
OR 5-ounce container baby kale, roughly chopped

3 tablespoons finely chopped fresh sage

4 ounces Gruyère cheese, finely shredded (1 cup), divided

1⅓ cups chopped walnuts, toasted

Cook the pasta in a large pot of boiling salted water until al dente. Drain, reserving the cooking water. In a 12-inch skillet, heat the oil until shimmering. Add the leeks, 2 teaspoons salt and ½ teaspoon pepper. Cover and cook, stirring occasionally, until softened. Add the cabbage; re-cover and cook, stirring occasionally, until tender. Add the pasta, sage and 1½ cups cooking water. Off heat, gradually stir in ¾ cup of the cheese. Stir in more cooking water as needed to form a creamy sauce; stir in 1 cup of nuts. Season with salt and pepper. Serve sprinkled with remaining cheese and nuts.

Korean-Style Noodle Soup with Shrimp

Start to finish: 35 minutes
Servings: 4

This is a simplified, not-too-spicy version of haemul jjampong, a typically fiery Korean seafood and noodle soup. Gochujang, or Korean chili paste, gives the broth a bright red hue as well as chili heat and a solid dose of umami. Look for gochujang in red bottles or tubs in the international aisle of the grocery store or in Asian markets. We cook the starchy udon noodles directly in the broth to add body to the soup, which also makes this a simple one-pot dinner.

3 tablespoons neutral oil

2 bunches scallions, cut into ½-inch lengths, whites and greens reserved separately

¼ cup gochujang

8 ounces savoy cabbage, cored and thinly sliced OR 8 ounces shiitake mushrooms, stemmed and thinly sliced OR a combination

2 tablespoons soy sauce

6 ounces dried udon noodles

1½ pounds extra-large shrimp, peeled and deveined OR 2 pounds mussels, scrubbed OR 12 ounces each

Kosher salt and ground black pepper

In a large pot, heat the oil until shimmering. Add the scallion whites and cook, stirring, until softened. Add the gochujang and cook, stirring, until the oil turns red. Add the cabbage, 8 cups water and the soy sauce. Cover and bring to a boil. Add the udon and cook, stirring, until tender. Add the shellfish, cover and remove from the heat. Let stand until the shrimp are opaque and/or the mussels have opened (discard any that do not open). Stir in the scallion greens, then season with salt and pepper.

Optional garnish: Toasted sesame seeds

141

Spaghetti with Spiced Beef and Tomato Sauce

Start to finish: 45 minutes
Servings: 4 to 6

The Greek dish called makaronia me kima is similar to pasta with an Italian meat ragù, but the sauce is flavored with warm spices and herbs that yield a different flavor profile—one that may even suggest all-American chili to some tasters. This is our version of the Greek classic, and it is best served with some of the optional garnishes, along with warm, crusty bread.

1 tablespoon extra-virgin olive oil, plus more to serve

6 medium garlic cloves, minced

6-ounce can tomato paste

1½ teaspoons ground cinnamon

½ teaspoon ground allspice

1½ pounds 80 percent lean ground beef

Kosher salt and ground black pepper

1 pound spaghetti

In a 12-inch skillet, cook the oil and garlic, stirring, until it begins to brown. Add the tomato paste and cook, stirring, until slightly darker in color, then stir in the cinnamon and allspice. Add 1½ cups water, the beef, 1 teaspoon salt and ½ teaspoon pepper. Simmer, stirring and breaking the meat into bits, until thickened; season with salt and pepper. Meanwhile, cook the pasta in a large pot of salted boiling water until al dente. Drain and return to the pot. Add the sauce and toss to combine. Serve drizzled with oil.

Optional garnish: Chopped fresh oregano **OR** chopped fresh mint **OR** crumbled feta cheese **OR** chopped pitted olives **OR** chopped tomato **OR** a combination

Pasta with Lentils and Thyme

Start to finish: 25 minutes
Servings: 4

Pasta e lenticchie, or pasta with lentils, is from Campania, Italy, where cooks sometimes make the hearty dish with multiple pasta shapes to use up leftovers in the pantry. In this version we pair ditalini (or mezze rigatoni pasta) with canned lentils to have dinner on the table in about half an hour. The consistency of this dish is somewhere between pasta with a loose sauce and a soupy stew—it's better served with a spoon than a fork. An arugula salad with a lemony vinaigrette is a perfect accompaniment.

¼ cup extra-virgin olive oil, plus more to serve

3 medium garlic cloves, minced

⅓ cup tomato paste

½ cup dry red wine

1 tablespoon minced fresh thyme

Two 15-ounce cans brown lentils, rinsed and drained

8 ounces ditalini OR mezze rigatoni pasta

Kosher salt and ground black pepper

In a large saucepan, heat the oil until shimmering. Add the garlic and cook, stirring, until fragrant. Stir in the tomato paste and cook until the oil turns red. Whisk in the wine and thyme, then cook, stirring, until the liquid has almost fully evaporated. Add 3 cups water, the lentils, pasta and 1 teaspoon each salt and pepper. Bring to a boil, then lower to simmer. Cook, uncovered and stirring occasionally, until the pasta is al dente. Season with salt and pepper. Serve drizzled with additional oil.

Optional garnish: Finely grated Parmesan cheese **OR** chopped fresh flat-leaf parsley **OR** both

Fettuccine with Fennel, Smoked Trout and Crème Fraîche

Start to finish: 30 minutes
Servings: 4

In this elegant pasta dish, bright, citrusy lemon zest and juice balance the richness of the smoked trout and crème fraîche. If your fennel bulb has fronds still attached, chop and sprinkle them on as a garnish just before serving; if not, use chopped fresh dill to add a fresh herbal flavor and vibrant color.

2 tablespoons extra-virgin olive oil

1 large fennel bulb, trimmed, halved lengthwise, cored and thinly sliced (see note)

Kosher salt and ground black pepper

½ teaspoon fennel seeds

8 ounces fettuccine OR tagliatelle

½ cup crème fraîche

4 ounces smoked trout, skin removed, broken into ½-inch pieces

1 tablespoon grated lemon zest, plus ¼ cup lemon juice

In a 12-inch skillet, heat the oil until shimmering. Add the fresh fennel and ¼ teaspoon salt, then cover and cook, stirring, until beginning to brown. Stir in the fennel seeds, cover and set aside. Cook the pasta in a large pot of salted water until al dente. Reserve 1 cup cooking water, then drain. Add the pasta, crème fraîche and ½ cup cooking water to the skillet. Toss over medium until coated, adding cooking water as needed to thin. Off heat, stir in the trout, lemon zest and juice, and 1 teaspoon pepper, then season with salt.

Optional garnish: Chopped fennel fronds OR chopped fresh dill

Pasta with Parmesan Cream

Start to finish: 25 minutes
Servings: 4 to 6

The key to this rich, simple pasta dish is starting with a good-quality chunk of true Parmesan cheese (Parmigiano-Reggiano). Domestic Parmesan or even real Parmesan that's pre-grated will not yield the right flavor and consistency. We simmer a piece of Parmesan rind into the cream for added flavor and umami; some supermarkets and cheese shops sell just rinds, or simply cut the rind off your chunk of Parmesan.

2½ cups heavy cream

2-inch Parmesan rind, plus 4 ounces Parmesan cheese, finely grated (2 cups)

2 bay leaves

3 tablespoons lemon juice

Kosher salt and ground black pepper

1 pound linguini fini OR spaghetti

In a saucepan, gently simmer the cream, cheese rind and bay, stirring, until slightly thickened and reduced to 2 cups. Off heat, remove and discard the cheese rind and bay. Whisk in the lemon juice; the mixture will thicken slightly. Whisk in the cheese a handful at a time until smooth, then whisk in 1 teaspoon salt and ½ teaspoon pepper; set aside uncovered. In a large pot of salted boiling water, cook the pasta until al dente. Reserve ½ cup cooking water; drain and return to the pot. Pour the sauce over the pasta; toss, adding cooking water to thin.

Optional garnish: Thawed frozen green peas OR chopped fresh herbs

Pasta with Cherry Tomato Sauce and Pistachios

Start to finish: 25 minutes
Servings: 4 to 6

Cooking whole cherry tomatoes in olive oil helps release their juices and melt them into a silky sauce. With chopped pistachios added for crunch, this pasta dish is bright and satisfying.

Kosher salt and ground black pepper

1 pound spaghetti OR linguine

¼ cup extra-virgin olive oil

2 pints cherry OR grape tomatoes

1½ tablespoons tomato paste

½ cup chopped roasted pistachios

Finely grated Parmesan OR pecorino Romano cheese, to serve

Cook the pasta in a large pot of salted boiling water until just shy of al dente. Reserve 3 cups cooking water, then drain. Meanwhile, in a 12-inch skillet, combine the oil and tomatoes. Cover and cook, stirring, until the tomatoes burst. Stir in the tomato paste and enough cooking water to almost cover. Cook covered, stirring, until a silky sauce forms. Add the pasta to the pan and cook uncovered, stirring often, until al dente. Off heat, stir in the pistachios and cheese, then season with salt and pepper.

Optional garnish: Chopped or torn fresh mint OR grated lemon zest OR both

147

Spicy Cumin-Beef Noodles

Start to finish: 30 minutes
Servings: 4

Hand-formed Chinese "belt" noodles called biang biang mian often are paired with warming spices and bold ingredients. For example, spicy cumin lamb is a common match for the broad ribbon-like noodles. This recipe is our simple beef-based riff on that. Italian pappardelle is the widest noodle commonly available in most grocery stores, so that's what we used to approximate biang biang mian. Balsamic vinegar may seem a peculiar ingredient, but it mimics the sweet-tart, lightly syrupy character of Chinese black vinegar.

9-ounce package dried pappardelle pasta

3 tablespoons chili-garlic sauce

2 tablespoons low-sodium soy sauce

2 tablespoons balsamic vinegar

3 tablespoons neutral oil, divided

1 pound beef steak tips OR flat iron steak, trimmed, cut into 1½-inch strips, thinly sliced against the grain

4 teaspoons cumin seeds, lightly crushed

Ground black pepper

Cook the noodles in a large pot of boiling water until tender. Reserve ¼ cup cooking water, then drain the noodles. Into the reserved cooking water, stir the chili-garlic sauce, soy, vinegar and 1 tablespoon of oil. In a 12-inch skillet, heat the remaining 2 tablespoons oil until shimmering. Add the steak, cumin seeds and ½ teaspoon pepper. Stir briefly, then cook without stirring until the meat no longer is pink. Add the noodles and sauce mixture, then toss.

Optional garnish: Chopped fresh cilantro OR chili oil OR both

PASTA

149

Stir-Fried Udon with Bacon and Cabbage

Start to finish: 25 minutes
Servings: 4

Thick, chewy Japanese udon noodles are great stir-fried. We combine them with smoky bacon and crisp-tender green cabbage. Use low-sodium soy sauce, as regular soy sauce may result in an overseasoned dish. Sliced scallions, though an optional garnish, bring fresh color and flavor, so sprinkle some on if you have a few in your refrigerator.

10 ounces dried udon noodles

8 ounces thick-cut bacon, chopped

12 ounces green cabbage, (¾ small head), cored and thinly sliced

3 medium cloves garlic, minced

½ cup low-sodium soy sauce

2 tablespoons hoisin sauce OR oyster sauce

Cook the noodles in a large pot of boiling water until tender. Drain, rinse and drain again. In a 12-inch nonstick skillet, cook the bacon, stirring, until crisp. Add the cabbage and cook, stirring, until it softens and starts to brown. Stir in the garlic and cook until fragrant. Add the noodles, soy and hoisin, then cook, tossing, until the noodles are heated through and evenly sauced.

Optional garnish: Thinly sliced scallions OR toasted sesame seeds OR shichimi togarashi OR a combination

Whole-Wheat Fusilli with Pancetta and Cauliflower

Start to finish: 25 minutes
Servings: 4 to 6

This recipe matches whole-wheat pasta with a whole head of cauliflower (chopped into small pieces), cooking them together in a single pot to yield a hearty, satisfying dish with minimal fuss. Pancetta and garlic infuse the mix with savory flavor, while rosemary (or thyme) adds herbal notes. Either pecorino or Parmesan works well here, so use whichever you prefer.

4 ounces pancetta, finely chopped

3 tablespoons extra-virgin olive oil, plus more to serve

6 medium garlic cloves, chopped

1 tablespoon minced fresh rosemary OR thyme

1 pound whole-wheat fusilli pasta

Kosher salt and ground black pepper

1½- to 2-pound head cauliflower, trimmed, cored and chopped into ½-inch pieces

1 ounce pecorino Romano OR Parmesan cheese, finely grated (½ cup)

In a large pot, cook the pancetta in the oil, stirring, until crisp; using a slotted spoon, transfer to a plate. Stir the garlic, rosemary, 4 cups water, the pasta and 1 teaspoon salt into the pot. Simmer, stirring, for 5 minutes. Add the cauliflower, cover and cook, stirring occasionally, until the pasta is al dente and the cauliflower is tender, adding water if needed to prevent sticking. Off heat, stir in half the cheese, then season with salt and pepper. Top with the pancetta, the remaining cheese and additional oil.

Optional garnish: Red pepper flakes

Seafood

Recipes

Seafood starts out simple. Cookish means it stays that way.

Seafood cooks fast and typically neither requires nor is improved by elaborate seasoning strategies. Getting the flavors and textures right does require some thought, but happily we had a world of options from which to draw inspiration.

Turkey's balik ekmek, or "fish bread," sold in Istanbul markets, gave us a starting point for our fish-and-tahini sandwich that pairs haddock, warm spices, nutty tahini and creamy yogurt. The Maldivian dish called mas bai served as the springboard for an aromatic one-pot dish of fish and rice—we use the residual heat of the rice to cook the fish, ensuring it stays moist and flavorful. And from Vietnam, we borrowed the technique of cooking pork, chicken or seafood in a savory-sweet caramel sauce—we opted for shrimp.

Sometimes it's a seasoning more than a particular dish that inspires us. In Mexico, we learned to make enchipotlada-style seafood using chipotle chilies in adobo to add smoky spice to tomato sauce. We use it to balance the richness of salmon.

Likewise, Spain's savory-spicy cured chorizo sausage adds chewy texture and flavor to our halibut with chorizo, tomatoes and green olives, and we use the tangy-herbal Middle Eastern spice blend known as za'atar to balance meaty swordfish.

And sometimes we focus on technique. Steaming is a great way to cook flaky fish because the moist heat cooks evenly from all sides, so no need to shift—and risk breaking up—the fillets. The problem with steaming is it can leave seafood tasting bland. So we employ robust seasonings from the Asian pantry like miso and hoisin. We also line the steamer basket with aromatic ingredients, such as lemon slices, which give us extra flavor and the bonus of fillets that don't stick to the bottom. In a twist on steam cooking, we wrap soy sauce-seasoned salmon fillets in foil and cook them on the stovetop in a skillet. For a finishing touch, we pair the fillets with any one of four brightly flavored salads that balance the richness of the salmon.

Salmon in Chipotle-Tomato Sauce

Start to finish: 25 minutes
Servings: 4

This recipe cooks fish fillets enchipotlada style—that is, in a tomato sauce made spicy and smoky by the addition of chipotle chilies in adobo. In Mexican kitchens, pork and shrimp are commonly prepared this way, but we use salmon. Its richness is balanced by the acidity and spiciness of the sauce. Try to purchase center-cut fillets that are of the same thickness so that they cook at the same rate.

2 tablespoons extra-virgin olive oil

3 medium garlic cloves, thinly sliced

1 tablespoon cumin seeds, lightly crushed

14½-ounce can crushed tomatoes

1 tablespoon honey

1 chipotle chili in adobo sauce, chopped, plus ½ teaspoon adobo sauce

Four 6-ounce center-cut salmon fillets

Kosher salt and ground black pepper

In a 12-inch skillet, heat the oil until shimmering. Add the garlic and cook, stirring, until golden. Add the cumin and cook until fragrant. Stir in the tomatoes, honey, chipotle and adobo sauce and ⅓ cup water. Simmer, then add the fillets skin up. Cover and gently simmer until the thickest part of the fillets reaches about 120°F, 6 to 8 minutes. Discard the skin, then transfer the fillets to a platter. Cook the sauce, stirring, until slightly thickened. Season with salt and pepper, then spoon over the salmon.

Optional garnish: Lime wedges OR chopped fresh cilantro OR both

Seared Za'atar Swordfish with Cucumber Salad

Start to finish: 30 minutes
Servings: 4

Swordfish has a sturdy, firm texture that withstands searing in a hot skillet until well browned and nicely crusted. For this recipe, we cut swordfish steaks into large chunks and season them with salt, pepper and za'atar (a Middle Eastern dried herb and spice blend) before placing them in a hot pan. A simple cucumber salad, served as a bed under the fish, counters the swordfish's meatiness with fresh flavor and crisp texture.

1 English cucumber, thinly sliced

1 large shallot, halved and thinly sliced

⅓ cup lightly packed fresh flat-leaf parsley

1 tablespoon red wine vinegar

4 tablespoons extra-virgin olive oil, divided, plus more to serve

5 teaspoons za'atar, divided, plus more to serve

Kosher salt and ground black pepper

1½ pounds swordfish steaks, cut into 1½-inch chunks

In a large bowl, toss the cucumber, shallot, parsley, vinegar, 3 table-spoons oil and 3 teaspoons za'atar, then season with salt and pepper. Transfer to a platter. Season the swordfish with salt and pepper and the remaining 2 teaspoons za'atar. In a 12-inch cast-iron or nonstick skillet, heat the remaining 1 tablespoon oil until shimmering. Add the fish and cook, turning once, until golden on the top and bottom, 3 to 4 minutes per side. Place on top of the salad, then sprinkle with za'atar and drizzle with oil.

Cod Soup with Cilantro, Garlic and Croutons

Start to finish: 30 minutes
Servings: 4

We got the idea for this simple one-pot meal from the Portuguese bread soup called açorda. Traditionally, eggs lend açorda substance and richness. This version gets heft from chunks of tender, buttery cod fillets. Bottled clam juice supplies the broth with a briny-sweet flavor. You'll need a large bunch of cilantro for this recipe; before tossing it into the blender, trim off and discard the bottoms of the stems, then wash and dry the bunch, picking out any damaged sprigs.

1 bunch (about 4 ounces) cilantro

4 medium garlic cloves, smashed and peeled

6 tablespoons extra-virgin olive oil, divided

Kosher salt and ground black pepper

6 ounces crusty bread, sliced ½ inch thick and torn into bite-size pieces (about 4 cups)

Two 8-ounce bottles clam juice

½ teaspoon red pepper flakes

1 pound skinless cod fillets, cut into 1½- to 2-inch chunks

In a blender, puree the cilantro, garlic, 4 tablespoons oil, ¼ cup water, 2 teaspoons salt and ½ teaspoon pepper. In a medium bowl, toss the bread with the remaining 2 tablespoons oil. In a large pot, toast the bread, stirring, until golden. Return the bread to the bowl and toss with 2 tablespoons of cilantro puree. In the pot, stir together 2 cups water, the clam juice, pepper flakes and remaining cilantro puree. Simmer, add the cod and cook, uncovered, until the fish flakes easily. Season with salt and pepper. Serve topped with the croutons.

159

Coconut-Curry Rice with Salmon and Cilantro

Start to finish: 40 minutes (15 minutes active)
Servings: 4

The Maldivian dish called mas bai gave us the idea for this rich, fragrant one-pot fish and rice dish. For ease, we use curry powder instead of a handful of individual spices to deliver both flavor and color. We cut the fish into small chunks and scatter them over the rice immediately after steaming; the rice's residual heat gently cooks the fish so the pieces, even if small, remain moist and flavorful.

3 tablespoons neutral oil OR coconut oil

1 bunch cilantro, chopped, stems and leaves reserved separately

2½ teaspoons curry powder

2 teaspoons finely grated fresh ginger

1½ cups long-grain white rice, rinsed and drained

1 cup coconut milk

Kosher salt and ground black pepper

8 ounces skinless salmon fillet OR tuna steak, cut into ½-inch pieces

In a large saucepan, cook the oil, cilantro stems, curry powder and ginger, stirring, until sizzling and fragrant. Stir in the rice, coconut milk and 1¼ cups water. Bring to a simmer. Cover, reduce to low and cook until the rice is tender and the liquid has been absorbed, 15 to 20 minutes. Uncover and scatter the fish over the rice. Re-cover, remove from the heat and let stand for 8 minutes. Fluff the rice with a fork, mixing in the fish. Stir in the cilantro leaves and season with salt and pepper.

Optional garnish: Lime wedges OR chopped Fresno or jalapeño chilies OR toasted unsweetened coconut OR a combination

Steamed Clams with Corn, Fennel and Crème Fraîche

Start to finish: 30 minutes
Servings: 4

Think of this as a chowder for eating with your fingers. Finished with a small measure of crème fraîche (or whole-milk yogurt), the briny-sweet liquid released by the clams becomes a subtly creamy broth that's as delicious as the clams themselves. If you can, use corn kernels cut from freshly shucked ears (you'll need two good-sized ears to get the 2 cups kernels called for in the recipe), but frozen corn works in the off-season. Serve with oyster crackers or with crusty bread for mopping up the broth.

2 tablespoons extra-virgin olive oil

1 medium fennel bulb, halved, cored and thinly sliced

1 medium yellow onion, halved and thinly sliced

2 teaspoons fennel seeds

Kosher salt and ground black pepper

2 cups corn kernels

2 pounds hard-shell clams (about 1½ inches diameter), such as littleneck or Manila, scrubbed

¼ cup crème fraîche OR plain whole-milk yogurt

In a Dutch oven, heat the oil until shimmering. Add the fennel, onion, fennel seeds and a pinch of salt, then cook, stirring, until the vegetables are lightly browned. Stir in the corn and 1 cup water. Bring to a boil and add the clams. Cover and cook over medium, stirring once or twice, until the clams have opened. Stir once more, then remove and discard any clams that haven't opened. Off heat, stir in the crème fraîche and ½ teaspoon pepper. Season with salt.

Optional garnish: Hot sauce OR chopped fresh flat-leaf parsley OR lemon wedges OR a combination

Fish Sandwiches with Tahini and Yogurt

Start to finish: 15 minutes
Servings: 4

For these easy fish sandwiches, we broil haddock fillets until tender and flaky. Haddock is lean and mild, so to boost flavor, we first season it with olive oil mixed with aromatic coriander and cumin. And to add richness, the toasted rolls are spread with a mixture of yogurt, tahini and additional spices. Leafy greens, sliced tomato, shaved red onion and fresh flat-leaf parsley are all delicious additions for these sandwiches.

½ cup plain whole-milk yogurt

¼ cup tahini

2 teaspoons ground coriander, divided

1½ teaspoons ground cumin, divided

Kosher salt and ground black pepper

2 tablespoons extra-virgin olive oil

Four 4-ounce skinless haddock fillets

4 French rolls OR Kaiser rolls, toasted

Heat the broiler with a rack about 4 inches from the element. Mix the yogurt, tahini, ½ teaspoon coriander, ½ teaspoon cumin and ½ teaspoon salt; set aside. In another bowl, mix the oil with the remaining 1½ teaspoons coriander, the remaining 1 teaspoon cumin, ½ teaspoon salt and 1 teaspoon pepper. Place the fillets on a wire rack set over a broiler-safe rimmed baking sheet, then brush with the spiced oil. Broil until the fish flakes easily, about 4 minutes. Serve on toasted rolls spread with the yogurt-tahini mixture.

Steamed Fish

Steaming is an ideal cooking method for mild, flaky white fish. Moist heat surrounds the fish, cooking it from all sides so that there's no need to move the delicate fillets. We line the steamer basket with ingredients that prevent the fish from sticking while also lending flavor. We prefer 1-inch-thick fillets of cod, haddock or halibut for this steaming technique.

Top left: Steamed Fish with Ginger and Shiitake Mushrooms; Bottom Left: Steamed Fish with Miso and Scallions; Top right: Steamed Fish with Hoisin, Cilantro and Orange

Steamed Fish with Miso and Scallions

Start to finish: 20 minutes
Servings: 4

Salty, subtly sweet white miso mixed with umami-rich soy sauce and pungent scallions add plenty of flavor to lean, mild white fish. We use lemon slices to line the steamer basket; they lend citrusy brightness without overwhelming with acidity.

¼ cup white miso

1 bunch scallions, thinly sliced, white and green parts reserved separately

2 tablespoons neutral oil

2 tablespoons honey

2 tablespoons low-sodium soy sauce

Four 6-ounce cod OR haddock OR halibut fillets (about 1 inch thick)

2 lemons, thinly sliced

In a large, shallow bowl, mix the miso, scallion whites, oil, honey and soy sauce. Add the fillets and turn to coat. Fill a Dutch oven with about 1 inch of water, cover and bring to a simmer. Line a steamer basket with half the lemon slices, place the fillets on top and lay the remaining lemon slices over the fish. Place the basket in the pot, cover, reduce to medium and steam until the fish flakes easily, about 10 minutes. Using a wide spatula, transfer the fish to a platter. Sprinkle with scallion greens.

Optional garnish: Toasted sesame seeds

Steamed Fish with Ginger and Shiitake Mushrooms

Start to finish: 20 minutes
Servings: 4

This recipe layers on the umami: fresh shiitake mushrooms under the fish, a ginger-soy mixture brushed onto the fillets, and sliced prosciutto placed on top. Prosciutto may seem like an odd ingredient here—it's an easy-to-find substitute for Chinese-style dry-cured ham.

2 tablespoons soy sauce, plus more to serve

2 tablespoons toasted sesame oil

1 tablespoon grated fresh ginger

8 ounces shiitake mushrooms, stemmed

Four 6-ounce cod OR haddock OR halibut fillets (about 1 inch thick)

Kosher salt and ground black pepper

4 slices prosciutto

In a small bowl, mix the soy sauce, sesame oil and ginger. Fill a Dutch oven with about 1 inch of water, cover and bring to a simmer. Arrange the mushrooms gills up in a steamer basket and place the fillets on top. Season the fish with salt and pepper, then spoon on all of the soy mixture. Lay a slice of prosciutto on each fillet. Place the steamer basket in the pot, cover, reduce to medium and steam until the fish flakes easily, about 10 minutes. Using a wide spatula, transfer the fish and mushrooms to a platter. Serve with additional soy sauce.

Optional garnish: Thinly sliced scallions

Steamed Fish with Hoisin, Cilantro and Orange

Start to finish: 20 minutes
Servings: 4

In this recipe, we balance the sweetness of hoisin with herbal cilantro, the sharpness of fresh ginger and the tang of rice vinegar. Grated orange zest in the flavoring paste and orange slices as liners for the steaming basket perk up the flavors. Be sure to grate the zest from the oranges before slicing them.

1 cup lightly packed fresh cilantro, chopped, plus more to serve

3 tablespoons hoisin sauce

2 tablespoons finely grated fresh ginger

1 tablespoon grated zest from 2 oranges, oranges thinly sliced

1 tablespoon neutral oil

2 teaspoons unseasoned rice vinegar

Ground black pepper

Four 6-ounce cod OR haddock OR halibut fillets (about 1 inch thick)

In a large shallow bowl, mix the cilantro, hoisin, ginger, orange zest, oil, vinegar and ½ teaspoon pepper. Add the fillets and turn to coat. Fill a Dutch oven with about 1 inch of water, cover and bring to a simmer. Line a steamer basket with half the orange slices, place the fillets on top and lay the remaining orange slices on the fish. Place the basket in the pot, cover, reduce to medium and steam until the fish flakes easily, about 10 minutes. Using a wide spatula, transfer the fish to a platter. Sprinkle with additional cilantro.

Optional garnish: Toasted sesame oil

Pasta with Shrimp and Browned Butter

Start to finish: 20 minutes
Servings: 4

We build big flavor into this dish by cooking tagliatelle or pappardelle—dried pastas made with egg—in a skillet, directly in the liquid that becomes the pasta sauce. The noodles' delicate texture pairs perfectly with sweet, briny shrimp and the nuttiness of browned butter. Use large or extra-large shrimp so they remain tender and plump. Red pepper flakes and lemon juice brighten and balance the richness of this dish.

6 tablespoons salted butter, cut into 1-tablespoon pieces, divided

1½ pounds large (26/30 per pound) or extra-large (21/25 per pound) shrimp, peeled, deveined and patted dry

Kosher salt and ground black pepper

Red pepper flakes

8 ounces dried tagliatelle OR pappardelle pasta

4 scallions, cut into 1-inch lengths

Juice of 2 lemons

In a 12-inch skillet, melt 2 tablespoons butter. Add the shrimp and sprinkle with salt and black pepper. Cook without stirring until browned on the bottom; transfer to a bowl. In the same skillet, cook the remaining 4 tablespoons butter, stirring often, until browned. Add 3 cups water, a pinch of pepper flakes and salt and black pepper, then bring to a simmer. Add the pasta, cover and cook, stirring occasionally, until al dente. Uncover and continue to cook until the liquid reduces slightly, then stir in the scallions and shrimp; cook for another minute. Off heat, stir in the lemon juice, then season with salt, black pepper and pepper flakes.

SEAFOOD

Foil-Wrapped Salmon

Start to finish: 35 minutes
Servings: 4

This unusual cooking method for salmon ensures moist, evenly cooked fillets cooked to medium doneness, but doesn't make a mess on the stovetop, nor does it require firing up the oven. A quick marination in soy sauce helps season the fish throughout. Fillets that are 1 to 1¼ inches thick work best; if yours are thinner or thicker, or if you prefer your salmon rarer or more fully cooked than medium, adjust the cooking time down or up, respectively. While the salmon marinates, prepare a fresh, colorful salad for serving alongside (recipes follow).

Four 6-ounce center-cut salmon fillets (1 to 1¼ inches thick)

¼ cup soy sauce

Neutral oil

Ground black pepper

In a pie plate, marinate the fillets, skin up, in the soy for 15 minutes. Heat a 12-inch skillet over high for 5 minutes. Place the salmon skin down on a lightly oiled 18-inch sheet of heavy-duty foil. Drizzle with oil and sprinkle with pepper. Cover with another sheet of foil and crimp the edges. Set the packet in the skillet, reduce to medium-high and cook for 5 minutes, rotating the pan. Remove the packet and cool for 5 minutes before opening carefully.

Avocado and Cilantro Salad

In a medium bowl, whisk 3 tablespoons extra-virgin olive oil and 2 teaspoons Dijon mustard. Add ¼ cup pickled sweet peppers (patted dry and thinly sliced) plus 1 tablespoon pickling liquid, 1 ripe avocado (halved, pitted, peeled and thinly sliced) and 2 cups lightly packed fresh cilantro. Toss to combine, then season with salt and pepper.

Apple, Carrot and Horseradish Salad

In a medium bowl, mix 3 tablespoons extra-virgin olive oil and 2 tablespoons prepared horseradish. Add 1 large carrot (peeled and shredded on the large holes of a box grater), 1 medium Granny Smith apple (unpeeled, cored and shredded on the large holes of a box grater) and 2 tablespoons poppy seeds. Toss to combine, then season with salt and pepper.

Cucumber and Scallion Salad

In a medium bowl, whisk 3 tablespoons neutral oil and 3 tablespoons unseasoned rice vinegar. Add 1 English cucumber (halved, seeded and shredded on the large holes of a box grater), 4 scallions (thinly sliced on the diagonal) and ¼ cup unsweetened wide-flake coconut (toasted). Toss to combine, then season with salt and pepper.

Fresh Fennel and Herb Salad

In a medium bowl, whisk 3 tablespoons extra-virgin olive oil, 2 tablespoons unseasoned rice vinegar, 2 teaspoons white miso and 1 teaspoon white sugar. Add 1 large fennel bulb (trimmed, halved lengthwise, cored and thinly sliced crosswise) and ½ cup lightly packed chopped fresh tarragon OR mint OR basil. Toss to combine, then season with salt and pepper.

171

Broiled Caribbean Mahi Mahi

Start to finish: 20 minutes
Servings: 4

This recipe was inspired by the grilled wahoo we learned to make in Barbados. To simplify prep, we narrowed the long list of herbs and aromatics used to season the fish to just scallions and fresh thyme. And instead of a pre-grill marinade, we keep the flavors clean and bright by finishing the fish with a vibrant sauce. Mahi mahi is a widely available stand-in for hard-to-find wahoo; you also can use grouper or snapper fillets. Rice and beans are excellent accompaniments.

4 scallions, minced

1½ tablespoons chopped fresh thyme

1 tablespoon grated lime zest, plus
2 tablespoons lime juice

¼ teaspoon ground allspice

3 tablespoons neutral oil, divided

Kosher salt and ground black pepper

1 tablespoon packed brown sugar

Four 6-ounce mahi mahi fillets
(about 1 inch thick), patted dry

Heat the broiler with a rack 6 inches from the element. Whisk together the scallions, thyme, lime zest and juice, allspice, 1 tablespoon of oil and ½ teaspoon each salt and pepper; set aside. In a pie plate, mix the sugar, 1 teaspoon salt, ½ teaspoon pepper and remaining 2 tablespoons oil; add the fish and turn to coat. Place the fillets on an oiled, broiler-safe rimmed baking sheet and broil until lightly browned at the edges, about 5 minutes, rotating about halfway through. Transfer to a platter. Spoon the herb-oil mixture over the fish.

Optional garnish: Fresno chilies, stemmed, seeded and minced

Spanish-Style Tuna Salad

Start to finish: 15 minutes
Servings: 4

This mayonnaise-free tuna salad was inspired by the colorful mixed vegetable and tuna salads served in Spain. For the richest flavor and silkiest texture, use good-quality tuna packed in olive oil. Our favorite widely available brands are Wild Planet and Genova. Serve the tuna over greens, with some or all of the optional garnishes.

2 tablespoons plus ⅓ cup extra-virgin olive oil, divided

2 medium shallots, finely chopped

1 tablespoon sweet paprika

¼ cup lemon juice

2 tablespoons Dijon mustard

Kosher salt and ground black pepper

Three 5-ounce cans olive oil-packed tuna, drained

1 cup pimento-stuffed green olives, chopped

In a small microwave-safe bowl, combine 2 tablespoons oil, the shallots and paprika. Cover and microwave on high until the shallots are sizzling, about 30 seconds; let cool. In a large bowl, whisk the remaining ⅓ cup oil, lemon juice, mustard and 1 teaspoon pepper, then stir in the cooled shallot-oil mixture. Fold in the tuna and olives. Taste and season with salt.

Optional garnish: Hard-cooked eggs, quartered, **OR** cherry or grape tomatoes, halved **OR** drained capers **OR** chopped fresh flat-leaf parsley **OR** lemon wedges **OR** a combination

Halibut with Chorizo, Tomatoes and Green Olives

Start to finish: 20 minutes
Servings: 4

Bold Spanish ingredients lend loads of smoky, briny, woodsy flavor to mild-tasting, firm but flaky halibut fillets. If you prefer, use cod instead. Either way, look for fillets that are at least 1 inch thick so they remain moist and flavorful and don't overcook. Serve with warm, crusty bread.

Four 6-ounce skinless halibut OR cod fillets (see note)

Kosher salt and ground black pepper

2 tablespoons extra-virgin olive oil, plus more to serve

1 cup cherry OR grape tomatoes

½ cup pitted green olives, chopped

2 ounces Spanish chorizo, thinly sliced

2 teaspoons chopped fresh thyme

2 tablespoons sherry vinegar

Season the fish with salt and pepper. In a 12-inch nonstick skillet, heat the oil until shimmering. Add the tomatoes, cover and cook, stirring occasionally, until they begin to split. Stir in the olives, chorizo and thyme, then cook until fragrant. Nestle the fish in the tomato mixture, cover and cook until it flakes easily, about 5 minutes. Transfer the fillets to a platter. Stir the vinegar into the sauce, then season with salt and pepper. Spoon the sauce over the fish and drizzle with additional oil.

Optional garnish: Chopped fresh flat-leaf parsley

Curried Shrimp Cakes

Start to finish: 20 minutes
Servings: 4

For these flavorful pan-fried shrimp cakes, look for shrimp that are free of sodium tripolyphosphate, a preservative that affects texture and adds salinity. If you purchase packaged frozen shrimp, check the ingredients on the label; if you purchase shrimp from the seafood counter, ask the fishmonger. As you form the shrimp mixture into patties, lightly moisten your hands with water to help prevent sticking. We like to serve these tucked into warm naan, with lettuce leaves for wrapping or on a leafy salad.

1 cup panko breadcrumbs

1½ pounds large (26/30 per pound) or medium (41/50 per pound) shrimp, peeled (tails removed) and deveined

2 tablespoons mayonnaise

¼ cup chopped fresh cilantro, plus more to serve

1 tablespoon hot sauce, plus more to serve

2 teaspoons curry powder

¼ cup neutral oil

In a food processor, process the panko to fine crumbs, then transfer to a large plate. Add half the shrimp to the processor and finely chop. Add the mayonnaise and remaining shrimp, then pulse until the second batch are roughly chopped. Transfer to a medium bowl and stir in the cilantro, hot sauce and curry powder. Form into four patties and coat with the panko. In a 12-inch nonstick skillet over medium, heat the oil until shimmering. Add the cakes and cook until golden on both sides. Serve sprinkled with cilantro and hot sauce.

Optional garnish: Chutney OR thinly sliced cucumber OR lemon wedges OR a combination

Seared Salmon with Chilies, Pickled Ginger and Snap Peas

Start to finish: 40 minutes
(25 minutes active)
Servings: 4

Briefly marinating salmon fillets in soy sauce adds seasoning and helps with browning. The sharp notes of sliced fresh chilies and pickled ginger (the type served with sushi) offset the fattiness of the fish. Snap or snow peas add color and crunch, and also turn this into a one-pan meal. When shopping, try to choose salmon fillets of the same thickness so they all cook at the same rate. This recipe yields medium-rare salmon (the centers are about 120°F); if you prefer yours a little more cooked through, after flipping the fillets, leave them in the pan for a minute or two longer.

**Four 6-ounce center-cut salmon fillets
(1 to 1¼ inches thick)**

¼ cup plus 1 tablespoon soy sauce

Ground black pepper

1 tablespoon neutral oil

**8 ounces sugar snap peas
OR snow peas, trimmed**

2 Fresno OR jalapeño chilies, stemmed, seeded and thinly sliced

½ cup chopped fresh mint OR thinly sliced scallions

¼ cup drained pickled ginger, chopped

In a pie plate, marinate the fillets, skin up, in ¼ cup soy sauce for 15 minutes. Remove the fillets, pat dry and sprinkle with pepper. In a 12-inch nonstick skillet over medium-high, heat the oil until barely smoking. Add the salmon skin up, reduce to medium and cook until well browned, about 6 minutes. Flip, cover, reduce to low and cook for 6 to 8 minutes. Transfer to a platter. Add the peas and chilies to the pan and cook over high, stirring, just until the peas are blistered. Off heat, stir in the mint, ginger and remaining 1 tablespoon soy sauce, then pour over the salmon.

Optional garnish: Toasted black or white sesame seeds OR chili oil

Mussels with Fregola, Tomatoes and Capers

Start to finish: 40 minutes (15 minutes active)
Servings: 4

Fregola is a tiny, pellet-shaped Sicilian pasta that cooks up with a nutty, wheaty flavor and distinctive chewiness. It resembles pearl couscous. In fact, pearl couscous is a reasonable substitute if fregola is not available, but keep in mind couscous cooks faster by a few minutes. Serve with crusty bread for soaking up the broth.

¼ cup extra-virgin olive oil

1 pint cherry OR grape tomatoes

½ cup dry white wine

½ cup fregola (see note)

¼ cup drained capers

½ teaspoon red pepper flakes, plus more to serve

Ground black pepper

2 pounds mussels, scrubbed

In a large Dutch oven over medium, cook the oil and tomatoes, covered and stirring once or twice, until the tomatoes burst. Add 1½ cups water, the wine, fregola, capers, pepper flakes and ½ teaspoon black pepper. Bring to a simmer, cover and cook, stirring occasionally, until the fregola is tender, 10 to 15 minutes. Bring to a boil and stir in the mussels. Cover and cook until the mussels just begin to open. Remove from the heat and let stand, covered, for 3 to 5 minutes, quickly stirring once halfway through. Remove and discard any mussels that haven't opened.

Optional garnish: Chopped fresh basil

Seared Scallop and Arugula Salad with Pomegranate Vinaigrette

Start to finish: 15 minutes
Servings: 4

Done right, scallops are deliciously rich and buttery. In this recipe, we sear them in a hot skillet and serve them on a salad that complements the scallops' natural sweetness and luxurious texture. Success depends on using "dry" sea scallops, ones that have not been treated with sodium tripolyphosphate, a chemical that forces water absorption. If purchasing frozen, check the ingredients on the label; at the seafood counter, make sure the scallops are not sitting in a pool of liquid, or inquire with the fishmonger. Another tell is color: dry scallops have a pale coral hue, whereas treated scallops are stark white.

1 pound dry jumbo sea scallops, patted dry, side tendons removed

Kosher salt and ground black pepper

2 tablespoons plus ¼ cup extra-virgin olive oil

¼ cup pomegranate molasses

5-ounce container baby arugula

½ medium red onion, thinly sliced

1 sweet, crisp apple (such as Honeycrisp), halved, cored and thinly sliced

½ cup chopped toasted hazelnuts OR pecans OR walnuts

Season the scallops with salt and pepper. In a 12-inch nonstick skillet, heat 2 tablespoons oil until barely smoking. Add the scallops and cook undisturbed until well browned. Flip and cook 1 to 2 minutes. Transfer to a plate. In a small bowl, whisk the remaining ¼ cup oil, the molasses and any accumulated juices from the scallops. In a large bowl, toss the arugula, onion, apple and nuts with half the dressing, 1 teaspoon salt and ½ teaspoon pepper; transfer to a platter. Arrange the scallops on top and drizzle with remaining dressing.

Optional garnish: Pomegranate seeds

Vietnamese-Style Caramel Shrimp

Start to finish: 25 minutes
Servings: 4

The classic Vietnamese method of cooking pork, chicken or fatty fish in a savory-sweet caramel sauce produces deep, umami-rich flavors. In this recipe, we apply the technique to shrimp. We liked the dish when made with both shallots and garlic, as well as with ginger and lemon grass, so use all those ingredients if you have them on hand. Serve with steamed jasmine rice and a stir-fried vegetable to round out the meal.

¼ cup white sugar

3 tablespoons fish sauce

1 or 2 Fresno **OR** serrano chilies, stemmed and sliced into thin rings

2 medium shallots, thinly sliced **OR** 4 medium garlic cloves, minced **OR** both

2 teaspoons finely chopped fresh ginger **OR** 1 lemon grass stalk, trimmed to the bottom 6 inches, bruised **OR** both

Ground black pepper

1½ pounds extra-large (21/25 per pound) shrimp, peeled (tails removed) and deveined

In a 12-inch skillet, combine the sugar and 2 table-spoons water. Cook over medium-high, occasionally swirling the pan, until the caramel is mahogany in color and smokes lightly. Off heat, add the fish sauce. Bring to a boil, stirring to dissolve any clumps, then add the chilies, shallots, ginger and ½ teaspoon pepper. Bring to a simmer and cook, stirring, for about 30 seconds. Add the shrimp and cook over high, stirring, just until opaque. Remove and discard the lemon grass, if used.

Optional garnish: Sliced scallions **OR** lime wedges **OR** both

Chicken

Recipes

For the best throw-it-together chicken, we add texture and flavor—but not effort.

We look for techniques that heighten flavor, such as broiling lemons alongside the chicken in our Moroccan-style skewers. Getting some char on the lemons before juicing them over the meat mellows their sharpness and acidity, adding a subtle sweetness to the sauce. Likewise, we use toasted walnuts to add both savory depth and crunch to our chicken salad with leafy greens. A splash of oil is a great way to bring the richness of long-cooked meat to a quick-cooking lean cut, such as chicken breast. We do this in our pulled chicken; oil and cilantro leaves go in at the end of cooking. In our stir-fried red curry, a glug of coconut oil is added up front.

Mild chicken pairs perfectly with assertive seasonings, so we search out ingredients that deliver one-stroke flavor solutions, like the red pepper jelly that livens up the rotisserie chicken in our chicken and bean salad or the garam masala spice mix that adds quick and complex flavor to our spicy ground chicken with currants. And we find ways to punch up the flavor of pantry staples. On their own, store-bought mayonnaise, ketchup and spicy Sriracha sauce are fine, but together they're bright and tangy, one of several flavor hacks we came up with for dipping sauces to pair with our crisp chicken cutlets.

Figuring out how to apply seasonings is important, too. We're always on the lookout for ways to get the most flavor from our ingredients while also really driving the seasonings into the chicken. We follow the lead of Andrea Nguyen, author of several cookbooks including "Vietnamese Food Any Day," and slash chicken legs to the bone so spices and other flavors permeate. In another flavor-boosting tactic, we do as "Season" author Nik Sharma does and slide seasonings directly under the skin where they stay put and have better contact with the meat.

Boneless, skinless chicken cuts lend themselves easily to casual cooking, but there's room for the whole bird, too. Our oven-roasted chicken and potato dish is cooked in an oven-safe skillet (the low sides promote good browning). Once the chicken's done, we take it out and transfer the pan to the stovetop. The drippings easily reduce, and the addition of lemon juice, tapenade and chopped oregano creates rich, complex flavor with stir-together ease.

Moroccan Chicken Skewers

Start to finish: 30 minutes
Servings: 4 to 6

These broiled chicken skewers are finished with the juice of charred lemon halves that have been drizzled with honey, along with a sprinkle of fresh herbs. Cilantro, flat-leaf parsley or mint are good choices, alone or in combination.

Grated zest and juice of 1 lemon, plus 2 lemons, halved

¼ cup extra-virgin olive oil

2 tablespoons honey, plus more for drizzling

1 tablespoon finely grated fresh ginger

2 tablespoons ground coriander OR cumin OR 1 tablespoon of each

Kosher salt and ground black pepper

2 pounds boneless, skinless chicken thighs, halved lengthwise

Fresh cilantro OR mint OR flat-leaf parsley, chopped

Heat the broiler with a rack 4 inches from the element. In a medium bowl, mix the lemon zest and juice, oil, honey, ginger, spices, 2 teaspoons salt and 1 teaspoon pepper; set aside 2 tablespoons. Toss the chicken with the remaining mixture. Scrunch the chicken onto metal skewers, then place on a foil-lined rimmed baking sheet. Add the 4 lemon halves. Broil until charred, about 12 minutes, flipping halfway through. Spoon the reserved lemon-oil mixture over the chicken. Sprinkle with herbs. Drizzle the lemon halves with honey and serve alongside for squeezing over the chicken.

Chicken Salad with Red Cabbage and Miso

Start to finish: 20 minutes
Servings: 4

For this simple chicken salad, miso (or soy sauce) lends savory depth to the mayo-based dressing while shredded red cabbage adds both crunch and color. For ease, use a store-bought rotisserie chicken; it will yield enough shredded meat for this recipe. Pile the salad onto leafy greens or a bowl of warm rice. This recipe can easily be scaled up or down.

3 tablespoons mayonnaise

5 teaspoons white miso OR soy sauce

5 teaspoons unseasoned rice vinegar OR chili-garlic sauce

4 teaspoons neutral oil

3 cups shredded cooked chicken

2 cups shredded red cabbage

1½ cups lightly packed fresh cilantro, chopped OR 4 scallions, thinly sliced

Kosher salt

In a large bowl, whisk together the mayonnaise, miso, vinegar and oil. Add the chicken, cabbage and cilantro, then toss. Season with salt. Serve at room temperature or cover, refrigerate and serve chilled.

Optional garnish: Toasted sesame seeds OR a drizzle of toasted sesame oil

185

Chicken and Bean Salad with Pepper Jelly Vinaigrette

Start to finish: 20 minutes
Servings: 4

This substantial, flavor-packed chicken salad can be on the table in under 30 minutes. An average-size store-bought rotisserie bird will yield enough shredded chicken for this recipe. To be efficient, shred the meat while the beans soak for 10 minutes in the dressing. The salad is especially good on top of leafy greens or served with a hunk of cornbread.

1 bunch scallions, thinly sliced
OR ½ red onion, thinly sliced

⅓ cup red pepper jelly

2 tablespoons white vinegar OR hot sauce

2 tablespoons neutral oil

Kosher salt and ground black pepper

15½-ounce can black-eyed peas OR kidney beans
OR black beans, rinsed and drained

3 cups shredded cooked chicken

In a large bowl, stir together the scallions, jelly, vinegar, oil and a pinch each of salt and pepper. Add the beans, stir and let stand for about 10 minutes. Stir in the chicken, then season with salt and pepper.

Chicken and Leafy Greens with Lemon-Dill Vinaigrette

Start to finish: 20 minutes
Servings: 4

Made with the meat from a store-bought rotisserie chicken, this satisfying salad comes together quickly and easily. Toasted walnuts not only lend richness and texture, they also add umami, making the flavors fuller and more complex. Steeping the chopped onion for a few minutes in lemon juice tempers their harshness, so don't skip this step.

1 tablespoon grated lemon zest, plus ¼ cup lemon juice

½ medium red onion, finely chopped

Kosher salt and ground black pepper

⅓ cup extra-virgin olive oil

½ cup walnuts, toasted and finely chopped

3 tablespoons finely chopped fresh dill

3 cups shredded cooked chicken

5-ounce container baby arugula OR baby spinach OR mixed greens

In a large bowl, combine the lemon juice and onion; let stand for 10 minutes. Add 1 teaspoon salt and ½ teaspoon pepper, then whisk in the oil. Stir in the walnuts, dill and lemon zest. Add the chicken and greens, then toss. Season with salt and pepper.

Optional garnish: Thinly sliced radishes

Spiced Ground Chicken with Currants and Pistachios

Start to finish: 25 minutes
Servings: 4

Ground or minced meat with aromatic spices is common to cuisines across the globe. Take, for instance, Latin American picadillo, Indian keema and all-American chili. Store-bought spice blends pack tons of flavor—and plenty of convenience—in a single jar. For this dish, we use either garam masala or za'atar to robustly season mild-tasting ground chicken. Serve with warm flatbread alongside.

1 pound ground chicken

¼ cup dried currants OR dried cranberries

2 tablespoons tomato paste

1 tablespoon garam masala OR za'atar, plus more to serve

Kosher salt and ground black pepper

2 tablespoons extra-virgin olive oil, plus more to serve

¼ cup roasted pistachios OR toasted slivered almonds OR toasted pine nuts

In a large skillet, combine the chicken, currants, tomato paste and garam masala. Season with salt and pepper, add enough water to barely cover the mixture, then drizzle with the oil. Simmer, uncovered and stirring occasionally to break up the meat, until the chicken is tender and the mixture is saucy. Season with salt, pepper and additional garam masala. Serve sprinkled with nuts and drizzled with oil.

Optional garnish: Sliced radishes OR baby arugula OR both

Poaching

Chinese cooks gently poach whole chickens in liquid flavored with a few aromatics to yield moist, tender meat. To make the approach a little easier, we use boneless, skinless chicken breasts and cut back on the liquid for concentrated flavor that becomes the basis for a simple sauce. We get the same tenderness minus the hassle of deboning the finished chicken.

Pictured: Sake and Citrus-Poached
Chicken with Miso Sauce

Cider-Poached Chicken with Mustard and Thyme

Start to finish: 30 minutes
Servings: 4 to 6

Hard cider adds a delicate fruitiness to poached chicken breasts but without the cloying sweetness of fresh cider or apple juice. Fresh thyme, garlic and mustard are perfect flavor companions to the cider, as are toasted walnuts. Serve this autumnal dish with roasted root vegetables and warm, crusty bread.

16-ounce can hard cider

4 large thyme sprigs, plus 1 tablespoon finely chopped fresh thyme

3 medium garlic cloves, smashed and peeled OR 4 scallions, cut into 1-inch lengths

Kosher salt and ground black pepper

2 pounds boneless, skinless chicken breasts, pounded ½ inch thick

3 tablespoons whole-grain mustard

2 tablespoons neutral oil

Chopped toasted walnuts, to serve

In a 12-inch skillet, simmer 2 cups water, the cider, thyme sprigs, garlic and 1 tablespoon salt. Add the chicken, cover and cook at a bare simmer until the chicken is opaque throughout, about 18 minutes; flip the breasts once halfway through. Transfer the chicken to a platter. Strain ¼ cup poaching liquid into a small bowl, then stir in the mustard, oil and chopped thyme; season with salt and pepper. Slice the chicken and serve sprinkled with walnuts and with the sauce.

Optional garnish: Chopped fresh flat-leaf parsley OR fresh tarragon

Coconut and Lemon Grass-Poached Chicken

Start to finish: 30 minutes
Servings: 4 to 6

Lean, mild chicken breasts get richness and subtle flavor and spiciness when poached in coconut milk infused with lemon grass and fresh chilies. If you wish to tone down or play up the chili heat, decrease or increase the amount of minced chili that goes into the sauce rather than adjust the halved chilies in the poaching liquid. Serve the chicken with rice and simple stir-fried vegetables.

14-ounce can coconut milk

3 stalks fresh lemon grass, trimmed to the bottom 6 inches and bruised

3 serrano chilies, halved, plus 1 serrano chili, stemmed, seeded and minced

Kosher salt and ground black pepper

2 pounds boneless, skinless chicken breasts, pounded ½ inch thick

2 tablespoons fish sauce

1 teaspoon grated lime zest, plus 3 tablespoons lime juice

Set aside 1 tablespoon of coconut milk. In a 12-inch skillet, simmer 2 cups water, the remaining coconut milk, lemon grass, halved chilies and 1 tablespoon salt. Add the chicken, cover and cook at a bare simmer until the chicken is opaque throughout, about 18 minutes; flip the breasts once halfway through. Transfer the chicken to a platter. Strain 3 tablespoons poaching liquid into the reserved coconut milk, then stir in the minced chili, fish sauce and lime juice and zest; season with salt and pepper. Slice and serve the chicken with the sauce.

Optional garnish: Chopped fresh cilantro OR thinly sliced scallions

Lager-Poached Chicken with Chipotle Sauce

Start to finish: 30 minutes
Servings: 4 to 6

Smoky, spicy chipotle chilies and earthy cumin simmer in lager to create a flavorful poaching liquid for chicken breasts. There's no need to seek out a craft brew for this—a 16-ounce can of Coors or Budweiser works just fine. We mix a few tablespoons of the poaching liquid with sour cream (or mayonnaise) to make a rich sauce. Serve with beans and rice or a fresh, crunchy salad.

16-ounce can lager beer (see note)

1½ teaspoons cumin seeds, toasted and lightly crushed

2 chipotle chilies in adobo sauce, torn, plus 4 teaspoons adobo sauce

Kosher salt and ground black pepper

2 pounds boneless, skinless chicken breasts, pounded ½ inch thick

2 tablespoons sour cream OR mayonnaise

1 teaspoon grated lime zest, plus 2 teaspoons lime juice, plus lime wedges to serve

In a 12-inch skillet, simmer 2 cups water, the beer, 1 teaspoon of cumin, the chilies and 1 tablespoon salt. Add the chicken, cover and cook at a bare simmer until the chicken is opaque throughout, about 18 minutes; flip the chicken once halfway through. Transfer the chicken to a platter. Strain 3 tablespoons poaching liquid into a small bowl, then stir in the sour cream, adobo sauce, remaining cumin and lime zest and juice; season with salt and pepper. Serve the chicken with the sauce and lime wedges.

Optional garnish: Roughly chopped fresh cilantro OR chopped fresh chives OR diced avocado

Sake and Citrus-Poached Chicken with Miso Sauce

Start to finish: 30 minutes
Servings: 4 to 6

The clean, delicate notes of sake and the brightness of citrus are ideal for chicken breasts. Savory-sweet furikake, a Japanese nori, sesame and bonito seasoning blend typically sprinkled on rice, is a delicious garnish for this dish, but toasted sesame seeds are excellent, too. Serve with rice and a lightly dressed slaw. Use freshly squeezed lemon or lime juice in this recipe; the juiced halves are used in the poaching liquid.

2 cups sake

3 tablespoons lemon juice OR lime juice, juiced halves reserved (see note)

3 medium garlic cloves, smashed and peeled OR 4 scallions, cut into 1-inch lengths

Kosher salt and ground black pepper

2 pounds boneless, skinless chicken breasts, pounded ½ inch thick

2 tablespoons white miso OR red miso

2 tablespoons neutral oil

Furikake OR toasted sesame seeds, to serve

In a 12-inch skillet, simmer 2 cups water, the sake, the juiced lemon halves, garlic and 1 tablespoon salt. Add the chicken, cover and cook at a bare simmer until the chicken is opaque throughout, about 18 minutes; flip the breasts once halfway through. Transfer the chicken to a platter. Strain ¼ cup poaching liquid into a small bowl, then whisk in the miso, oil and lemon juice; season with salt and pepper. Serve the chicken sprinkled with furikake and with the sauce.

CHICKEN

193

Vietnamese-Style Chicken Meatballs

Start to finish: 25 minutes
Makes 15 to 18 meatballs

These flavor-packed, quick-and-easy meatballs were inspired by traditional Vietnamese pork meatballs. They can be served with lettuce leaves for wrapping, piled onto cooked rice to make rice bowls, added to Southeast Asian soups or tucked into a baguette with pickled vegetables and a smear of mayo. The meatballs also make great appetizers. The recipe doubles easily, but form and cook the meatballs in two batches.

3 tablespoons neutral oil, divided

1 pound ground chicken

1 scallion, minced OR 1 medium garlic clove, minced

¼ cup lightly packed fresh cilantro, finely chopped
OR ¼ cup lightly packed fresh mint, finely chopped

1 serrano chili, stemmed, seeded and minced
OR 1 tablespoon finely grated fresh ginger

Grated zest of 1 lime

4 teaspoons fish sauce

¼ teaspoon ground black pepper

In a 12-inch nonstick skillet, swirl together 2 tablespoons oil and 2 tablespoons water. In a medium bowl, combine all remaining ingredients. Mix with your hands, then shape into ping-pong sized balls and place in the skillet. Heat over medium-high until simmering, then cover and cook until the outsides are no longer pink. Uncover and cook without stirring until deeply browned. Stir and cook, stirring occasionally, until well browned.

Optional garnish: Sweet chili sauce

Chicken and Orzo Soup with Garlic and Paprika

Start to finish: 40 minutes (15 minutes active)
Servings: 4

For this simple Turkish-inspired soup, browning a generous amount of tomato paste with chopped garlic builds a complex, deeply savory base. Sweet paprika lends bold color and earthy notes and dried mint infuses the dish with its unique herbaceousness. Simmering the orzo in the broth after the chicken is fully tender ensures perfectly cooked pasta, and also adds body to the broth. If you like, serve with crusty bread or a simple salad dressed with lemon vinaigrette.

3 tablespoons extra-virgin olive oil, plus more to serve

⅓ cup tomato paste

4 medium garlic cloves, finely chopped

1 tablespoon sweet paprika

2 teaspoons dried mint

Kosher salt and ground black pepper

1½ pounds boneless, skinless chicken thighs, halved

1 cup orzo pasta

In a large saucepan, combine the oil, tomato paste and garlic. Cook, stirring, until several shades darker. Add the paprika and mint, then cook, stirring, just until fragrant. Add the chicken, 7 cups water and 2½ teaspoons salt. Simmer, uncovered, until a skewer inserted into the chicken meets no resistance. Transfer the chicken to a bowl. Add the orzo to the pan and cook until al dente. Shred the chicken. When the orzo is done, add the chicken and season with salt and pepper. Serve drizzled with additional oil.

Optional garnish: A dollop of yogurt OR squeeze of lemon OR torn fresh mint OR a sprinkle of Aleppo pepper OR a combination

195

Citrus-Cilantro Chicken Skewers

Start to finish: 30 minutes (20 minutes active)
Servings: 4 to 6

Cuban mojo, a multipurpose blend of garlic, citrus and olive oil, inspired these tangy-sweet chicken skewers. We combine citrus zest and juice, cilantro, vinegar and garlic; the mixture doubles as quick marinade and sauce for serving on the side. Grapefruit or oranges work equally well here; when zesting the fruit make sure to remove only the colored peel, not the bitter pith underneath. For easiest cleanup, line the baking sheet with foil before placing the skewers on top.

Grated zest of 1 grapefruit OR 2 medium oranges, plus 4 tablespoons juice, divided

1 cup lightly packed fresh cilantro, chopped

¼ cup packed brown sugar OR honey

3 tablespoons neutral oil, divided

2 tablespoons white wine vinegar

2 medium garlic cloves, finely grated

Kosher salt

2 pounds boneless, skinless chicken thighs, halved lengthwise

Heat the broiler with a rack 4 inches from the element. In a medium bowl, stir together the zest, 2 tablespoons juice, cilantro, sugar, 2 tablespoons oil, vinegar, garlic and 2 teaspoons salt. Transfer 2 tablespoons of the mixture to a small bowl. Add to it the remaining 1 tablespoon oil and remaining 2 tablespoons juice; set aside. Toss the chicken with the original mixture, then scrunch onto metal skewers. Place on a broiler-safe rimmed baking sheet. Broil until lightly charred, about 12 minutes, flipping once halfway through. Serve with the sauce.

Pan-Fried Chicken and Vegetable Patties

Start to finish: 20 minutes
Servings: 4

Dark meat ground chicken will give you the juiciest, most flavorful patties, but white meat works well, too. Make sure to shred the turnip or carrot on the small holes of box grater, as fine shreds combine better with the chicken and turn tender with cooking. Made with horseradish, the patties are great served on buns, with cheese and other burger toppings. Spiced with harissa, we liked the patties stuffed into flatbread, along with fresh tomato and feta cheese. Or serve either version with vinaigrette-dressed baby greens.

1 pound ground chicken, preferably dark meat

½ cup finely shredded peeled turnip OR carrot (see note)

1 medium garlic clove, finely grated

4 teaspoons soy sauce

1 tablespoon honey OR maple syrup

1½ teaspoons prepared horseradish OR harissa paste

3 tablespoons neutral oil, divided

Kosher salt and ground black pepper

In a medium bowl, combine the chicken, turnip, garlic, soy sauce, honey, horseradish, 1 tablespoon of oil and ¼ teaspoon each salt and pepper. Mix well, then shape into eight 4-inch patties. In a 12-inch nonstick skillet, heat 1 tablespoon of the remaining oil until shimmering. Add 4 patties and cook until well browned on both sides, flipping once. Transfer to a paper towel-lined plate, then wipe out the skillet. Repeat with the remaining oil and remaining patties.

Crisp-Breaded Chicken Cutlets

Start to finish: 30 minutes
Servings: 4 to 6

We use Japanese panko breadcrumbs for these pan-fried chicken cutlets. Panko has a coarse, fluffy texture that cooks up remarkably light and crisp. We add flavor by mixing a spice blend into the panko before coating the chicken. Look for cutlets that are about ¼ inch thick so they cook through at the same speed the breading browns. Serve with lemon or lime wedges or with a simple sauce (see our flavor hacks for dipping sauces p. 199). The cutlets also are terrific made into sandwiches, along with a crisp cabbage slaw.

2 large eggs

Kosher salt

½ cup all-purpose flour

2 cups panko breadcrumbs

2 tablespoons chili powder OR curry powder OR harissa spice blend OR shichimi togarashi

Six 4-ounce chicken cutlets (about ¼ inch thick)

½ cup neutral oil, divided

In a bowl, beat the eggs with 1 teaspoon salt. Place the flour in a second bowl and the panko in a third; stir 1 teaspoon salt into each, then stir the chili powder into the panko. One at a time, coat the cutlets on both sides with flour, dip into the eggs, then coat both sides with panko, pressing to adhere. In a 12-inch nonstick skillet, heat ¼ cup of oil until shimmering. Add 3 cutlets and brown on both sides, then transfer to a wire rack. Add the remaining ¼ cup oil and cook the remaining cutlets in the same way.

Dipping Sauces for Crispy Cutlets

Tangy Soy-Sesame Sauce

In a small bowl, stir together ½ cup soy sauce, ¼ cup unseasoned rice vinegar and 1 teaspoon toasted sesame oil.

Makes ¾ cup

Yogurt-Chutney Sauce

In a small bowl, stir together 1 cup whole-milk plain yogurt, 3 tablespoons mango chutney, ½ teaspoon kosher salt and ½ teaspoon ground black pepper.

Makes 1¼ cups

Sour Cream and Lime Sauce

In a small bowl, stir together 1 cup sour cream, the grated zest and juice of 1 lime, ½ teaspoon kosher salt and ½ teaspoon ground black pepper.

Makes 1 cup

Yogurt-Tahini Sauce

In a small bowl, stir together 1 cup whole-milk plain yogurt, 2 tablespoons tahini, ½ teaspoon kosher salt and ½ teaspoon ground black pepper.

Makes 1 cup

Sriracha-Mayo Sauce

In a small bowl, stir together 2 tablespoons Sriracha and ⅓ cup each mayonnaise and ketchup.

Makes ¾ cup

Foil-Roasted Chicken with Ginger and Thyme

Start to finish: 45 minutes
(15 minutes active)
Servings: 4

Sealing chicken thighs and a few aromatics in a foil packet allows for a two-step cooking technique. To start, the ingredients steam with their own moisture. Then, after the packet is cut open, the chicken roasts until browned, developing deeper flavor. To serve, offer slices of warm, crusty baguette on the side.

2 medium yellow onions, halved and sliced

1 bunch fresh thyme

3-inch piece fresh ginger, peeled and chopped

3 pounds bone-in, skin-on chicken thighs, trimmed

Kosher salt and ground black pepper

1 to 1½ teaspoons cayenne pepper

Lemon wedges OR lime wedges, to serve

Heat the oven to 500°F with a rimmed baking sheet on the middle rack. Layer the onions, thyme and ginger in the center of an 18-inch sheet of extra-wide, heavy-duty foil. Set the chicken, skin up, over them, then season with salt, pepper and cayenne. Cover with a second sheet of foil and fold the edges to seal. Carefully place the packet on the hot baking sheet and cook for 15 minutes. Cut open the packet to expose the chicken and roast until the thighs reach 175°F, about another 20 minutes. Serve with lemon wedges.

Optional garnish: Hot sauce

Chicken and Rice Noodles in Ginger-Hoisin Broth

Start to finish: 45 minutes
Servings: 4

Browning the aromatics—ginger and shallots—and briefly cooking a few tablespoons of hoisin sauce develops a solid flavor base for this simple soup. You can use flat, wide rice sticks or thin rice vermicelli. Either way, cook the noodles according to the package directions, then immediately divide them among individual bowls; if left to stand, the drained noodles may stick together. If you like, serve with lime wedges and Sriracha hot sauce.

2 tablespoons neutral oil

3-inch piece fresh ginger, peeled and thinly sliced

3 medium shallots, halved and sliced

3 tablespoons hoisin sauce

2½ pounds bone-in, skin-on chicken thighs, skin removed

8 ounces rice noodles, cooked according to package directions and divided among 4 serving bowls

1 cup lightly packed fresh basil, torn

In a large pot, heat the oil until shimmering. Add the ginger and shallots, then cook, stirring, until well browned. Add the hoisin and cook, stirring, until it coats the bottom of the pot. Add 2 quarts water and bring to a simmer. Add the chicken and cook for 35 minutes. Remove from the heat. Transfer the chicken to a plate and shred into bite-size pieces; discard the bones. Return the meat to the pot and cook until heated. Ladle over the noodles and top with the basil.

Slashed

Cutting slashes into bone-in chicken parts allows seasonings to flavor the meat deeply, and the cuts grip the paste or rub that's applied for bigger flavor impact. The chicken cooks a little more quickly, too.

Left to right: Chipotle-Lime Slashed Chicken, Thai-Inspired Slashed Chicken, Chili-Garlic Slashed Chicken with Ginger and Honey, Slashed Chicken with Grainy Mustard and Fennel Seed

Slashed Chicken with Chili-Garlic Sauce and Honey

Start to finish: 50 minutes (15 minutes active)
Servings: 4

In this recipe, the flavorings strike a balance of sweet, spicy, garlicky and tangy, with fresh ginger adding pungency. Prep and season the chicken as the first step, then let stand at room temperature while the oven heats. For easier cleanup, line the baking sheet with foil.

3 tablespoons chili-garlic sauce

3 tablespoons honey

1½ tablespoons unseasoned rice vinegar

1 tablespoon finely grated fresh ginger

Kosher salt

3 pounds bone-in, skin-on chicken leg quarters OR bone-in, skin-on chicken thighs

1 tablespoon sesame seeds, toasted

Place a wire rack in a rimmed baking sheet. Mix the chili-garlic sauce, honey, vinegar, ginger and 1 tablespoon salt. Using a sharp knife, cut parallel slashes about 1 inch apart all the way to the bone on both sides of each chicken leg. Rub the mixture onto the chicken and into the slashes, then place skin side up on the rack. Heat the oven to 450°F. Roast until the chicken is well browned and reaches 175°F, 20 to 25 minutes. Transfer to a platter and sprinkle with sesame seeds.

Optional garnish: Sliced scallions OR lime wedges OR both

Chipotle-Lime Slashed Chicken

Start to finish: 50 minutes (15 minutes active)
Servings: 4

Mexican mole negro gave us the idea to combine cocoa and chilies to make a seasoning paste for roasted chicken. Chipotle chilies in adobo sauce lend their earthy, smoky heat and tomatoey tang, while brown sugar and lime round out the flavors. The toasted almonds sprinkled on top before serving are a nod to the nuts used to make mole negro. For easy cleanup, line the baking sheet with foil.

3 chipotle chilies in adobo sauce, minced, plus 1 tablespoon adobo sauce

2 tablespoons packed brown sugar

2 tablespoons unsweetened cocoa powder

Grated zest and juice of 1 lime, plus lime wedges to serve

Kosher salt

3 pounds bone-in, skin-on chicken leg quarters OR bone-in, skin-on chicken thighs

Sliced almonds, toasted, to serve

Place a wire rack in a rimmed baking sheet. Mix the chipotles and adobo sauce, sugar, cocoa, lime juice and 2 teaspoons salt. Using a sharp knife, cut parallel slashes about 1 inch apart all the way to the bone on both sides of each chicken leg. Rub the mixture onto the chicken and into the slashes, then place skin side up on the rack. Heat the oven to 450°F. Roast until the chicken is well browned and reaches 175°F, 20 to 25 minutes. Transfer to a platter and sprinkle with the lime zest and almonds.

Slashed Chicken with Whole Grain Mustard and Fennel

Start to finish: 50 minutes (15 minutes active)
Servings: 4

Whole-grain mustard not only seasons this chicken, the seeds also add pops of texture. The sharp acidity of the mustard is kept in check by the sweetness of brown sugar, and fennel seeds and herbs round out the flavors. The fastest way to grind the fennel seeds is with an electric spice grinder; if you can find already ground fennel seed at the grocery store, use an equal amount. Foil placed under the rack on the baking sheet will catch drips and make cleanup easier.

⅓ cup whole-grain mustard

4 medium garlic cloves, minced

2 tablespoons packed brown sugar

2 teaspoons fennel seeds, ground

Kosher salt and ground black pepper

3 pounds bone-in, skin-on chicken leg quarters OR bone-in, skin-on chicken thighs

2 tablespoons chopped fresh tarragon OR 1 tablespoon chopped fresh sage

Place a wire rack in a rimmed baking sheet. Mix the mustard, garlic, sugar, fennel, 2 teaspoons salt and 1 teaspoon pepper. Using a sharp knife, cut parallel slashes about 1 inch apart all the way to the bone on both sides of each chicken leg. Rub the mixture onto the chicken and into the slashes, then place skin side up on the rack. Heat the oven to 450°F. Roast until the chicken is well browned and reaches 175°F, 20 to 25 minutes. Transfer to a platter and sprinkle with the tarragon.

Optional garnish: Lemon wedges

Thai Slashed Chicken

Start to finish: 50 minutes (15 minutes active)
Servings: 4

We borrowed some of the flavors from the Thai dish called gai yang and applied them to chicken parts that have been slashed for better seasoning and quicker cooking. Cilantro is used two ways here—the stems are minced for the marinade and the leaves go on as garnish. To simplify cleanup, line the baking sheet with foil.

4 medium garlic cloves, minced

3 tablespoons packed brown sugar

2 tablespoons fish sauce

2 tablespoons finely chopped fresh cilantro stems, plus chopped fresh cilantro leaves, to serve

1 tablespoon grated lime zest, plus 2 tablespoons lime juice

1½ teaspoons ground black pepper

3 pounds bone-in, skin-on chicken leg quarters OR bone-in, skin-on chicken thighs

Place a wire rack in a rimmed baking sheet. Mix the garlic, sugar, fish sauce, cilantro stems, lime zest and juice and pepper. Using a sharp knife, cut parallel slashes about 1 inch apart all the way to the bone on both sides of each chicken leg. Rub the mixture onto the chicken and into the slashes, then place skin side up on the rack. Heat the oven to 450°F. Roast until the chicken is well browned and reaches 175°F, 20 to 25 minutes. Transfer to a platter and sprinkle with chopped cilantro leaves.

CHICKEN

205

Chicken and Rice Soup with Napa Cabbage

Start to finish: 25 minutes
Servings: 4

For this meal in a bowl, store-bought chicken broth gets a big flavor boost and a good dose of umami from either Chinese black bean garlic sauce or spicy chili-bean sauce (called toban djan); look for jars of these ingredients in the international aisle of the supermarket. We also add powdered gelatin to approximate the richness of long-simmered chicken stock. If you prefer, you can skip the gelatin and simply add the broth, bean sauce, cabbage and rice to the pot, then bring to a boil. To make the soup heartier, add diced tofu or top servings with a soft-boiled egg.

2 quarts low-sodium chicken broth

Three ¼-ounce packets unflavored powdered gelatin (see note)

4 teaspoons black bean garlic sauce OR chili-bean sauce (toban djan)

2 cups chopped napa cabbage OR 8 ounces cremini mushrooms, thinly sliced

1 cup long-grain white rice OR short-grain white rice

3 cups shredded cooked chicken

Kosher salt and ground black pepper

In a large saucepan, combine the broth and gelatin; let stand for 6 minutes. Add the bean sauce, cabbage and rice. Bring to a boil, then reduce to a steady simmer and cook, stirring occasionally, until the cabbage and rice are tender, 10 to 15 minutes. Add the chicken and cook, stirring, just until warmed through. Season with salt and pepper.

Optional garnish: Cilantro leaves OR sliced scallions OR both

Pulled Chicken with Tomatoes, Chilies and Cilantro

Start to finish: 25 minutes
Servings: 4

Mild and lean chicken breasts have long muscle fibers that are great for shredding. In this recipe, a tomato-based sauce spiked with chilies adds savory-sweet-spicy flavor, and a splash of oil at the end of cooking boosts richness. If using canned green chilies, don't drain off the liquid—add it to the pan along with the chilies. This is great tucked into tacos or burritos, served with rice and refried beans, or spooned over a salad.

3 tablespoons neutral oil, divided

2 pounds boneless, skinless chicken breasts

4 plum tomatoes, cored and chopped

1 cup lightly packed fresh cilantro, chopped, stems and leaves reserved separately

6 medium garlic cloves, chopped
OR 1 small yellow onion, chopped

2 teaspoons dried oregano

1 chipotle chili in adobo sauce, finely chopped, plus 2 teaspoons adobo sauce OR one 4-ounce can diced green chilies, with liquid

Kosher salt and ground black pepper

In a 12-inch skillet, heat 1 tablespoon of oil until shimmering. Add the chicken and cook until well-browned, then flip and add the tomatoes, cilantro stems, garlic, oregano and chili and sauce. Reduce the heat, cover and cook until the tomatoes soften. Transfer only the chicken to a bowl. Increase the heat and cook the sauce until slightly reduced. Shred the chicken, then return it to the pan. Cook until thickly coated. Stir in the cilantro leaves and the remaining 2 tablespoons oil. Season with salt and pepper.

Almond, Caper and Herb-Crusted Chicken Cutlets

Start to finish: 25 minutes
Servings: 4

Chopped capers and fresh herbs create a flavorful undercoat for the nutty, crunchy crust on these chicken cutlets. Look for cutlets that weigh about 4 ounces each and are about ¼ inch thick. This way, they'll cook quickly and evenly. As an accompaniment, we suggest a lemony arugula salad or roasted sweet potatoes. Or, sandwich the cutlets and baby greens in bread smeared with mayonnaise.

¾ cup sliced almonds, finely chopped

½ cup panko breadcrumbs

Kosher salt and ground black pepper

Four 4-ounce chicken cutlets (about ¼ inch thick)

¼ cup drained capers, finely chopped

¼ cup lightly packed fresh tarragon OR fresh dill, chopped

6 tablespoons neutral oil, divided

Lemon wedges OR Dijon mustard OR sour cream, to serve

Combine the almonds, panko, 1 teaspoon salt and ½ teaspoon pepper. Season the cutlets on both sides with salt and pepper, then sprinkle with the capers and tarragon, pressing to adhere. Coat both sides of each cutlet with the almond mixture, pressing firmly. In a 12-inch skillet, heat 3 tablespoons of oil. Add 2 cutlets and cook until golden brown on both sides. Transfer to a paper towel-lined plate and wipe out the skillet. Repeat with remaining cutlets and oil. Serve with lemon wedges.

Spiced Chicken and Cashew Meatballs

Start to finish: 30 minutes
Makes 13 to 15 meatballs

Roasted cashews ground in a food processor with a few seasonings add richness and bold flavor to these oven-cooked meatballs. Ground cardamom lends subtle citrus and floral notes, while garam masala adds a warm, well-rounded spiciness; use whichever you have or prefer. Serve with warmed flatbread.

1 cup lightly packed fresh cilantro, plus cilantro leaves to serve

¾ cup roasted cashews, plus chopped cashews to serve

1 tablespoon extra-virgin olive oil, plus more for brushing

1½ teaspoons ground cardamom OR garam masala

Grated zest from 1 lime

Kosher salt and ground black pepper

1 pound ground chicken

Heat the oven to 450°F. Line a rimmed baking sheet with kitchen parchment. In a food processor, combine the cilantro, cashews, oil, cardamon, lime zest, 1 teaspoon salt and 2 teaspoons pepper; process to a coarse paste. In a large bowl, mix with the chicken, then form into 1½-inch balls and place on the prepared baking sheet. Brush generously with oil and bake until well browned, about 16 minutes. Serve sprinkled with chopped cashews and cilantro leaves.

Optional garnish: Whole-milk plain yogurt

Charred Ginger-Lime Chicken

Start to finish: 30 minutes
Servings: 4 to 6

We use a broiler to add char to boneless chicken thighs, then toss the just-cooked chicken with a few aromatics. As the chicken cools, it absorbs some of the flavors and its heat slightly softens the sharp notes of the ginger. For a bit of chili heat, use pickled jalapeños; for a little sweetness and vibrant color, opt for red cherry peppers. Serve with a rice or grain pilaf, or cut the thighs into smaller pieces and serve on leafy greens.

2 pounds boneless, skinless chicken thighs, halved lengthwise

2 teaspoons white sugar

4 tablespoons neutral oil, divided

Kosher salt and ground black pepper

Grated zest and juice from 2 limes

1 tablespoon finely grated fresh ginger

3 tablespoons chopped fresh cilantro
OR mint OR basil

2 tablespoons chopped pickled jalapeños
OR pickled red cherry peppers, plus
2 teaspoons pickling liquid

Heat the broiler with a rack 4 inches from the element. In a medium bowl, toss the chicken with the sugar, 1 tablespoon of the oil, 1 teaspoon salt and ½ teaspoon pepper. Set a wire rack in a broiler-safe rimmed baking sheet; arrange the chicken on it. Broil until charred, 13 to 16 minutes, flipping once halfway through. Immediately transfer to a clean bowl and toss with the remaining 3 tablespoons oil, lime zest and juice, ginger, herbs, and jalapeños and pickling liquid. Let stand for 10 minutes before serving.

Optional garnish: Chopped roasted peanuts

Maple and Soy-Glazed Chicken Skewers

Start to finish: 40 minutes
Servings: 4

For these savory-sweet chicken skewers loosely based on Japanese yakitori, we layer on the flavors—first as a quick marinade for the chicken, then as a basting sauce. The final coating helps the sesame seeds or scallions—or both—adhere to the chicken. Serve with rice and a crunchy slaw or make into a sandwich or wrap with shredded vegetables and a smear of mayonnaise. For easy clean up, line the baking sheet with foil.

½ cup soy sauce

1 tablespoon finely grated fresh ginger OR 3 medium garlic cloves, finely grated OR both

2 tablespoons neutral oil

¼ cup maple syrup

1½ teaspoons sherry vinegar OR cider vinegar

2 pounds boneless, skinless chicken thighs, halved lengthwise

Thinly sliced scallions OR sesame seeds, toasted OR both

In a medium bowl, stir together the soy sauce, ginger and oil. In a small bowl, combine 3 table-spoons of the mixture with the maple and vinegar. Toss the chicken with the remaining soy mixture. Heat the broiler with a rack 4 inches from the element. Scrunch the chicken onto metal skewers, then set on a broiler-safe rimmed baking sheet. Broil until well browned, about 12 minutes, flipping once. Brush lightly with the soy-maple mixture, then broil until lightly charred, 2 to 3 minutes per side. Brush with the remaining soy-maple mixture, then sprinkle with the scallions.

Traybakes

In Britain, meat and vegetables are placed on a baking
sheet (tray) along with some seasonings and go into
the oven together. The chicken is flavored as it cooks, and
with the right cut of meat and the right vegetables they
all are done at the same time. The low-sided baking
sheet allows the chicken to cook quickly and
brown evenly.

Top left: Cumin-Caraway Chicken and Tomato Traybake; Bottom
Left: Za'atar Chicken and Eggplant Traybake; Top Right: Jerk-Spiced
Chicken and Pineapple Traybake; Bottom right: Fennel-Crusted
Chicken and Scallion Traybake

Za'atar Chicken and Eggplant Traybake

Start to finish: 50 minutes (20 minutes active)
Servings: 4

Za'atar is a Middle Eastern seed, herb and spice blend. We use it as a seasoning for chicken and eggplant roasted together on the same baking sheet. Surrounded by the chicken and eggplant, garlic cloves at the center of the baking sheet become soft and creamy. To finish the dish, we create a flavorful sauce by mashing the cloves then deglazing the pan with water and lemon juice.

3 tablespoons za'atar (see note)

1 teaspoon white sugar

Kosher salt and ground black pepper

10 medium garlic cloves, peeled

3 pounds bone-in, skin-on chicken breasts or thighs

1-pound eggplant, cut into 2-inch chunks

Extra-virgin olive oil, for drizzling

Juice of 1 lemon

Heat the oven to 450°F. Stir together the za'atar, sugar, 1 tablespoon salt and 2 teaspoons pepper. Place the garlic in the center of a rimmed baking sheet. Arrange the chicken, skin up, and eggplant around the garlic. Drizzle with oil, then sprinkle with the za'atar mixture. Roast until the breasts reach 160°F or the thighs reach 175°F, 30 to 40 minutes. Transfer the chicken and eggplant to a platter. Mash the garlic on the baking sheet, then add ¼ cup water and the lemon juice; scrape up any browned bits. Spoon the sauce over the chicken.

Optional garnish: Chopped fresh cilantro OR chopped fresh oregano OR sliced scallions

Fennel-Crusted Chicken and Scallion Traybake

Start to finish: 50 minutes (15 minutes active)
Servings: 4

Tender, silky, lightly charred scallions serve as an accompaniment to spice-crusted chicken, as well as a flavoring for the roasted lemon pan sauce. For best texture, crush the fennel seeds with a mortar and pestle or with the bottom of a skillet—don't pulverize them to a powder in a spice grinder. A sprinkle of fresh herbs at the end keeps the dish bright and lively. Tarragon plays up the licorice notes of the fennel seed; cilantro will bring out the coriander. Serve with a grain or rice pilaf, crusty bread or over polenta.

2 teaspoons fennel seeds, crushed

1½ teaspoons ground coriander

Kosher salt and ground black pepper

3 pounds bone-in, skin-on chicken breasts or thighs

1 bunch scallions, cut into 1½-inch pieces

1 lemon, halved

Extra-virgin olive oil, for drizzling

Chopped fresh tarragon OR fresh cilantro, to serve

Heat the oven to 450°F. Mix the fennel, coriander, 1 tablespoon salt and ½ teaspoon pepper. Set the chicken skin up on a rimmed baking sheet. Arrange the scallions and lemon halves around it. Drizzle with oil, then sprinkle with the spices. Roast until the breasts reach 160°F or the thighs reach 175°F, 30 to 40 minutes. Transfer the chicken to a platter. Squeeze the juice of the lemon halves onto the pan and stir to combine with the scallions. Spoon the sauce around the chicken and sprinkle with tarragon.

Jerk-Spiced Chicken and Pineapple Traybake

Start to finish: 50 minutes (20 minutes active)
Servings: 4

Chunks of fresh pineapple and whole habanero chilies roast alongside bone-in, skin-on chicken parts, the whole lot seasoned with a mixture of dried thyme and Jamaican jerk spice. After roasting, the lightly caramelized fruit and softened chilies are tossed with lime juice and pan juices to make a sweet-savory accompaniment. The final sprinkle of lime zest is key—it perks up the dish with fruity flavor but without added acidity. To simplify prep, purchase an already peeled and cored pineapple.

2 teaspoons dried thyme

2 teaspoons jerk seasoning

Kosher salt and ground black pepper

3 pounds bone-in, skin-on chicken breast or thighs

1 pineapple, peeled, cored and cut into 1-inch chunks

4 habanero chilies, stemmed

1 lime, zest grated, then halved

Extra-virgin olive oil, for drizzling

Heat the oven to 450°F. Mix the thyme, jerk seasoning, 1 tablespoon salt and 1½ teaspoons pepper. Set the chicken skin up on a rimmed baking sheet. Set the pineapple, chilies and lime halves around it. Drizzle with oil, then sprinkle with the spices. Roast until the breasts reach 160°F or the thighs reach 175°F, 30 to 40 minutes. Transfer the chicken to a platter. Chop the chilies and add to the pineapple along with the juice from the lime halves. Stir with the pan juices, then spoon the mixture around the chicken. Sprinkle with the lime zest.

Cumin-Caraway Chicken and Tomato Traybake

Start to finish: 50 minutes (15 minutes active)
Servings: 4

For this recipe, we've used some of the ingredients that give character to harissa, a North African spice paste. Crushing the cumin and caraway in a mortar with a pestle or with the bottom of a skillet, rather than grinding the seeds to a fine powder, makes sprinkling easier and creates a more interesting texture. The tomatoes and jalapeños turn soft and silky with roasting but are firm enough to hold their shape. Serve with crusty bread to mop up the flavorful pan juices.

2 teaspoons cumin seeds, crushed

1½ teaspoons caraway seeds, crushed

Kosher salt and ground black pepper

3 pounds bone-in, skin-on chicken breasts or thighs

3 jalapeño chilies, stemmed, seeded and quartered

4 medium tomatoes, cored and halved

Extra-virgin olive oil, for drizzling

Heat the oven to 450°F. Mix the cumin, caraway, 1 tablespoon salt and 1½ teaspoons pepper. Set the chicken skin up on a rimmed baking sheet and arrange the jalapeños and tomato halves, cut side up, around it. Drizzle with oil, then sprinkle with the spice mix. Roast until the breasts reach 160°F or the thighs reach 175°F, 30 to 40 minutes. Transfer the chicken and vegetables to a platter, then spoon on the juices from the baking sheet.

CHICKEN

217

Steamed Lemon Chicken with Scallions and Oyster Sauce

Start to finish: 20 minutes
Servings: 4

In this dish, the clean, mild flavor of chicken breasts meets salty-sweet oyster sauce, tangy lemons and pungent scallions that are tempered by moist steam heat. Use a Dutch oven or a similar wide cooking vessel so the chicken is in a single layer in the steamer and cooks evenly. A tight-fitting lid is essential for trapping heat in the pot. Serve with rice and a crunchy cabbage slaw.

¼ cup oyster sauce

2 tablespoons mirin

1 teaspoon toasted sesame oil

Grated zest and juice of 1 lemon, plus 1 lemon, sliced into thin rounds

Ground black pepper

4 boneless, skinless chicken breasts (about 6 ounces each)

1 bunch scallions, whites thinly sliced, greens cut into 1-inch pieces, reserved separately

In a small bowl, mix the oyster sauce, mirin, oil, lemon zest and ¾ teaspoon pepper. Measure 2 tablespoons of the mixture into a medium bowl, add the chicken to it and turn to coat. Into the remaining mixture, stir the lemon juice; set aside. In a large Dutch oven, bring 1 inch of water to a boil. Place the chicken in a steamer basket, then top with the scallion whites and lemon slices. Add to the pot, cover and cook until the thickest part of the breasts reach 160°F, about 12 minutes. Remove from the heat and let stand, covered, for 5 minutes. Sprinkle with the scallion greens and serve with reserved sauce.

Ginger-Peanut Sautéed Chicken

Start to finish: 20 minutes
Servings: 4

The inspiration for this quick sauté of chunked chicken thighs was West African beef suya, or skewers of meat seasoned with spices and ground or chopped peanuts. Stir only occasionally while the chicken cooks so the pieces brown well, which results in richer, deeper flavor in the finished dish. Serve the chicken with rice and braised greens.

1½ pounds boneless, skinless chicken thighs, trimmed and cut into 1-inch chunks

¼ cup roasted peanuts, finely chopped

1 tablespoon ground ginger

Kosher salt and ground black pepper

2 tablespoons neutral oil

1 teaspoon packed brown sugar

Juice of 1 lime OR lemon

Fresh flat-leaf parsley, roughly chopped OR sliced scallions, to serve

In a medium bowl, toss the chicken with the peanuts, ginger, 1 teaspoon salt and 1½ teaspoons pepper. In a 12-inch nonstick skillet, heat the oil until barely smoking. Add the chicken and cook, stirring infrequently, until well browned and the chicken is opaque throughout, about 10 minutes. Off heat, add the sugar and lime juice, stirring until lightly glazed. Season with salt and pepper, then stir in the parsley.

220

Spicy Stir-Fried Chicken and Snow Peas

Start to finish: 20 minutes
Servings: 4

A combination of Chinese oyster sauce and Korean gochujang (fermented red chili paste) add complex savoriness to this stir-fry; lime zest and juice add brightness. Fresno chilies add a little heat that reinforces the spiciness of the gochujang; if you prefer a milder dish, use a red bell pepper instead. Serve with steamed rice.

3 tablespoons oyster sauce

2 tablespoons gochujang

2 teaspoons grated lime zest, plus
3 tablespoons lime juice

1½ pounds boneless, skinless chicken breasts, cut crosswise into thin slices

Kosher salt and ground black pepper

2 tablespoons neutral oil

4 ounces snow peas, trimmed

2 large Fresno chilies OR 1 medium red bell pepper, stemmed, seeded and sliced into thin strips

In a small bowl, mix the oyster sauce, gochujang and lime zest and juice. In a medium bowl, toss the chicken with ¼ teaspoon salt and 1 teaspoon pepper. In a 12-inch skillet, heat the oil until barely smoking. Add the chicken in an even layer and cook without stirring until lightly browned. Add the snow peas and chilies, then cook, stirring, until the chicken is almost opaque throughout. Add the sauce and cook, stirring, until the vegetables are crisp-tender. Season with salt and pepper.

Spicy Butter-Soy Chicken

Start to finish: 20 minutes (10 minutes active)
Servings: 4

This simple stir-fry was inspired by Filipino salpicao, a dish that dresses tender cubes of beef with a garlicky soy-butter sauce. Lean, mild-tasting chicken breasts get a big savory-sweet flavor boost from just a few high-impact ingredients. We like the mild burn that results when the seeds are left in the serranos, but you can remove the seeds for less heat. Serve with rice to soak up the sauce.

3½ teaspoons light brown OR dark brown sugar

3 tablespoons soy sauce

1½ pounds boneless, skinless chicken breasts, cut into ½- to ¾-inch chunks

1 tablespoon neutral oil

2 medium garlic cloves, finely chopped

5 tablespoons salted butter, cut into 5 pieces

2 serrano chilies, stemmed and sliced into thin rings (see note)

Kosher salt

In a medium bowl, mix the sugar and soy sauce. Add the chicken, toss, then let stand for 10 minutes. Drain the marinade into a small bowl and reserve. In a 12-inch skillet, heat the oil until barely smoking. Add the chicken and cook, stirring, until almost no pink remains. Add the garlic and marinade, then cook, stirring, until the chicken is opaque throughout. Off heat, add the butter and half the chilies, stirring until the butter melts. Season with salt. Serve sprinkled with the remaining chilies.

Optional garnish: Scallions, thinly sliced on the diagonal OR flaky sea salt OR both

Stir-Fried Red Curry Chicken with Green Beans and Herbs

Start to finish: 25 minutes
Servings: 4

Pad prik king, a Thai stir-fry seasoned with aromatic red curry paste, inspired this quick-cooking chicken and vegetable dish. A quarter cup of coconut oil may sound like a lot, but it adds richness to lean boneless, skinless chicken breasts. If using basil, leave the leaves whole; if using mint or cilantro, it's fine to use the tender stems in addition to the whole leaves. Serve with steamed jasmine rice.

¼ cup coconut oil

1½ pounds boneless, skinless chicken breasts, cut crosswise into thin strips

8 ounces green beans, halved diagonally OR 1 bell pepper, stemmed, seeded and thinly sliced

3 tablespoons Thai red curry paste

2 cups fresh basil OR mint OR cilantro

Kosher salt and ground black pepper

Juice of ½ lime

In a 12-inch skillet, heat the coconut oil until barely smoking. Add the chicken and cook without stirring until lightly browned, about 2 minutes. Add the green beans and curry paste, then cook, stirring, until the paste is lightly browned. Add ⅓ cup water and cook, stirring, until the chicken is opaque and the beans are crisp-tender. Add the herbs and stir until just wilted. Off heat, stir in the lime juice, then season with salt and pepper.

Orange-Ginger Chicken

**Start to finish: 1 hour 10 minutes
(15 minutes active), plus marinating
Servings: 4**

The marinade for this recipe is made in a blender with a quartered whole orange—skin and all—and the ginger does not need to be peeled, either. When transferring the chicken to the wire rack, allow a good amount of the marinade to cling to the pieces for deep browning and crusting. Rice and steamed or stir-fried vegetables are good accompaniments. For easier cleanup, line the baking sheet with foil before setting the rack on top.

1 navel orange, not peeled, cut into quarters, plus orange wedges to serve

½ cup orange juice

1 cup low-sodium soy sauce

7 ounces fresh ginger, not peeled, thinly sliced

½ cup packed brown sugar

3 pounds bone-in, skin-on chicken thighs, trimmed

In a blender, puree the orange, juice, soy sauce, ginger and sugar until smooth. Transfer to a large bowl, add the chicken and turn to coat. Cover and refrigerate for at least 1 hour or up to 24 hours. Heat the oven to 400°F. Set a wire rack in a rimmed baking sheet, then arrange the chicken, with marinade clinging, skin side up on the rack. Bake until the thighs reach 170°F, about 45 minutes. Turn the oven to broil and broil until the chicken is deep golden brown and lightly charred, 2 to 4 minutes. Serve with orange wedges.

Optional garnish: Sliced scallions

Jalapeño-Apricot Glazed Chicken Thighs

**Start to finish: 50 minutes
(15 minutes active)**
Servings: 4

These glazed chicken thighs feature an addictive combination of sweet, savory and spicy flavors. We first roast the thighs in a hot oven, then finish them under the broiler to caramelize the glaze. Use either apricot or peach preserves—whichever you prefer or have on hand. For easy cleanup, line the baking sheet with foil before setting the wire rack on top.

2 tablespoons ground cumin

Kosher salt and ground black pepper

3 pounds bone-in, skin-on chicken thighs

½ cup apricot preserves OR peach preserves

3 tablespoons cider vinegar, divided

1 jalapeño chili OR 2 Fresno chilies, stemmed and sliced into thin rounds

Heat the oven to 450°F. Set a wire rack in a broiler-safe rimmed baking sheet. Stir together the cumin, 2 teaspoons salt and 1 teaspoon pepper; use to season the chicken on all sides. Place the thighs, skin up, on the rack. Roast until the chicken reaches 175°F, about 35 minutes. In a small bowl, mix the preserves, 2 tablespoons vinegar and the jalapeño. Brush the chicken with some of the mixture, then broil until bubbling. Stir the remaining 1 tablespoon vinegar into the remaining preserves mixture and serve with the chicken.

Italian Chicken Sausage and White Beans with Escarole

Start to finish: 30 minutes
Servings: 6

This one-pot meal pairs leafy, subtly bitter escarole with creamy white beans, fennel seeds and fresh chicken sausage (not the fully cooked kind). We drain only one can of the cannellini beans; the liquid in the second can is added to the pot to create a full-bodied broth. Serve with hunks of warm, crusty bread.

2 tablespoons extra-virgin olive oil, plus more to serve

1 tablespoon fennel seeds

1 pound hot OR **sweet fresh Italian chicken sausage, casing removed**

1 teaspoon red pepper flakes

2 heads escarole, chopped

Two 15½-ounce cans cannellini beans, 1 can rinsed and drained

Kosher salt and ground black pepper

Finely grated Parmesan cheese OR **pecorino Romano cheese, to serve**

In a large Dutch oven, heat the oil until shimmering. Add the fennel seeds and stir until fragrant. Add the sausage and cook, breaking it into bite-size pieces, until lightly browned. Stir in the pepper flakes, escarole, the beans (and the liquid from 1 can). Cover and cook, stirring occasionally, until the escarole is wilted and tender. Season with salt and pepper. Serve drizzled with additional oil and sprinkled with cheese.

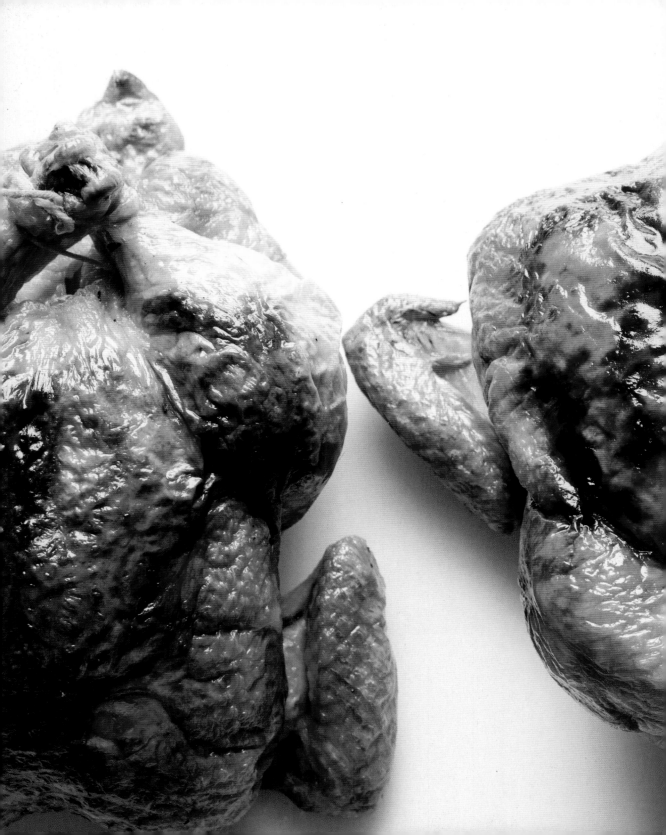

Seasoned Under the Skin

Sliding spices and aromatic seasonings beneath the skin boosts flavor by putting the ingredients directly in contact with the meat. The skin also helps them stay put during cooking.

Left to right: Green Chili and Herb Roasted Chicken, Red Curry and Lime Roasted Chicken, Garam Masala and Tamarind Roasted Chicken

Garam Masala and Tamarind Roasted Chicken

Start to finish: 2 hours (15 minutes active)
Servings: 4

Garam masala is an Indian spice blend containing cumin, bay, fennel, cinnamon, dried chilies and black pepper, along with an assortment of other spices. To make the seasoning paste for this chicken, we supplement with extra cinnamon and black pepper to bring added warmth that balances the tangy sweetness of the chutney. Serve with warmed flatbread and dal.

4 tablespoons salted butter, softened

1 tablespoon garam masala

**1 tablespoon tamarind chutney,
plus more to serve**

½ teaspoon ground cinnamon

Kosher salt and ground black pepper

4-pound whole chicken

Heat the oven to 425°F. Set a wire rack in a rimmed baking sheet. Mix the butter, chutney, garam masala, cinnamon, 1 teaspoon salt and ½ teaspoon pepper. Using your fingers, loosen the skin from the meat on the chicken's breast and thigh areas, then smear the mixture evenly under the skin. Season all over with salt, then tuck the wings to the back and tie the legs. Set the bird breast up on the rack and roast until the thighs reach 175°F, 60 to 80 minutes. Let rest for about 30 minutes, then carve. Drizzle with additional chutney.

Red Curry and Lime Roasted Chicken

Start to finish: 2 hours (15 minutes active)
Servings: 4

We temper pungent, spicy Thai red curry paste with butter and add freshness with lime zest before smearing the paste under the skin of a whole chicken just before roasting. Serve with rice, along with mango salad, stir-fried vegetables or boiled sweet potatoes.

4 tablespoons salted butter, softened

**2 tablespoons grated lime zest,
plus lime wedges to serve**

1½ to 2 tablespoons Thai red curry paste

½ teaspoon ground ginger

Kosher salt

4-pound whole chicken

Heat the oven to 425°F. Set a wire rack in a rimmed baking sheet. Mix the butter, lime zest, curry paste, ginger and 1 teaspoon salt. Using your fingers, loosen the skin from the meat on the chicken's breast and thigh areas, then smear the mixture evenly under the skin. Season all over with salt, then tuck the wings to the back and tie the legs. Set the bird breast up on the rack and roast until the thighs reach 175°F, 60 to 80 minutes. Let rest for about 30 minutes, then carve. Serve with lime wedges.

Green Chili and Herb Roasted Chicken

Start to finish: 2 hours (20 minutes active)
Servings: 4

With flavors that are herbal, fresh and subtly spicy, this roasted chicken was inspired in large part by adjika, an aromatic green chili, fresh herb and spice paste from the country of Georgia. Make sure to seed the serranos to moderate the heat. Serve with rice pilaf, roasted potatoes or a crunchy salad.

4 tablespoons salted butter, softened

⅓ cup finely chopped fresh mint

2 serrano chilies, stemmed, seeded and finely chopped

2 scallions, finely chopped

1 teaspoon ground coriander

Kosher salt and ground black pepper

4-pound whole chicken

Heat the oven to 425°F. Set a wire rack in a rimmed baking sheet. Mix the butter, mint, chilies, scallions, coriander, 1 teaspoon salt and ½ teaspoon pepper. Using your fingers, loosen the skin from the meat on the chicken's breast and thigh areas, then smear the mixture evenly under the skin. Season all over with salt, then tuck the wings to the back and tie the legs. Set the bird breast up on the rack and roast until the thighs register 175°F, 60 to 80 minutes. Let rest for about 30 minutes, then carve.

Optional garnish: Lemon wedges

Stir-Fried Turmeric Chicken

Start to finish: 25 minutes
Servings: 4

This simple stir-fry is earthy and golden with turmeric and sweetened with honey that caramelizes and builds flavor. Don't slice the onion too thinly—the slivers should be about ½ inch thick so they soften only slightly and offer a crunchy textural contrast to the tender chicken. The shot of lime zest and juice at the end keeps flavors bright and lively.

2 tablespoons honey

2 teaspoons soy sauce

¾ teaspoon ground turmeric

2 tablespoons neutral oil, divided

Kosher salt and ground black pepper

1½ pounds boneless, skinless chicken thighs, cut into 1-inch chunks

1 small red onion **OR** yellow onion, halved and sliced ½ inch thick

2 tablespoons grated lime zest, plus 1 tablespoon lime juice, plus lime wedges to serve

In a medium bowl, stir the honey, soy sauce, turmeric, 1 tablespoon of oil and ¾ teaspoon salt. Stir in the chicken. In a 12-inch nonstick skillet, heat the remaining 1 tablespoon oil until shimmering. Add the chicken and cook, stirring, until well browned. Add the onion and cook, stirring, until the chicken is opaque throughout and the onion is wilted but still crunchy. Off heat, stir in the lime juice and half the zest. Season with salt and pepper, then sprinkle with the remaining zest. Serve with lime wedges.

Optional garnish: Thinly shredded red cabbage

West African Peanut Chicken

Start to finish: 40 minutes
Servings: 4 to 6

Inspired by Senegalese mafe, this recipe seasons boneless, skinless chicken thighs with the bold flavors of West African peanut stew. A single chili adds just enough spice and fruitiness. Try not to move the thighs until they've browned long enough to release easily from the pan; the browning contributes flavor. It is delicious with warm naan or other flatbread.

2 pounds boneless, skinless chicken thighs, halved crosswise and patted dry

Kosher salt and ground black pepper

1 tablespoon neutral oil

14½-ounce can diced tomatoes

2 tablespoons fish sauce

1 habanero chili **OR** serrano chili, halved and seeded

¼ cup creamy peanut butter

Grated zest and juice of 1 lemon **OR** 1 lime

Season the chicken with salt and pepper. In a 12-inch skillet, heat the oil until shimmering. Add the chicken and cook, undisturbed, until browned. Stir, then add the tomatoes with juices, fish sauce and chili; scrape the skillet. Cover and cook until the chicken is opaque throughout. Stir in the peanut butter and simmer uncovered until thickened. Season with salt and pepper and stir in the lemon zest and juice.

Optional garnish: Chopped fresh flat-leaf parsley

233

Korean Fire Chicken

Start to finish: 1 hour (25 minutes active)
Servings: 4 to 6

For this simple spin on Korean buldak, which translates as "fire chicken," you will need a large broiler-safe skillet. Gochujang, or Korean fermented chili paste, is a key ingredient. Look for it in the international aisle in supermarkets or in Asian grocery stores. Different brands can vary in spiciness, so you may want to start with the smaller amount, then taste after whisking with the vinegar and soy. If desired, whisk in additional gochujang, keeping in mind that the flavors in the finished dish will be slightly more concentrated. Serve with rice and, if you like, lettuce leaves for wrapping.

⅓ to ½ cup gochujang (see note)

¼ cup unseasoned rice vinegar

¼ cup low-sodium soy sauce

½ teaspoon toasted sesame oil

3 pounds boneless, skinless chicken thighs, each trimmed and cut crosswise into 3 pieces

1 bunch scallions, cut into 1-inch lengths

In a 12-inch broiler-safe skillet, whisk the gochujang, vinegar, soy sauce and oil. Stir in the chicken, then let stand 15 to 20 minutes. Heat the broiler with a rack about 6 inches from the element. Place the skillet in the oven and broil until the edges of the chicken are deeply charred, about 30 minutes, stirring halfway through. Transfer to the stovetop (the handle will be hot), bring to a simmer and cook, stirring, until the sauce thickly coats the chicken, 3 to 5 minutes. Off heat, stir in the scallions.

Optional garnish: Toasted sesame seeds

Chutney-Glazed Spatchcocked Chicken

Start to finish: 1 hour 20 minutes
(20 minutes active)
Servings: 4 to 6

Spatchcocking a chicken—that is, cutting out its backbone and opening up and flattening the bird—allows for even browning and relatively quick cooking. We make a simple glaze with fruity, tangy-sweet chutney mixed with butter for richness and turmeric for savoriness. Before cooking, we mix citrus juice into a portion of the glaze to serve as a sauce alongside the carved chicken. An herbed grain pilaf is a perfect accompaniment.

½ cup tamarind chutney **OR** mango chutney

4 tablespoons salted butter, melted

1 teaspoon ground turmeric **OR** ground ginger

Juice of 1 lemon **OR** 1 lime

4-pound whole chicken

Kosher salt and ground black pepper

Heat the oven to 425°F. Set a wire rack in a rimmed baking sheet. Stir together the chutney, butter and turmeric; measure ⅓ cup into a small bowl, then stir the juice into it; set aside for serving. Using kitchen shears, cut along each side of the chicken's backbone and discard. Place the bird skin side up flat on the rack. Season with salt and pepper, then brush with half the chutney mixture. Roast for 40 minutes. Brush with the remaining chutney mixture and roast until the thighs reach 175°F, another 10 to 15 minutes. Let rest for 10 minutes. Carve and serve with the sauce.

Portuguese-Style Pot-Roasted Chicken

Start to finish: 1 hour (10 minutes active)
Servings: 4

This is a much-simplified version of Portuguese frango na púcara, or chicken cooked with wine and tomatoes in a terra cotta pot. The recipe couldn't be much easier, but the flavors are complex and smoky. Tawny port or brandy—both of which have woodsy notes from aging and a subdued fruitiness—is key for depth and richness in the sauce. Bone-in chicken thighs, leg quarters or breasts all work well, but if using breasts, select ones no larger than 12 ounces each or they may not fit comfortably in the pot and may be slow to cook. Serve with roasted potatoes and plenty of crusty bread.

14½-ounce can diced fire-roasted tomatoes

1 cup tawny port OR brandy (see note)

1½ teaspoons smoked paprika

4 ounces thick-cut bacon, chopped

3 pounds bone-in, skin on chicken thighs, leg quarters or breasts (see note)

Kosher salt and ground black pepper

1 bunch fresh cilantro OR flat-leaf parsley, chopped

In a large Dutch oven, stir the tomatoes with juices, port, paprika and bacon. Season the chicken with salt and pepper, then nestle skin up in the pot. Heat the oven to 400°F. Roast, uncovered, until the dark meat reaches 175°F or the white meat reaches 160°F, about 50 minutes. Transfer the chicken to a serving dish. Stir the cilantro into the sauce, then season with salt and pepper. Spoon around the chicken.

Roasted Chicken and Potatoes with Olives and Oregano

Start to finish: 1¾ hours (15 minutes active)
Servings: 4

An oven-safe skillet offers two advantages for roasting a whole chicken. The low sides mean better heat circulation, which results in good browning. When the chicken is done, the pan can go directly onto the stovetop so that the drippings are easily reduced. We add fingerling potatoes to the skillet, so main dish and side cook together. Keep in mind that the skillet's handle will be hot when the pan is removed from the oven and while on the stovetop.

2 pounds fingerling potatoes

2 lemons, halved

4 oregano sprigs, plus 2 tablespoons chopped fresh oregano

Extra-virgin olive oil

Kosher salt and ground black pepper

4-pound whole chicken, legs tied

2 tablespoons black olive tapenade
OR ½ cup chopped pitted Kalamata olives

Heat the oven to 450°F. In a 12-inch oven-safe skillet, toss the potatoes, lemon halves and oregano sprigs with oil, salt and pepper. Set the chicken on top and season with salt and pepper. Roast until the thighs reach 175°F, about 1½ hours. Transfer the chicken and lemons to a cutting board. Set the pan on the stovetop (the handle will be hot) and cook the drippings and potatoes, stirring, until mostly dry. Squeeze in the juice from the lemons, then stir in the tapenade and chopped oregano. Serve with the chicken. Let rest for 30 minutes.

Pork

Recipes

Kick up the flavor of mild, sweet pork with warm spices and robust seasonings.

Spit-roasting a whole suckling pig slathered with myriad spices, as is done for Bali's famous babi guling, is a bit much for us, even on a weekend. But whipping up a bold paste of lightly citrusy lemon grass paired with garam masala and turmeric, slapping it on a well-scored pork shoulder and shoving it in a medium oven to roast untroubled while we go about our business for a few hours? That's the kind of casual feasting we can get behind.

Pork pairs well with robust seasonings, like the ancho chili powder we use to up the flavor of our tacos. The spice, made from dried ripe poblanos, is earthy and warm. And because it's not a blend, like regular chili powder, the flavor comes through cleanly. Gochujang, the high-impact chili paste, warms up our Korean-style spicy pork, and we toast and grind Sichuan peppercorns to add a pop of heat to our take on mapo tofu, the classic Chinese dish of ground pork and silky tofu. A touch of tang is another good comple-ment to pork. Tart Granny Smith apples and fresh fennel add flavor to our chops, while orange and yogurt produce tangy-sweet skewers.

Pork chops are great, and get even better when we take a cue from the popular Macau street food "pork chop bun." We pound the chops thin (so they better absorb flavors and cook faster) and give them a brief soak in bottled teriyaki sauce and five-spice powder. For a Mexican-inspired take on chops, we make a sauce inspired by salsa macha, a blend of dried chilies, garlic, nuts, seeds and olive oil. We use honey-roasted peanuts for sweet crunch and California or New Mexico chilies for heat.

Ground pork is another good option for fuss-free and flavorful cooking. It shines in our Southeast Asian–inspired meatballs brightened by lemon grass and ginger, and in our spicy-sweet burgers which have a little Asian chili-garlic sauce and brown sugar mixed in.

Delicious, tender pulled pork may sound like a project, but we've come up with an easy way. We use pork butt or shoulder, cut the meat into chunks and throw them in a Dutch oven along with seasonings to cook to succulent tenderness with little input from us, just the way we like it.

PORK

Ancho-Spiced Pork and Potato Tacos

Start to finish: 25 minutes
Servings: 4

Potatoes and pork seasoned with ancho chili powder and cumin make an easy, flavorful filling for tacos. Be sure to use a nonstick skillet, as the potatoes' starch makes them prone to sticking. If you like, offer a few of the garnishes suggested and allow diners to top their own tacos.

1½ teaspoons ancho chili powder

1 teaspoon ground cumin

Kosher salt and ground black pepper

1 pound Yukon Gold OR russet potatoes, not peeled, cut in ½-inch pieces

3 tablespoons extra-virgin olive oil

1 pound boneless pork loin chops, trimmed and cut into ½-inch pieces

4 medium garlic cloves, thinly sliced

8 corn tortillas, warmed

Mix the chili powder, cumin and ½ teaspoon each salt and pepper. In 2 separate bowls, toss half the spice mixture with the potatoes and the remaining half with the pork. In a 12-inch nonstick skillet, heat the oil until shimmering. Add the potatoes, then cover and cook, stirring occasionally, until well browned and tender. Stir in the pork and garlic, then cover and cook, stirring occasionally, until the pork is lightly browned and cooked through. Season with salt and pepper and serve with the tortillas.

Optional garnish: Chopped fresh cilantro OR thinly sliced radishes OR thinly sliced red onion OR diced avocado OR lime wedges OR sour cream OR a combination

Pork Skewers with Garlic, Orange and Yogurt

Start to finish: 20 minutes
Servings: 4

Greek yogurt seasoned with coriander, garlic and orange zest does double duty in this recipe. It's used as a sauce for serving and also creates a flavorful coating for chunks of pork loin. The yogurt-tossed pork is speared onto skewers and cooked quickly under the broiler; the char they develop adds flavor to the lean, mild-tasting meat. Serve with a rice or orzo pilaf and a simple leafy salad.

1 cup plain whole-milk Greek yogurt

1 tablespoon ground coriander

2 medium garlic cloves, finely grated

Grated zest and juice from 1 orange

1 tablespoon extra-virgin olive oil

1 tablespoon honey

Kosher salt and ground black pepper

1½ pounds 1-inch-thick boneless pork loin chops, cut into 1-inch chunks

Mix the yogurt, coriander, garlic, orange zest, oil, honey, 1½ teaspoons salt and 1 teaspoon pepper. In a small bowl, combine half the yogurt mixture and 1 tablespoon of orange juice; set aside. Toss the pork with the remaining yogurt mixture. Heat the broiler with a rack 6 inches from the element. Thread the pork onto metal skewers and place on a wire rack set in a broiler-safe rimmed baking sheet. Broil until lightly charred, about 7 minutes, turning once halfway through. Drizzle with the remaining orange juice and serve with the yogurt sauce.

Optional garnish: Chopped fresh flat-leaf parsley **OR** cilantro

245

Smoky Chili-Garlic Pork Burgers

Start to finish: 30 minutes
Servings: 4

To give these burgers spicy-sweet flavor and mild garlickiness, we mix Asian chili-garlic sauce and a little brown sugar into the ground pork. We also smear the buns with a chili-garlic mayonnaise. Pillow-soft, subtly sweet buns are a particularly good match for the tender, juicy burgers—we especially like potato buns or rolls. Serve with lettuce, sliced tomato, pickles or any of your favorite burger toppings.

⅓ cup mayonnaise

5 teaspoons plus 2 tablespoons chili-garlic sauce, divided

3 teaspoons packed brown sugar, divided

1 pound ground pork

2 teaspoons smoked paprika

Kosher salt and ground black pepper

1 tablespoon neutral oil

4 hamburger buns, preferably potato buns

Mix the mayonnaise, 5 teaspoons chili-garlic sauce and 1 teaspoon sugar. In a medium bowl, mix the pork, paprika, the remaining 2 tablespoons chili-garlic sauce, the remaining 2 teaspoons sugar, 1 teaspoon salt and ½ teaspoon pepper. Form into 4 patties. In a 12-inch nonstick skillet, heat the oil until shimmering. Add the patties and cook, flipping once, until well browned on both sides and the centers reach 160°F, 8 to 10 minutes total. Serve in buns spread with the mayonnaise mixture.

Pork Chops with Apples and Fennel Seed

Start to finish: 25 minutes
Servings: 4

This play on the classic pairing of pork chops and applesauce gets a big flavor boost from ground fennel, whole-grain mustard and a generous dose of butter. To grind the fennel seeds, use a mortar with a pestle or pulse them in an electric spice grinder. If you can find ground fennel at the grocery store, use an equal amount. Serve the chops with mashed or roasted potatoes.

5 teaspoons fennel seeds, ground (see note), divided

Kosher salt and ground black pepper

Four 1-inch-thick bone-in, center-cut pork loin chops (about 8 ounces each), patted dry

2 tablespoons neutral oil

2 medium Granny Smith apples, quartered, cored and thinly sliced

¾ cup apple cider

4 tablespoons salted butter, cut into 4 pieces

2 tablespoons whole-grain mustard

Mix 1 tablespoon ground fennel, 4 teaspoons salt and 2 teaspoons pepper, then sprinkle the mixture onto the chops. In a 12-inch skillet, heat the oil until barely smoking. Add the chops and cook until well browned, then flip and continue to cook until the centers reach 130°F. Transfer to a platter. Add the apples to the pan and cook, stirring, until softened. Add the cider and remaining ground fennel, then cook, stirring, until slightly syrupy. Off heat, stir in the butter and mustard, then season with salt and pepper. Pour over the chops.

Optional garnish: Chopped fresh rosemary

Spice-Crusted Pork Tenderloin Bites

Start to finish: 20 minutes
Servings: 4

This recipe was inspired by Spanish pinchos morunos, or grilled skewers of seasoned meat. For ease, we skip the skewers and cook the spiced chunks of pork tenderloin in a hot skillet. Serve this as a tapa or appetizer, or make it into a meal by offering garlicky braised greens and crusty bread alongside.

1 tablespoon honey

1 tablespoon lemon juice

1¼-pound pork tenderloin, trimmed of silver skin and cut into 1- to 1½-inch chunks

1½ teaspoons ground coriander

1½ teaspoons ground cumin

1½ teaspoons smoked paprika

Kosher salt and ground black pepper

1 tablespoon neutral oil

In a small bowl, mix the honey and lemon juice. In a medium bowl, toss the pork with the coriander, cumin, paprika and ¾ teaspoon each salt and pepper. In a 12-inch skillet, heat the oil until barely smoking. Add the pork and cook undisturbed until well browned on the bottom. Flip the pieces and cook, occasionally turning, until browned on all sides. Off heat, drizzle with the honey-lemon mixture.

Ground Pork with Ginger and Miso

Start to finish: 30 minutes
Servings: 4

Japanese nikumiso is considered a sauce, topping or small dish to accompany steamed rice and vegetables. This is our riff, and it requires only a small handful of high-impact ingredients and a few minutes of cooking to infuse ground pork with deep, umami-rich flavor. White miso is sweeter and milder than bolder, more assertive red miso; use whichever you prefer, or mix them if you happen to have both. Serve on steamed short-grain rice, on simply cooked cooked vegetables such as roasted eggplant or even in lettuce leaves.

3 tablespoons minced fresh ginger

4 scallions, thinly sliced, whites and greens reserved separately

3 tablespoons neutral oil

3 tablespoons white miso
OR red miso OR a combination

1½ pounds ground pork

3 tablespoons mirin

2 tablespoons soy sauce

In a 12-inch nonstick skillet over medium-high, cook ginger and scallion whites in the oil, stirring, until fragrant. Add the miso and cook, stirring constantly, until the miso darkens slightly. Add the pork, mirin, soy sauce and ⅓ cup water, then cook, stirring to break up the meat, until the liquid evaporates and the meat begins to crisp. Remove from the heat and stir in 2 tablespoons water. Serve sprinkled with the scallion greens.

Optional garnish: Toasted sesame seeds

PORK

Shredded Pork

Cut into chunks, tossed into a Dutch oven with seasonings and cooked slowly for several hours in a 325°F oven, tough and chewy pork butt (or shoulder) becomes succulent and tender enough to shred. The technique involves little hands-on work, and once the pot is in the oven it requires almost no attention.

Left to right: Miso-Gochujang Shredded Pork, Coconut-Red Curry Shredded Pork, Rosemary-Balsamic Shredded Pork, Star Anise and Soy Shredded Pork, (recipes next page)

Miso-Gochujang Shredded Pork

Start to finish: 3¾ hours (30 minutes active)
Servings: 6 to 8

For an Asian-inflected take on pulled pork, a trio of high-powered ingredients—gochujang (Korean red pepper paste), hoisin and white miso—adds loads of umami-rich, savory-sweet flavor. We like the pork piled onto soft buns with pickled jalapeños on the side. It's also great with a crisp cabbage slaw.

3 to 4 pounds boneless pork butt OR shoulder, trimmed and cut into 1½-inch chunks

¾ cup gochujang

¼ cup hoisin sauce

1 medium yellow onion, halved and thinly sliced

¼ cup white miso

Heat the oven to 325°F with a rack in the lower-middle position. In a large Dutch oven, stir together the pork, gochujang and hoisin. In a bowl, toss the onion with the miso, then distribute over the pork. Cover and cook for 2 hours. Uncover and cook until the pork is fork-tender, another 1½ to 2 hours, stirring once or twice. Skim off and discard the fat, then shred the pork.

Optional garnish: Thinly sliced scallions OR toasted sesame seeds OR both

Rosemary-Balsamic Shredded Pork

Start to finish: 3¾ hours (30 minutes active)
Servings: 6 to 8

Think of this as a pulled-pork version of Italian porchetta. Fresh rosemary and fennel seeds lend fragrance and flavor, and tangy-sweet balsamic vinegar helps balance the richness of the meat. Piled onto crusty rolls and topped with baby arugula, the pork makes delicious sandwiches. Or, spoon it on top of soft polenta.

3 to 4 pounds boneless pork butt OR shoulder, trimmed and cut into 1½-inch chunks

3 tablespoons balsamic vinegar

2 tablespoons packed brown sugar

2 tablespoons chopped fresh rosemary

1 tablespoon fennel seeds

Kosher salt and ground black pepper

1 medium yellow onion, halved and thinly sliced

Heat the oven to 325°F with a rack in the lower-middle position. In a large Dutch oven, stir together the pork, ¼ cup water, vinegar, sugar, rosemary, fennel seeds, and 2 teaspoons each salt and pepper. Scatter the onion over the pork. Cover and cook for 2 hours. Uncover and cook until the pork is fork-tender, another 1½ to 2 hours, stirring once or twice. Skim off and discard the fat, then shred the pork. Season with salt and pepper.

Optional garnish: Lemon wedges OR chopped fresh flat-leaf parsley OR both

Coconut-Red Curry Shredded Pork

Start to finish: 3¾ hours (30 minutes active)
Servings: 6 to 8

Thai red curry paste packs a handful of intense, aromatic ingredients, so it allows you to achieve complex flavor with just a few spoonfuls. Some brands are spicier than others, so if you're sensitive to chili heat, use the lesser amount; you can stir in a little more curry paste at the end, if desired. Serve the shredded pork over steamed jasmine rice or mounded onto buns with quick-pickled vegetables.

3 to 4 pounds boneless pork butt OR shoulder, trimmed and cut into 1½-inch chunks

½ cup coconut milk

3 to 4 tablespoons Thai red curry paste

2 tablespoons packed brown sugar

3 stalks lemon grass, trimmed to bottom 6 inches, bruised

Kosher salt and ground black pepper

1 medium yellow onion OR 2 large shallots, halved and thinly sliced

Heat the oven to 325°F with a rack in the lower-middle position. In a large Dutch oven, stir together the pork, coconut milk, curry paste, sugar, lemon grass and 2 teaspoons each salt and pepper. Scatter the onion over the pork. Cover and cook for 2 hours. Uncover and cook until the pork is fork-tender, another 1½ to 2 hours, stirring once or twice. Remove and discard the lemon grass. Skim off and discard the fat, then shred the pork. Season with salt and pepper.

Optional garnish: Chopped fresh cilantro OR lime wedges OR both

Star Anise and Soy Shredded Pork

Start to finish: 3¾ hours (30 minutes active)
Servings: 6 to 8

In this take on pulled pork, star anise perfumes the meat with its warm, sweet fragrance, while soy sauce adds savory depth. To balance the richness, we include a little vinegar—rice vinegar is good, but balsamic vinegar adds sweet notes that mimic Chinese black vinegar. Serve this over steamed rice, with lettuce leaves for wrapping or pile it onto buns and top with quick-pickled cucumbers.

3 to 4 pounds boneless pork butt OR shoulder, trimmed and cut into 1½-inch chunks

¼ cup soy sauce

2 tablespoons rice vinegar OR balsamic vinegar

2 tablespoons packed brown sugar

2 whole star anise

Kosher salt and ground black pepper

1 medium yellow onion, halved and thinly sliced

Heat the oven to 325°F with a rack in the lower-middle position. In a large Dutch oven, stir together the pork, soy sauce, vinegar, sugar, star anise and 2 teaspoons each salt and pepper. Scatter the onion over the pork. Cover and cook for 2 hours. Uncover and cook until the pork is fork-tender, another 1½ to 2 hours, stirring once or twice. Remove and discard the star anise. Skim off and discard the fat, then shred the pork. Season with salt and pepper.

Optional garnish: Thinly sliced scallions OR hoisin OR both

PORK

255

Garlic and Five Spice Pork Chop Sandwiches

Start to finish: 30 minutes
Servings: 4

We got the idea for these tasty sandwiches from the Macanese street food called "pork chop bun." We use boneless thin-cut pork chops (look for ones about ½ inch thick), pound them even thinner and give them a quick marinade in bottled teriyaki sauce boosted with garlic and five-spice powder. A broiler makes quick work of cooking the pork. For added flavor and richness, butter the cut sides of the buns before toasting. And if you like, tuck lettuce leaves, pickled red onions or pickled jalapeños into the sandwiches for serving.

¼ cup teriyaki sauce

6 medium garlic cloves, finely grated

½ teaspoon Chinese five-spice powder

Ground black pepper

8 thin-cut boneless pork loin chops (about 1 pound total; see note), trimmed and pounded to ⅛-inch thickness

4 Kaiser rolls OR potato buns, toasted (see note)

Mayonnaise, to serve

In a bowl, mix the teriyaki sauce, garlic, five-spice and ½ teaspoon pepper. Add the pork and turn to coat, then set aside. Heat the broiler with a rack about 4 inches from the element. Arrange the pork in a single layer on a broiler-safe rimmed baking sheet. Broil until sizzling and browned at the edges, 4 to 5 minutes, flipping the pieces halfway through. Serve in buns spread with mayonnaise.

Pork and Chorizo with Roasted Peppers

Start to finish: 35 minutes
Servings: 4

This is a simplified skillet version of the Spanish tapa called carcamusa. Traditionally, the dish is slow-simmered to tenderize the pork, but we chose to use tenderloin to speed the cooking. Spanish chorizo is a key ingredient here—it suffuses the dish with a smoky, meaty, garlicky flavor while offering a chewy counterpoint to the velvety tenderloin. Serve crusty bread alongside for dipping in the sauce.

6 ounces Spanish chorizo, casing removed, halved lengthwise and thinly sliced

2 tablespoons extra-virgin olive oil

1 cup roasted red peppers, patted dry and finely chopped

1 small yellow onion, grated on the large holes of a box grater

3 tablespoons tomato paste

1¼-pound pork tenderloin, trimmed of silver skin and cut into ½-inch chunks

½ cup frozen peas, thawed

Kosher salt and ground black pepper

In a 12-inch skillet over medium, cook the chorizo in the oil, stirring, until it has rendered some fat and the oil is red. Using a slotted spoon, transfer the chorizo to a plate. Into the skillet, stir the peppers, onion and tomato paste. Cover and cook, stirring, until the mixture is lightly browned. Add the pork, chorizo and ¾ cup water. Cover and simmer, stirring occasionally, until the pork is just cooked through. Stir in the peas, then season with salt and pepper.

Pork, Sweet Pepper and Cabbage Stew

Start to finish: 1 hour
(25 minutes active)
Servings: 4

This simple, hearty stew was inspired by a Peloponnese recipe from Diane Kochilas, an expert on Greek cuisine. We borrowed her technique of grating the onion so that it breaks down completely, adding silky texture and quickly relinquishing all of its flavor to the braising liquid. The cabbage and tomato paste are browned to develop depth and complexity. Serve with garlicky braised greens and crusty bread.

2 tablespoons extra-virgin olive oil, plus more to serve

1 pound green cabbage (1 small head), cored and cut into 1-inch ribbons

¼ cup tomato paste

2 pounds boneless pork shoulder, trimmed and cut into 1-inch chunks

1 small yellow onion, grated on the large holes of a box grater

1 red bell pepper OR orange bell pepper, stemmed, seeded and thinly sliced

1 tablespoon honey, plus more to serve

Kosher salt and ground black pepper

In a large Dutch oven, heat the oil until shimmering. Add the cabbage and cook, stirring, until charred in spots. Add the tomato paste and cook, stirring, until it clings to the pot and browns. Add the pork, onion, bell pepper, honey, 2 cups water and a generous pinch each of salt and pepper. Simmer, cover and cook, stirring occasionally, until the pork is tender, 30 to 40 minutes. Season with salt and pepper. Serve drizzled with additional oil and honey.

Optional garnish: Chopped fresh oregano

Breaded Pork Cutlets with Caraway and Dill

Start to finish: 30 minutes
Servings: 4

To achieve an ultra-crisp crust on these cutlets, we opt for the classic combination of flour, egg and panko (Japanese-style breadcrumbs). Our cut of choice for pork cutlets is tenderloin because it is easily pounded to an even thinness and its texture is dependably tender. But to add flavor to mild-tasting pork tenderloin, we generously season the panko with caraway and dill, as well as with salt and pepper. Serve with greens or potato salad, or make them into sandwiches.

¼ cup all-purpose flour

1½ cups panko breadcrumbs

Kosher salt and ground black pepper

1½ teaspoons caraway seeds

2 tablespoons chopped fresh dill,
plus more to serve

2 large eggs

1¼-pounds pork tenderloin, trimmed
of silver skin, cut into 4 evenly sized pieces
and pounded to ¼-inch thickness

6 tablespoons neutral oil, divided

Place the flour and panko in separate bowls. Stir ½ teaspoon salt into each; stir the caraway, dill and 1 teaspoon pepper into the panko. In a third bowl, beat the eggs with ½ teaspoon salt. Coat the cutlets on both sides with flour, then eggs, then panko, pressing to adhere. In a 12-inch nonstick skillet, heat 3 tablespoons of oil until shimmering. Add 2 cutlets and cook until browned on both sides, then transfer to a rack. Repeat with the remaining oil and cutlets.

Optional garnish: Lemon wedges **OR** whole-grain mustard **OR** both

Pork Chops with Peanut-Red Chili Salsa

Start to finish: 30 minutes
Servings: 4

The salsa in this recipe was inspired by Mexican salsa macha, an unusual blend of dried chilies, garlic, nuts, seeds and olive oil. We use honey-roasted peanuts to give our version sweetness. California or New Mexico chilies work best here, as they offer mild heat, subtle fruitiness and vivid color. The spicy-nutty-sweet-tangy flavor of the salsa is a perfect match for simply cooked pork chops.

6 California OR New Mexico dried chilies, stemmed, seeded and torn into rough 1-inch pieces

2 medium garlic cloves, smashed and peeled

2 tablespoons black OR white sesame seeds

Four 1-inch-thick bone-in, center-cut pork loin chops (each about 8 ounces), patted dry

Kosher salt and ground black pepper

1 tablespoon neutral oil

¾ cup honey-roasted peanuts

¼ cup lime juice

In a 12-inch skillet over medium, toast the chilies, garlic and sesame seeds, stirring, until fragrant. Transfer to a food processor and let cool. Season the chops with salt and pepper. In the same skillet, heat the oil until barely smoking. Add the chops and cook until well browned, then flip and cook until 130°F at the center. Transfer to a platter. Add the peanuts to the processor and pulse until finely chopped. Transfer to a bowl. Stir in the lime juice and enough water to yield a spreadable consistency. Season with salt and pepper and serve with the chops.

Pork Meatballs with Lemon Grass and Dill

Start to finish: 25 minutes
Servings: 4

The inspiration for these meatballs comes from Southeast Asia (dill, though more a Western herb, is used in the cooking of northern Vietnam). If you can find ground galangal, it's great in place of the ground ginger; it lends a citrusy, uniquely Southeast Asian flavor and aroma. Serve with rice or lettuce leaves for wrapping, and with a simple dipping sauce of fish sauce, lime juice, sugar and garlic. Or tuck them into a baguette with pickled vegetables, banh mi style.

2 stalks fresh lemon grass, trimmed to the lower 5 or 6 inches, dry outer layers discarded, thinly sliced

1½ teaspoons ground ginger
OR ground galangal

3 tablespoons chopped fresh dill

3 medium garlic cloves, roughly chopped

1 large egg

3 tablespoons neutral oil, divided

Kosher salt and ground black pepper

1 pound ground pork

In a food processor, process the lemon grass, ginger, dill, garlic, egg, 1 tablespoon oil, 1 teaspoon salt and ½ teaspoon pepper until the lemon grass is finely chopped. Add the pork and process until paste-like. In a 12-inch nonstick skillet, swirl the remaining 2 tablespoons oil and 2 tablespoons water. Shape the pork mixture into 1½-inch balls and place in the pan. Cook without stirring over medium-high until the water simmers, then cover and cook until the exterior of the meatballs is no longer pink. Uncover and continue to cook, stirring occasionally, until browned on all sides.

Roasted Pork Shoulder with Turmeric and Lemon Grass

Start to finish: 4¾ hours (20 minutes active)
Servings: 8 to 10

When developing this recipe, we had in mind the Balinese spit-roasted pig called babi guling, which is seasoned with a long list of spices and aromatics. We start by making a paste with fresh lemon grass, shallots and turmeric, then add garam masala to layer in more complex spicing. Don't trim the fat off the surface of the pork roast—scoring it with a knife creates a surface to which the seasoning paste can adhere. For easy cleanup, line the baking sheet with foil before setting the roast on top.

4 medium shallots, peeled and quartered

3 stalks fresh lemon grass, trimmed to the lower 5 or 6 inches, dry outer layers discarded, thinly sliced

3 tablespoons packed brown sugar

2 tablespoons neutral oil

1 tablespoon garam masala

1 tablespoon ground turmeric

Kosher salt and ground black pepper

5-pound boneless pork shoulder roast, untrimmed

Heat the oven to 300°F. In a food processor, process the shallots, lemon grass, sugar, oil, garam masala, turmeric, 1 tablespoon salt and 2 teaspoons pepper to form a paste. With a knife, score a crosshatch pattern into the surface fat on top of the roast. Rub the paste onto all sides of the roast and into the cuts. Place the pork fat side up on a rimmed baking sheet and roast until the center reaches 195°F, about 4 hours. Let rest for 30 minutes, then cut into slices for serving.

Optional garnish: Thinly sliced scallions OR chopped fresh cilantro OR lime wedges OR sambal OR a combination

263

Spicy Pork and Tofu with Sichuan Pepper

Start to finish: 30 minutes
Servings: 4

Sichuan peppercorns give this simple dish a tongue-tingling quality, while the Chinese chili-bean sauce called toban djan provides spiciness and umami. To bring out the flavor and aroma of the peppercorns, toast them in a small skillet over medium until fragrant, about 2 minutes. Cool, then finely grind in an electric spice grinder. If you can't find chili-bean paste, chili-garlic sauce is a decent substitute. And if you're sensitive to spiciness, reduce the chili-bean sauce to 2 tablespoons or so. Serve with steamed jasmine rice.

8 ounces ground pork

3 tablespoons chili-bean sauce (toban djan) OR chili-garlic sauce

2 tablespoons neutral oil

1 tablespoon finely grated fresh ginger

2 bunches scallions, thinly sliced, white and green parts reserved separately

1 tablespoon Sichuan peppercorns, toasted and ground (see note)

Kosher salt

14-ounce container extra-firm OR firm tofu, drained, cut into ¾-inch cubes

In a 12-inch nonstick skillet, mix the pork, bean sauce, oil, ginger, scallion whites, Sichuan pepper, 1 teaspoon salt and ½ cup water. Cook over medium-high, stirring, until the meat no longer is pink. Stir in the tofu and an additional 1 cup water. Bring to a simmer and cook, stirring occasionally, until the liquid has evaporated and the mixture begins to sizzle. Stir in the scallion greens.

Optional garnish: Toasted sesame oil OR toasted sesame seeds OR chili oil

Korean-Style Spicy Pork

Start to finish: 30 minutes
Servings: 4

In dwaeji bulgogi, or Korean spicy grilled pork, thinly sliced pork, often fatty pork belly, is marinated in a savory-sweet mixture of gochujang and soy sauce. We, however, opt for easier-to-find pork shoulder, cook it in a skillet on the stovetop and add the flavorings last. Like pork belly, shoulder is well marbled and flavorful. If the shoulder you purchase has an exterior layer of fat thicker than ½ inch, trim some off so the dish doesn't wind up greasy. Serve this with steamed short-grain rice or with lettuce leaves for wrapping.

¼ cup gochujang

3 tablespoons soy sauce

1 tablespoon white sugar

3 tablespoons neutral oil

1 pound boneless pork shoulder, untrimmed (see note), cut into 2-inch strips and sliced ¼ to ⅛ inch thick against the grain

1 medium yellow onion, halved and thinly sliced

3-inch piece fresh ginger, peeled, quartered lengthwise and thinly sliced OR 4 cloves garlic, minced OR both

Mix the gochujang, soy sauce and sugar. In a 12-inch skillet, heat the oil until shimmering. Add the pork and cook, stirring occasionally, until no longer pink. Add the onion and ginger, then cook, stirring, until the ginger is fragrant. Stir in the gochujang mixture. Cover and cook, stirring occasionally, until the pork is tender and the sauce clings to the meat, about 10 minutes.

Optional garnish: Thinly sliced scallions OR toasted sesame oil OR toasted sesame seeds OR a combination

265

Beef

Recipes

To give beef the Cookish treatment we skip high-priced cuts or elaborate methods, and we aren't afraid to break some rules.

Rich beef calls out for robust seasoning. We looked at classic dishes from around the world—then simplified them for everyday ease. From China's Sichuan province we got the idea for an orange beef stir-fry, but we used marmalade instead of orange zest and juice; it gave us bitter, sweet and tangy flavors in one step. Tacos are hard to beat; we take ours up a notch by rubbing skirt steak with cumin for warm, spicy flavor and toss with lime juice after browning for a splash of acidity that balances the richness of the meat.

The best beef dishes start with the right technique, whether that's giving steak a good sear and slicing it thin or letting chunkier cuts like pot roast cook low and slow. For our Sichuan-inspired stir-fried beef and celery we dry-fry beef (cook it in oil but without seasoning), then add aromatics and spices, which cling well to the browned meat. And we're not shy about tweaking traditional methods. We give standard marinades a miss and add seasoning as the meat rests—the flavors of the sauce stay fresher and brighter.

Tougher cuts like chuck often are braised—browned, then cooked in a covered pan on the stovetop. We like the results, but not the effort. So we don't brown, use little or no added liquid, and use the oven, not the stovetop, to produce even, tender meat that makes its own concentrated sauce. We came up with four variations, including an olive- and orange-flavored version based on a traditional Provençal dish.

Expensive tenderloin doesn't fit our template for casual suppers. Ground beef does—but we make sure it's never stodgy or bland. We use smoked paprika to flavor the meat and sauce in our Spanish-style meatballs. And caramelized shallots and the curry spice mix garam masala lend quick, intense flavor to our Indian-style curried beef and peas. We've also got a dish inspired by Vietnam's canh, a brothy soup. Ours is modeled on a meatball version, but to save a step we don't bother to mold the meat into balls and instead simmer ground beef along with aromatics and umami-rich fish sauce; it produces a deeply flavorful broth.

BEEF

Curried Beef Skewers

Start to finish: 30 minutes
Servings: 4

These beef skewers were inspired by Burmese flavors, and get complexity from curry spices, savory fish sauce and the bite of fresh ginger. If you like, trim the ends off 2 medium shallots, then peel and halve them lengthwise; before cooking, cap each beef skewer with a shallot. Broiling will char the shallots' outer layers and the interiors will be sweet and tender, a nice complement to the beef. Serve with fragrant basmati or jasmine rice.

¼ cup neutral oil

2 tablespoons fish sauce

1½ tablespoons finely grated fresh ginger

8 medium garlic cloves, finely grated

1½ teaspoons curry powder

Grated zest of 1 lime, plus lime wedges to serve

Ground black pepper

1½ pounds beef flat iron steak OR boneless short ribs, trimmed and sliced against the grain into ½-inch-thick strips

Stir together the oil, fish sauce, ginger, garlic, curry powder, lime zest and a pinch of pepper. In a medium bowl, toss the steak with half the seasoning paste. Heat the broiler with a rack 4 inches from the element. Scrunch the meat onto metal skewers, then arrange on a wire rack in a broiler-safe rimmed baking sheet. Broil until charred on both sides, 6 to 10 minutes, flipping once. Brush the skewers with the remaining seasoning paste, then let stand for 10 minutes. Serve with lime wedges.

Optional garnish: Fried shallots **OR** hot sauce **OR** chopped roasted peanuts **OR** a combination of Fresno or jalapeño chilies, stemmed and thinly sliced

Skirt Steak and Green Chili Tacos

Start to finish: 25 minutes
Servings: 4

We turn sautéed onion, poblano chilies and cumin-seasoned skirt steak into an easy, flavorful taco filling. Dousing it with lime juice after cooking keeps the flavors bright and balanced. For the tenderest texture, slice the rested steak thinly and against the grain. And use a nonstick skillet, otherwise the steak's seasoning may stick to the pan and scorch.

1 pound skirt steak, trimmed

1 tablespoon ground cumin

Kosher salt and ground black pepper

2 teaspoons neutral oil

1 large yellow onion, halved and thinly sliced

2 poblano chilies, stemmed, seeded and cut into thin strips

¼ cup lime juice

Warmed corn tortillas, to serve

Rub the steak with cumin, 2 teaspoons salt and 1 teaspoon pepper, then cut into 5-inch sections. In a 12-inch nonstick skillet, heat the oil until barely smoking. Add the meat and brown on both sides; transfer to a plate. To the skillet, add the onion, chilies and ½ teaspoon salt. Cover and cook, stirring, until slightly softened, then uncover and cook until lightly browned; remove from heat. Thinly slice the steak against the grain and toss with its juices and the lime juice, then toss with the vegetables. Serve with tortillas.

Optional garnish: Thinly sliced radishes **OR** chopped fresh cilantro **OR** both

Steak Salad with Walnuts and Goat Cheese

Start to finish: 30 minutes
Servings: 4

We use pomegranate molasses in the dressing for this main-course salad. Its fruity, tangy-sweet flavor pairs well with the savory meat and peppery watercress. Take the time to finely chop the toasted walnuts; broken down into small pieces, the nuts better cling to the greens, rather than fall to the bottom of the bowl. Serve with warm, crusty bread.

1 pound beef flat iron steak, trimmed

Kosher salt and ground black pepper

5 tablespoons extra-virgin olive oil, divided

2 teaspoons ground coriander

3 tablespoons pomegranate molasses

4-ounce package baby watercress
OR 5-ounce container baby arugula

½ cup walnuts, toasted and finely chopped

2 ounces fresh goat cheese (chèvre), crumbled (½ cup)

Season the steak with salt and pepper. In a 12-inch skillet, heat 1 tablespoon of oil until barely smoking. Brown the steak on both sides until the center reaches 120°F (for medium-rare). Transfer to a platter. In a large bowl, whisk the remaining 4 tablespoons oil, the coriander, pomegranate molasses and ¼ teaspoon each salt and pepper. Thinly slice the steak and return to the platter. Whisk the accumulated juices from the steak and 2 tablespoons water into the dressing; toss in the watercress and walnuts. Top the steak with the salad and sprinkle with cheese.

BEEF

273

Spanish-Style Meatballs

Start to finish: 25 minutes
Servings: 4

These tapas-style meatballs, called albondigas, are rich and satisfying. Smoked paprika not only spices the meatballs, it also flavors the sauce and helps thicken it to a glaze-like consistency. For this recipe, look for firm, meaty green olives such as Castelvetrano olives. Serve with plenty of warm, crusty bread.

1 pound 90 percent lean ground beef

⅔ cup panko breadcrumbs

5 medium garlic cloves, 2 minced,
3 thinly sliced

2 tablespoons smoked paprika, divided

2 teaspoons minced fresh thyme,
plus 3 thyme sprigs

Kosher salt and ground black pepper

2 tablespoons extra-virgin olive oil

½ cup pitted green olives, chopped

Mix together the beef, panko, minced garlic, 1 tablespoon paprika, minced thyme, 2 teaspoons salt and 1 teaspoon pepper; form into 16 meatballs. In a 12-inch nonstick skillet, heat the oil until shimmering. Add the meatballs and brown on the bottom. Add 2 tablespoons water, cover and cook until the exteriors are no longer pink. Uncover and cook, turning often, until the centers reach 160°F. Add ½ cup water, the sliced garlic, remaining 1 tablespoon paprika, thyme sprigs and olives. Cook, stirring, until the sauce lightly glazes the meatballs.

Optional garnish: Toasted sliced almonds

Beef, Spinach and Feta Gozleme

Start to finish: 40 minutes
Servings: 4

Gozleme is a Turkish stuffed flatbread. Made the traditional way, large, thin sheets of unbaked dough are filled then cooked on a griddle-like pan. For ease, we use flour tortillas, fill them with a simple mixture of beef, spinach and feta, then toast them in the same skillet used to make the filling. To make this into a meal, serve a simple salad alongside.

1 pound 90 percent lean ground beef

3 tablespoons tomato paste

2½ teaspoons ground cumin

Kosher salt and ground black pepper

5-ounce container baby spinach, roughly chopped

4 ounces feta cheese, crumbled (1 cup)

Four 10-inch flour tortillas

2 teaspoons extra-virgin olive oil, divided

In a 12-inch nonstick skillet, cook the beef, tomato paste, cumin, 1 teaspoon salt, ½ teaspoon pepper and ½ cup water, until the beef is no longer pink. Add the spinach and cook, stirring, until the pan is dry. Transfer to a bowl; cool for 10 minutes, then stir in the feta. Wipe out the skillet. Divide the mixture among the tortillas, spreading it over the center third; fold each like a business letter. In the skillet, heat 1 teaspoon oil until shimmering. Add 2 filled tortillas and cook until golden on both sides, then transfer to plates. Repeat with the remaining oil and filled tortillas.

Beef and Pine Nut Kofte

Start to finish: 30 minutes
Servings: 4

These kofte (meatballs—or, in this case, patties) get their fine, tender texture and rich flavor from processing the beef with pine nuts, parsley and spices. Moistening your hands when shaping the mixture helps minimize sticking. Serve with warmed flatbread, sliced onion, diced tomato and/or cucumber, as well as yogurt mixed with a little tahini.

½ cup pine nuts

½ cup lightly packed fresh flat-leaf parsley, plus chopped parsley to serve

1 large shallot, roughly chopped

2 teaspoons ground cumin

½ teaspoon ground allspice

Kosher salt and ground black pepper

2 tablespoons extra-virgin olive oil, divided

1 pound 80 percent lean ground beef

In a food processor, process the pine nuts, parsley, shallot, cumin, allspice, 2 teaspoons salt, 1 teaspoon pepper and 1 tablespoon of the oil until coarsely ground, about 30 seconds. Add the beef and process until finely ground, 30 to 40 seconds. Form into patties. In a 12-inch nonstick skillet, heat 1 tablespoon oil until shimmering. Cook the patties until well browned on both sides and the centers reach 160°F. Transfer to a plate and sprinkle with chopped parsley.

Low-Liquid Braise

Low-liquid braising is an unconventional, but easy beef-stew method that yields deep flavor. We skip the step of browning the meat, add only a minimal amount of liquid (sometimes none at all) and use the steady heat of the oven instead of the stovetop for simmering. Because the ingredients cook gently in their own juices, the finished stew is meaty and concentrated in flavor, and the liquid does not require thickening.

Left to right: Beef Stew with Olives and Orange, (bottom) Nihari-Inspired Beef Stew, (top) Cumin-Garlic Beef Stew, Beef and Leek Stew with Smoked Paprika

Beef Stew with Olives and Orange

Start to finish: 3½ hours (30 minutes active)
Servings: 6

A Provençal-inspired braise combines savory olives and sweet oranges in this hearty dish. A Y-style vegetable peeler is the best tool for removing the zest strips from the orange. Serve with crusty bread or soft polenta.

4 to 5 pounds boneless beef chuck roast, trimmed and cut into 1½-inch chunks

2 medium red onions, ends trimmed, each cut into 8 wedges

1 cup pitted Kalamata olives, roughly chopped

Zest strips from 1 orange (see note), plus ⅓ cup orange juice

2 teaspoons dried oregano OR herbes de Provence

Kosher salt and ground black pepper

½ cup dry white wine

Heat the oven to 325°F. In a large Dutch oven, combine the beef, onions, half the olives, the zest strips, oregano, 1 tablespoon salt and 2 teaspoons pepper. Cover and cook in the oven for 2 hours. Stir in the wine and cook uncovered until a skewer inserted into the beef meets no resistance, about another hour. Stir in the remaining olives, then cover and let stand for 10 minutes. Skim off and discard the fat. Remove and discard the zest. Stir in the orange juice and season with salt and pepper.

Optional garnish: Chopped fresh basil OR flat-leaf parsley

Beef and Leek Stew with Smoked Paprika

Start to finish: 3½ hours (30 minutes active)
Servings: 6

Smoked paprika lends rich color and a complexity that makes this dish taste as though it demanded far more effort than it actually did. Woodsy sherry vinegar and an infusion of additional smoked paprika at the end brightens and rounds out the long-cooked flavors. Serve rustic bread and steamed or roasted vegetables alongside.

4 to 5 pounds boneless beef chuck roast, trimmed and cut into 1½-inch chunks

2 pounds leeks, white and light green parts halved lengthwise, cut crosswise into 1½-inch pieces, rinsed and drained

1 tablespoon plus ¼ teaspoon smoked paprika, divided

2 teaspoons dried thyme

Kosher salt and ground black pepper

½ cup dry red wine

2 tablespoons sherry vinegar

Heat the oven to 325°F. In a large Dutch oven, combine the beef, leeks, 1 tablespoon smoked paprika, thyme, 1 tablespoon salt and 1 teaspoon pepper. Cover and cook in the oven for 2 hours. Stir in the wine and cook uncovered until a skewer inserted into the beef meets no resistance, about 1 hour. Cover and let stand for 10 minutes. Skim off and discard the fat. Stir in the vinegar and remaining ¼ teaspoon smoked paprika; season with salt and pepper.

Optional garnish: Chopped fresh flat-leaf parsley OR chopped fresh chives

Cumin-Garlic Beef Stew

Start to finish: 3½ hours (30 minutes active)
Servings: 6

The Moroccan dish called tangia is named for the urn-like clay vessel in which it traditionally is cooked. It's a meat-centric dish typically seasoned with saffron and cumin but not herbs, and it gave us the idea for this recipe. Dried apricots absorb the beef's juices during braising, creating a velvety, sweet-savory sauce that coats the meat. Serve with steamed couscous, hunks of crusty bread or warmed flatbread.

4 to 5 pounds boneless beef chuck roast, trimmed and cut into 1½-inch chunks

⅔ cup dried apricots, sliced

6 medium garlic cloves, smashed and peeled

1 teaspoon ground cumin

½ teaspoon saffron threads

Kosher salt and ground black pepper

3 tablespoons lemon juice, plus lemon wedges to serve

Heat the oven to 325°F. In a large Dutch oven, combine the beef, apricots, garlic, cumin, saffron, 1 tablespoon salt and 1 teaspoon pepper. Cover and cook in the oven for 2 hours. Stir in ½ cup water and cook uncovered until a skewer inserted into the beef meets no resistance, about 1 hour. Cover and let stand for 10 minutes. Skim off and discard the fat. Stir in the lemon juice; season with salt and pepper. Serve with lemon wedges.

Optional garnish: Chopped pitted green olives OR chopped toasted pistachios

Nihari-Inspired Beef Stew

Start to finish: 3½ hours (30 minutes active)
Servings: 6

Nihari is a richly spiced South Asian stew, often made with a special spice blend called nihari masala, and with generous amounts of browned onions and fresh ginger. Our much-simplified version depends on readily available garam masala (an Indian spice blend) for warmth and complexity, supplemented by the earthy, fruity notes of sweet paprika. We add grated fresh ginger and lemon juice at the very end to sharpen all the flavors. Serve with basmati rice or warmed flatbread.

4 to 5 pounds boneless beef chuck roast, trimmed and cut into 1½-inch chunks

2 large red onions, halved and thickly sliced

2 teaspoons garam masala

1½ teaspoons sweet paprika

Kosher salt and ground black pepper

2 tablespoons lemon juice

1 tablespoon finely grated fresh ginger

Heat the oven to 325°F. In a large Dutch oven, combine the beef, onions, garam masala, paprika, 1 tablespoon salt and 2 teaspoons pepper. Cover and cook in the oven for 2 hours. Stir, return to the oven uncovered and cook until a skewer inserted into the beef meets no resistance, about 1 hour. Cover and let stand for 10 minutes. Skim off and discard the fat. Stir in the lemon juice and ginger; season with salt and pepper.

Optional garnish: Chopped fresh cilantro OR plain yogurt OR Fresno or jalapeño chilies, stemmed and thinly sliced

BEEF

281

Vietnamese-Style Beef, Watercress and Cilantro Soup

Start to finish: 30 minutes
Servings: 4

Canh is a broad category of simple home-style Vietnamese soups. In this version, we simmer softened shallots, fresh lemon grass and ground beef mixed with fish sauce and cilantro stems to yield a clean-tasting yet surprisingly flavorful broth. Serve with steamed jasmine rice.

1 pound 80 percent lean ground beef

3 tablespoons fish sauce, divided, plus more to serve

2 cups lightly packed fresh cilantro, stems minced and leaves chopped, reserved separately

Kosher salt and ground black pepper

3 tablespoons neutral oil

4 medium shallots, halved and thinly sliced

2 stalks lemon grass, trimmed to the bottom 6 inches, dry outer layers discarded, bruised and halved crosswise

2 cups lightly packed baby watercress, roughly chopped

Mix the beef, 2 tablespoons fish sauce, the cilantro stems and 1 teaspoon pepper. In a large saucepan, heat the oil until shimmering. Add the shallots and lemon grass and cook, stirring, until the shallots have softened. Add the beef mixture and cook, breaking it up, until only some pink remains. Add 6 cups water and 1 teaspoon salt. Boil, reduce to a simmer and cook uncovered for 10 minutes. Off heat, discard the lemon grass, then stir in the remaining 1 tablespoon fish sauce, the cilantro leaves and watercress.

Optional garnish: Lime wedges **OR** hot sauce **OR** both

Gochujang Skirt Steak and Noodles with Kimchi

Start to finish: 25 minutes
Servings: 4

For this meal in a bowl, use sturdy dried Asian wheat noodles, such as non-instant ramen or lo mein. Cook the noodles according to package directions, then drain and rinse; they don't need to be hot for serving. Gochujang is a fermented Korean chili paste; look for it sold in small red tubs or squeeze bottles in the international aisle of supermarkets or in Asian grocery stores.

1 pound skirt steak, trimmed

5 tablespoons gochujang, divided

Kosher salt

1 tablespoon neutral oil

1 tablespoon mirin

2 teaspoons toasted sesame oil, plus more to serve

1½ cups drained napa cabbage kimchi, roughly chopped, plus 3 tablespoons kimchi juice

10 ounces dried non-instant ramen OR lo mein noodles, cooked, drained and rinsed

Rub the steak with 2 tablespoons of gochujang and season with 2 teaspoons salt, then cut into 3-inch sections. In a 12-inch skillet, heat the neutral oil until shimmering. Add the steak and brown well on both sides. Transfer to a plate. In a large bowl, whisk together the remaining 3 tablespoons gochujang, mirin, sesame oil and kimchi juice. Thinly slice the steak against the grain and add to the bowl along with any juices, the noodles and kimchi, then toss. Season with salt and drizzle with additional sesame oil.

Optional garnish: Thinly sliced cucumber OR thinly sliced scallions OR both

BEEF

283

Pastrami Hash with Pickled Beets

Start to finish: 20 minutes
Servings: 6

This colorful, flavor-packed hash isn't just for breakfast or brunch—it also makes a satisfying dinner. To parcook the potatoes, we use the microwave, which is neater and faster than boiling on the stovetop. Serve the hash topped with sunny-side-up fried eggs.

1 pound red **OR** Yukon Gold potatoes, unpeeled, cut into ½-inch cubes

Kosher salt and ground black pepper

¼ cup neutral oil

1 medium yellow onion, chopped

2 medium carrots, peeled and chopped

8 ounces deli sliced pastrami, chopped

1 cup lightly packed fresh dill, chopped

1 cup drained pickled beets, chopped

In a large microwave-safe bowl, toss the potatoes with 1 teaspoon salt. Cover and microwave on high until tender, about 5 minutes; stir once halfway through. Drain off any moisture. In a 12-inch nonstick skillet, heat the oil until barely smoking. Add the potatoes, onion and carrots, then cook, stirring, until well browned and the carrots are tender. Add the pastrami and 1 teaspoon each salt and pepper. Cook, stirring, until the pastrami browns. Off heat, stir in the dill and beets.

Optional garnish: Sour cream

Beer-Braised Short Ribs with Mustard and Dill

Start to finish: 3½ hours (20 minutes active)
Servings: 4 to 6

This recipe borrows flavors from classic Belgian carbonnade à la flamande, a hearty stew of beef, onions and ale. A full-flavored, medium-bodied beer such as Fat Tire Amber Ale or Newcastle Brown Ale works well here. Or if you're willing to spend a little more, try a Belgian Trappist ale such as Chimay. Serve the ribs with spaetzle, egg noodles, mashed potatoes or crusty bread.

3 pounds boneless beef short ribs, trimmed

Kosher salt and ground black pepper

10 bay leaves

8 medium shallots, halved and sliced

12-ounce bottle amber ale OR brown ale OR 330-ml bottle Trappist ale (see note)

½ cup Dijon mustard

¼ cup lightly packed fresh dill, chopped

In a 13-by-9-inch baking dish, season the ribs with 1 tablespoon salt and 1 teaspoon pepper. Tuck in the bay and shallot, then add the beer. Cover tightly with foil and bake at 325°F for 2½ hours. Remove from the oven and increase the temperature to 425°F. Spread the mustard over the ribs and cook, uncovered, until the mustard has browned, about 30 minutes. Remove and discard the bay. Skim off and discard the fat from the surface of the liquid, then season with salt and pepper. Serve with sauce, sprinkled with dill.

BEEF

285

Braised Beef with Chilies and Mexican Chocolate

Start to finish: 4½ hours (15 minutes active)
Servings: 4 to 6

Making authentic Mexican mole is a labor of love. This recipe, though, captures some of the flavors of mole negro and pairs them with a fork-tender pot roast. Tablets of Mexican chocolate flavored with sugar and spices are usually used for making Mexican hot chocolate; here we add some to the pot to enrich the sauce with roasty, bittersweet notes. Look for Mexican chocolate sold in small hexagonal boxes; Ibarra and Abuelita are common brands. Serve the beef with warmed tortillas or rice.

2 large yellow onions, halved and sliced

2 ancho chilies, stemmed, seeded and torn into pieces

½ cup dried apricots, chopped **OR** raisins

¼ cup smooth almond butter

3-ounce tablet Mexican chocolate (see note), chopped

3- to 4-pound boneless beef chuck roast, trimmed

Kosher salt and ground black pepper

Heat the oven to 325°F. In a Dutch oven, toss together the onions, chilies, apricots, almond butter and chocolate. Season the roast with 1 tablespoon each salt and pepper, then place in the pot, nestling it into the onion mixture. Cover, place in the oven and cook for 3½ hours. Remove from the oven and let rest, covered, for 30 minutes. Transfer the roast to a cutting board, cut into slices against the grain and place on a platter. Mash the solids in the pot into a chunky sauce, then season with salt and pepper and spoon over the roast.

Optional garnish: Toasted sliced almonds **OR** lime wedges **OR** chopped fresh cilantro **OR** a combination

Ginger-Soy Beef with Watercress

Start to finish: 30 minutes
Servings: 4

This unusual cooking method skips browning the meat and instead gets flavor from reducing and concentrating a mixture of soy sauce, sugar, mirin, ginger and the juices released by the beef. We serve the beef on a bed of peppery watercress. To simplify prep, look for prewashed baby watercress sold in bags; if not available, baby arugula is a good option. Serve with steamed rice.

⅓ cup soy sauce

3 tablespoons white sugar

2 tablespoons mirin

3-inch piece fresh ginger, peeled, quartered lengthwise and thinly sliced

1 pound boneless beef short ribs OR flat iron steak, trimmed and sliced ¼ inch thick against the grain

4-ounce bag baby watercress OR 5-ounce container baby arugula

In a 12-inch skillet, boil the soy sauce, sugar, mirin and ginger, stirring to dissolve the sugar. Add the beef, reduce to low and cook, stirring occasionally and adjusting the heat to maintain a simmer, until the meat releases its juices. Increase to high and cook, stirring, until the liquid forms a light glaze that clings to the meat. Arrange the watercress on a platter and top with the beef.

Optional garnish: Thinly sliced scallions

Pan-Seared Steak

When it comes to steak, we skip marinades (which don't impart much flavor) and opt instead to apply bold flavorings immediately after cooking, keeping the flavors of the sauces fresh and bright. After slicing, we finish the steak with additional sauce or relish for a fresh infusion of flavor.

Top Left: Pan-Seared Steak with Red Chimichurri; Bottom Left: Pan-Seared Steak with Zhoug; Top Right: Pan-Seared Steak with Black Pepper-Lime Sauce; Bottom Right: Pan-Seared Steak with Spiced Scallion Radish

Pan-Seared Steak with Red Chimichurri

Start to finish: 30 minutes
Servings: 4

Argentinian red chimichurri—the lesser-known sibling of green chimichurri—adds rich, spicy, herbal notes to a simple pan-seared steak. If using flank or skirt steak, cut the meat into two or three pieces that fit comfortably in the skillet.

¼ cup plus 2 teaspoons neutral oil

1 tablespoon sweet paprika

1 tablespoon red pepper flakes

1 tablespoon dried oregano

1 medium garlic clove, finely grated

2 tablespoons balsamic vinegar

1½ pounds beef flat iron steak OR flank steak OR skirt steak (see note), trimmed

Kosher salt and ground black pepper

In a microwave-safe bowl, combine the ¼ cup oil, paprika, pepper flakes and oregano. Microwave on high for 30 seconds, then stir the garlic and vinegar; set aside. Season the steak with salt and pepper. In a 12-inch skillet, heat the remaining 2 teaspoons oil until barely smoking. Add the steak and cook until well browned on both sides and the center reaches 120°F (for medium-rare), flipping once. Transfer to a platter and spoon on half of the sauce. Let rest for 10 minutes, then thinly slice the steak against the grain, return to the platter and spoon on the remaining sauce.

Optional garnish: Chopped fresh oregano

Pan-Seared Steak with Spiced Scallion Relish

Start to finish: 30 minutes
Servings: 4

This simple stir-together relish gets umami from soy sauce, brightness from lemon juice and fragrance from fennel and cumin seeds. To crush the seeds, use a mortar and pestle or the bottom of a heavy skillet; alternatively, pulse them a few times in a spice grinder. Whatever your method, leave them with some texture—don't pulverize them to a powder. If using flank or skirt steak, cut the meat into two or three pieces that fit comfortably in the skillet.

1 bunch scallions, thinly sliced

2 tablespoons soy sauce

2 tablespoons lemon juice

1½ tablespoons fennel seeds, crushed

1½ tablespoons cumin seeds, crushed

1½ pounds beef flat iron steak OR flank steak OR skirt steak (see note), trimmed

Kosher salt and ground black pepper

2 teaspoons neutral oil

In a small bowl, mix the scallions, soy sauce, lemon juice, fennel and cumin. Season the steak with salt and pepper. In a 12-inch skillet, heat the oil until barely smoking. Add the steak and cook until well browned on both sides and the center reaches 120°F (for medium-rare), flipping once. Transfer to a platter and spoon on half the sauce. Let rest for 10 minutes, then thinly slice the steak against the grain, return to the platter and spoon on the remaining sauce.

Optional garnish: Toasted sesame seeds

Pan-Seared Steak with Black Pepper-Lime Sauce

Start to finish: 30 minutes
Servings: 4

The Khmer dipping sauce called tuk meric is made with just a few ingredients and has as its flavor base a generous amount of coarsely ground black pepper and freshly squeezed lime juice. Its tangy, peppery notes complement the meatiness of simply seared steak. A mortar and pestle or the bottom of a heavy skillet work best for coarsely grinding the peppercorns; you also could pulse them in a spice grinder, but their consistency will be slightly more uneven. If using flank or skirt steak, cut the meat into two or three pieces that fit comfortably in the skillet.

¼ cup lime juice

¼ cup coarsely ground black pepper

2 teaspoons packed light brown sugar

1 teaspoon fish sauce

Kosher salt

1½ pounds beef flat iron steak OR flank steak OR skirt steak (see note), trimmed

2 teaspoons neutral oil

In a small bowl, mix the lime juice, pepper, sugar, fish sauce and 2 teaspoons salt. Season the steak with salt. In a 12-inch skillet, heat the oil until barely smoking. Add the steak and cook until well browned on both sides and the center reaches 120°F (for medium-rare), flipping once. Transfer to a platter and spoon on half the sauce. Let rest for 10 minutes, then thinly slice the steak against the grain, return to the platter and spoon on the remaining sauce.

Optional garnish: Lime wedges OR chopped roasted peanuts OR chopped fresh cilantro OR a combination

Pan-Seared Steak with Zhoug

Start to finish: 30 minutes
Servings: 4

Zhoug is a Middle Eastern condiment made with herbs, fresh green chilies, lemon juice and spices. Its spiciness and bright, fresh, grassy flavors perfectly counter the richness of steak. We use a food processor to minimize the knifework for making zhoug, but if you prefer you can mince the herbs, garlic and chili by hand. If using flank or skirt steak, cut the meat into two or three pieces that fit comfortably in the skillet.

⅓ cup extra-virgin olive oil

1 bunch fresh cilantro OR flat-leaf parsley

3 tablespoons lemon juice

2 medium garlic cloves, smashed and peeled

1 teaspoon ground coriander

1 jalapeño chili, stemmed and seeded

1½ pounds beef flat iron steak OR flank steak OR skirt steak (see note), trimmed

Kosher salt and ground black pepper

2 teaspoons neutral oil

In a food processor, puree the olive oil, cilantro, lemon juice, garlic, coriander and chili. Transfer to a small bowl and season with salt and pepper; set aside. Season the steak with salt and pepper. In a 12-inch skillet, heat the neutral oil until barely smoking. Add the steak and cook until well browned on both sides and the center reaches 120°F (for medium-rare), flipping once. Transfer to a platter and spoon on half the sauce. Let rest for 10 minutes, then thinly slice the steak against the grain, return to the platter and spoon on the remaining sauce.

Optional garnish: Lemon wedges and fresh herbs

BEEF

Spicy Dry-Fried Beef and Celery

Start to finish: 40 minutes
Servings: 4

In Sichuan cooking, dry-frying, or gan-bian, is a technique in which a protein or vegetable first is browned, then is stir-fried with aromatics and seasonings that cling to the browned surfaces. The result is more or less sauce-free but boasts concentrated flavors. We use salty, savory fermented chili-bean paste called toban djan as a flavoring (chili-garlic sauce is a good alternative), along with tongue-tingling Sichuan peppercorns. Serve with steamed rice.

4 or 5 medium celery stalks, thinly sliced on the diagonal (about 3 cups)

Kosher salt

1 pound strip steak, trimmed of fat and silver skin, thinly sliced crosswise, slices stacked and cut against the grain into matchsticks

¼ cup neutral oil

2-inch piece fresh ginger, peeled, quartered lengthwise and thinly sliced

1 tablespoon Sichuan peppercorns, finely ground

2 tablespoons chili-bean sauce (toban djan) OR chili-garlic sauce

2 tablespoons low-sodium soy sauce

In a colander, toss the celery with 1 teaspoon salt; set aside. In a 12-inch skillet, heat the oil until shimmering. Add the meat and cook, stirring, until deeply browned. Squeeze the celery to remove excess moisture and add to the pan along with the ginger. Cook, stirring, until the celery is just tender. Stir in the Sichuan pepper, chili-bean sauce and soy sauce, then cook, stirring, until fragrant, about 1 minute. Remove from the heat, taste and season with salt.

Optional garnish: Chopped celery leaves

BEEF

Steak with Soy-Citrus Sauce

Start to finish: 20 minutes
Servings: 4

The Japanese dish called saikoro steak cooks chunks of beef (saikoro translates as "diced") in a skillet and sauces the meat with ponzu, a sauce of soy and citrus. For our version, we call for lemon, lime or orange, so use whichever fruit you prefer or that you happen to have. Grated daikon is a classic garnish for this dish—it adds an earthy, radish-like piquancy and subtle sweetness—but we've kept it optional here. Serve the beef with steamed rice.

1½ pounds beef steak tips OR flat iron OR tri tip, trimmed and cut into ¾-inch chunks

Ground black pepper

1 tablespoon neutral oil

2 tablespoons salted butter, cut into 2 pieces

2 medium garlic cloves, minced

2 tablespoons soy sauce

1 teaspoon grated lemon zest OR lime zest OR orange zest, plus 1½ tablespoons lemon OR lime OR orange juice

Scallions, thinly sliced on the diagonal, to serve

Season the beef with 1 teaspoon pepper. In a 12-inch skillet, heat the oil until barely smoking. Add the beef and cook, stirring, until evenly browned. Using a slotted spoon, transfer to a medium bowl. Add the butter and garlic to the skillet, then cook, stirring, until fragrant. Add the soy sauce and citrus juice. Cook, stirring, until syrupy. Off heat, add the beef and accumulated juices to the pan, then toss. Transfer to a serving dish and sprinkle with the citrus zest, additional pepper and scallions.

Optional garnish: Daikon radish, peeled, finely grated and squeezed of excess moisture

Portuguese-Style Beef with Pickled Vegetables

Start to finish: 10 minutes
Servings: 4 to 6

The Portuguese small plate called pica pau—which translates as "woodpecker"—inspired this recipe. The name is a reference to the toothpicks used to eat the dish. For pickled vegetables, we use Italian-style giardiniera; look for it in the super-market next to the jarred roasted peppers and olives. Serve with hunks of crusty bread for sopping up the sauce, and cold beer to wash it all down.

1 pound beef steak tips OR flat iron steak OR tri-tip, trimmed and cut into 1-inch chunks

Kosher salt and ground black pepper

2 teaspoons neutral oil

6 medium garlic cloves, finely grated

½ teaspoon red pepper flakes

2 tablespoons sherry vinegar

2 tablespoons cold salted butter, cut into 2 pieces

1 cup drained giardiniera OR mixed pitted olives

Season the beef with 1½ teaspoons salt and ½ teaspoon black pepper. In a 12-inch skillet, heat the oil until barely smoking. Add the beef and brown on all sides. Transfer to a serving dish. Add the garlic and pepper flakes to the pan and cook, stirring, just until fragrant. Stir in the vinegar, then remove from the heat. Add the butter and stir, scraping up any browned bits, until melted. Season with salt and pepper, stir in the giardiniera and spoon over the steak.

Optional garnish: Peperoncini OR chopped fresh flat-leaf parsley OR both

Curried Ground Beef and Peas

Start to finish: 25 minutes
Servings: 4 to 6

Keema matar, from the Indian subcontinent, is a simple, flavor-packed curry that can be on the table in minutes. We sauté a good amount of sliced shallots until caramelized at the edges to create a rich flavor base. Adding the beef at the end and cooking it gently prevents it from drying out and becoming tough and mealy. Serve with warm naan, basmati rice or potatoes.

2 tablespoons neutral oil

4 medium shallots, halved and sliced

4 teaspoons garam masala

Kosher salt and ground black pepper

14½-ounce can crushed tomatoes OR tomato puree

1 tablespoon finely grated fresh ginger

1 pound 80 percent lean ground beef

1½ cups frozen peas, thawed

In a 12-inch skillet over medium-high, heat the oil until shimmering. Add the shallots and cook, stirring, until deeply browned at the edges. Reduce to medium and stir in the garam masala and 1 teaspoon each salt and pepper. Stir in the tomatoes, ginger and 1 cup water. Simmer, uncovered and stirring occasionally, until thick. Add the beef and cook, breaking it up, just until no pink remains. Stir in the peas, then season with salt and pepper.

Optional garnish: Plain yogurt **OR** chopped fresh mint **OR** chopped fresh cilantro **OR** a combination

BEEF

Steak with Shallot and White Wine Pan Sauce

Start to finish: 30 minutes
Servings: 4

In this simple seared steak with a shallot-infused, butter-enriched pan sauce we balance the richness of the beef by keeping the sauce on the light side. We use white wine instead of red, lemon juice for acidity and fresh parsley for freshness. Serve with roasted potatoes and a simple salad to complete the meal.

Two 1-pound beef strip steaks
OR ribeye steaks

Kosher salt and ground black pepper

2 tablespoons neutral oil

4 tablespoons salted butter, cut into 1-tablespoon pieces, divided

2 medium shallots, minced

½ cup dry white wine

1 tablespoon lemon juice

1 cup lightly packed fresh flat-leaf parsley, finely chopped

Season the steaks with salt and pepper. In a 12-inch skillet, heat the oil until barely smoking. Add the steaks and brown on both sides until the centers reach 120°F for medium-rare. Transfer to a platter and set aside. To the pan, add 2 tablespoons butter and the shallots. Cook, stirring, until the shallots have softened. Add the wine, lemon juice and parsley. Cook, stirring, until the liquid has reduced to a couple tablespoons. Off heat, whisk in the remaining 2 tablespoons butter and 2 tablespoons water, then season with salt and pepper. Slice the steaks against the grain, return to the platter and pour on the sauce.

Chili and Herb Spiced Beef

Start to finish: 30 minutes
Servings: 4

Gently simmering ground beef, rather than searing it until browned, keeps the meat tender and moist. In this recipe, simmering also draws out the essential oils from the chilies and coriander. Cooking off the moisture then concentrates the flavors. If you like, reduce the chilies' heat by seeding them before slicing. Serve dolloped with tahini-spiked yogurt or drizzled with additional pomegranate molasses, accompanied by buttery rice pilaf or warmed flatbread.

2 teaspoons extra-virgin olive oil

1 pound 85 percent lean ground beef
OR ground lamb

2 or 3 serrano chilies OR jalapeño chilies, stemmed and sliced into thin rounds

2½ teaspoons ground coriander

Kosher salt and ground black pepper

1 small red onion, halved and thinly sliced
OR 1 cup chopped tomatoes

1 bunch flat-leaf parsley OR cilantro, roughly chopped

2 tablespoons pomegranate molasses
OR lemon juice

In a 12-inch nonstick skillet, heat the oil until shimmering. Add the beef, chilies, coriander, a pinch each of salt and pepper and enough water to just barely cover. Bring to a simmer and cook, stirring to break up the beef, until the water has evaporated and the mixture sizzles. Add the onion and cook, stirring, just until slightly softened, then stir in the parsley and pomegranate molasses. Season with salt and pepper.

Stir-Fried Orange Beef with Scallions

Start to finish: 25 minutes
Servings: 4

This stir-fried spin on Chinese orange beef, a perennial favorite that typically calls for deep-frying the meat, uses orange marmalade to add layers of sweetness, bitterness and citrusy brightness. Five-spice powder adds to the complexity with its warm spiciness. Finish the stir-fry with scallions, or use basil to accentuate the anise notes of the five-spice. This is great with steamed white or brown rice.

1½ pounds beef flat iron steak
OR boneless beef short ribs, trimmed
and sliced ¼ inch thick against the grain

1½ teaspoons Chinese five-spice powder

Ground black pepper OR ground white pepper

1 tablespoon neutral oil

3 tablespoons orange marmalade

2 tablespoons soy sauce

1 bunch scallions, cut into 1-inch lengths
OR 1 cup lightly packed fresh basil, torn if large

Juice from ¼ orange, plus more to serve

Toss the beef with the five-spice and ½ teaspoon pepper. In a 12-inch skillet, heat the oil until barely smoking. Add the beef in an even layer and cook without stirring until browned on the bottom, about 3 minutes. Stir, then add the marmalade and soy sauce. Cook, stirring, until the beef is lightly glazed. Off heat, stir in the scallions and orange juice. Season with pepper and additional orange juice.

Low-and-Slow Eye of Round

Eye of round is a big, inexpensive beef roast that, cooked slowly with gentle heat, yields tender results with little effort. To ensure the meat turns out flavorful, we first rub it with a high-impact seasoning paste, one that can stand up to a long roast.

Left to right: Curry-Roasted Eye of Round, (bottom) Roasted Eye of Round with Miso, Orange and Five-Spice, (top) Roasted Eye of Round with Berbere Spice, Roasted Eye of Round with Black Olives and Anchovies

Roasted Eye of Round with Miso, Orange and Five-Spice

Start to finish: 2¾ hours (20 minutes active)
Servings: 8 to 10

For our first take on eye of round, we chose salty, subtly sweet, umami-rich miso as a base, then added ginger, five-spice powder and orange zest for flavor complexity. Be sure to carve the roast into thin slices for the most tender texture.

¼ cup red miso OR white miso

2 tablespoons finely grated fresh ginger

2 tablespoons neutral oil

1 tablespoon Chinese five-spice powder

1 tablespoon grated orange zest

Kosher salt and ground black pepper

4-pound beef eye of round roast, trimmed of silver skin

4 tablespoons salted butter, cut into 4 pieces

Heat the oven to 275°F. Set a wire rack in a rimmed baking sheet. In a small bowl, mix the miso, ginger, oil, five-spice, orange zest, 1 tablespoon salt and 2 teaspoons pepper. Set aside 2 tablespoons of the mixture. Rub the remaining paste over the beef, set on the rack and roast until the center reaches 125°F, 1¾ to 2 hours. Let rest for 30 minutes on the rack, then thinly slice. In a small saucepan, melt the butter, then whisk in the reserved seasoning paste and accumulated beef juices; serve with the roast.

Optional garnish: Thinly sliced scallions

Roasted Eye of Round with Berbere Spice

Start to finish: 2¾ hours (20 minutes active)
Servings: 8 to 10

The Ethiopian spice blend called berbere is a mix of dried chilies, garlic, ginger and spices, and it's a key ingredient in the seasoning paste for this roast. Look for it in the spice section of well-stocked grocery stores. The spiciness of berbere tends to vary blend to blend, so we give a range for how much to use.

6 medium garlic cloves, smashed and peeled

2-inch piece fresh ginger, peeled and thinly sliced

2 to 3 tablespoons berbere seasoning (see note)

2 tablespoons neutral oil

1 tablespoon fresh rosemary

Kosher salt and ground black pepper

4-pound beef eye of round roast, trimmed of silver skin

4 tablespoons salted butter, cut into 4 pieces

Heat the oven to 275°F. Set a wire rack in a rimmed baking sheet. In a food processor, pulse the garlic, ginger, berbere, oil, rosemary, 1 tablespoon salt and 2 teaspoons pepper to a smooth paste. Set aside 2 tablespoons of the mixture. Rub the remaining paste on the beef, set on the rack and roast until the center reaches 125°F, 1¾ to 2 hours. Let rest for 30 minutes, then thinly slice. In a small saucepan, melt the butter, then whisk in the reserved seasoning paste and accumulated beef juices; serve with the roast.

Optional garnish: Fresno chilies or jalapeño chilies, stemmed and finely chopped

Curry-Roasted Eye of Round

Start to finish: 2¾ hours (20 minutes active)
Servings: 8 to 10

Tomato paste is the base for this seasoning mix; its sweetness and acidity accentuate the warm, spicy notes of the curry powder. It also adds color to the roast, which does not develop dark caramelization because of the low oven temperature. For best texture, be sure to slice the roast very thinly for serving.

¼ cup tomato paste

3 tablespoons finely grated fresh ginger

2 tablespoons curry powder

2 teaspoons ground coriander

Kosher salt and ground black pepper

4-pound beef eye of round roast, trimmed of silver skin

4 tablespoons salted butter, cut into 4 pieces

Heat the oven to 275°F. Set a wire rack in a rimmed baking sheet. Mix together the tomato paste, ginger, curry powder, coriander, 4 teaspoons salt and 2 teaspoons pepper. Set aside 2 tablespoons of the mixture. Rub the remaining paste on the beef, set on the rack and roast until the center reaches 125°F, 1¾ to 2 hours. Let rest on the rack for 30 minutes, then thinly slice. In a small saucepan, melt the butter, then whisk in the reserved seasoning paste and accumulated beef juices; serve with the roast.

Optional garnish: Chopped fresh cilantro **OR** lime wedges **OR** both

Roasted Eye of Round with Black Olives and Anchovies

Start to finish: 2¾ hours (20 minutes active)
Servings: 8 to 10

Black olive tapenade made into a seasoning paste with anchovies, garlic and thyme lends this roast bold Mediterranean flavor. If you prefer, instead of tapenade, use 6 tablespoons chopped pitted black olives plus 2 tablespoons chopped drained capers. Cut the meat into thin slices to optimize tenderness.

½ cup black olive tapenade (see note)

2 tablespoons extra-virgin olive oil

4 oil-packed anchovy filets

4 medium garlic cloves, smashed and peeled

2 teaspoons dried thyme

Kosher salt and ground black pepper

4-pound beef eye of round roast, trimmed of silver skin

4 tablespoons salted butter, cut into 4 pieces

Heat the oven to 275°F. Set a wire rack in a rimmed baking sheet. In a food processor, pulse the tapenade, oil, anchovies, garlic, thyme, 1 tablespoon salt and 2 teaspoons pepper to a smooth paste. Set aside 2 tablespoons of the mixture. Rub the remaining paste on the beef, set on the rack and roast until the center reaches 125°F, 1¾ to 2 hours. Let rest on the rack for 30 minutes, then thinly slice. In a small saucepan, melt the butter, then whisk in the reserved seasoning paste and accumulated beef juices; serve with the roast.

Optional garnish: Grated lemon zest **OR** chopped fresh flat-leaf parsley **OR** both

BEEF

305

Sautéed Beef with Mushrooms and Tarragon

Start to finish: 15 minutes
Servings: 4

This sauté was inspired by a Georgian beef and tomato stew called chashushuli. We took a few liberties to make this a simple one-pan dinner, but the flavors remain rich and satisfying. We opted to use a beef strip or ribeye steak because these cuts don't require long, slow cooking to become tender. Serve with rice or egg noodles.

3 tablespoons neutral oil

1 pound white mushrooms, trimmed and quartered

3 medium shallots, chopped

3 medium garlic cloves, thinly sliced

1-pound beef strip steak OR ribeye steak, trimmed of silver skin, halved lengthwise and sliced crosswise ½ inch thick

¼ cup tomato paste

Kosher salt and ground black pepper

1 bunch tarragon, chopped

In a 12-inch skillet, heat the oil until shimmering. Add the mushrooms, shallots and garlic, then cook, stirring, until browned. Add the beef and cook, occasionally turning with tongs, until lightly seared. Add the tomato paste, 2 teaspoons salt and 1 teaspoon pepper. Cook, stirring, until the tomato paste has darkened slightly. Add 1 cup water and cook, stirring, until the liquid thickens slightly. Off heat, stir in the tarragon, then season with salt and pepper.

Optional garnish: Sour cream

Desserts

Recipes

Desserts can be demanding, but they don't have to be.

Baking isn't a particularly forgiving medium. But by sticking to our fundamentals of cooking—foundation, contrast, embellishment—we were able to come up with a selection of desserts that are both simple and satisfying.

Our butterscotch pudding starts with the classic richness of brown sugar and butter, then gets more interesting with salt to contrast the sweet caramel, ginger for a warm layer of flavor and black pepper for savory-spicy depth. We add the optional garnish of whipped cream and finely chopped crystallized ginger with just a bit more pepper for the finishing touch. And our take on bananas Foster, that uniquely American creation, uses five-spice powder, not the usual cinnamon, to add complexity. For salty-savory contrast we use a bit of white miso. Likewise, we take stovetop rice pudding way beyond its typical milky blandness. We start by cooking the rice in water, which reduces overall cooking time as well as lets us use less dairy by releasing the natural creaminess of the rice. Then we add unexpected flavor pairings such as cardamom with orange and bourbon, and Earl Grey tea with blueberries.

Even baked goods can fit into casual cooking; we often make things easier by using gussied-up supermarket staples. Our dessert inspired by Britain's Eton mess starts with store-bought meringues—we toast them briefly for extra flavor and depth. Purchased Marie biscuits go into our easy, elegant semifreddo inspired by serradura, a Portuguese dessert found in Macau. We use frozen puff pastry for our quartet of freeform tarts, which leaves us free to focus on toppings, such as chocolate and spiced pear; we add Chinese five-spice powder for a warm, peppery kick. Likewise, our berry crisp—frozen berries work fine—gets rich, nutty flavor from tahini added to the crumbly topping—the sesame paste caramelizes as it bakes. We even have a from-scratch chocolate cake in the mix. Based on Sweden's "sticky cake," it can be stirred together with about 20 minutes' effort, for the perfect no-fuss ending to a thrown together supper.

Yogurt Panna Cotta with Honey and Turmeric

**Start to finish: 3½ hours
(20 minutes active)
Servings: 6**

Panna cotta usually is made with cream, but we add Greek yogurt, which heightens the creaminess and lends a tangy, more nuanced flavor than cream alone. Golden milk, an Indian beverage, is spiced with earthy turmeric and black pepper; cinnamon is a common ingredient, too. The fragrant brew gave us the idea for this colorful take on panna cotta. This is an excellent make-ahead dessert—after three hours of chilling, the ramekins can be covered with plastic wrap and refrigerated up to three days.

**1½ teaspoons unflavored
powdered gelatin**

1 cup heavy cream

½ cup honey

1 tablespoon ground turmeric

1 teaspoon ground black pepper

½ teaspoon ground cinnamon

½ teaspoon kosher salt

2 cups plain whole-milk Greek yogurt

In a small bowl, sprinkle the gelatin over 2 table-spoons water; let stand for 10 minutes. In a medium saucepan, combine the cream, honey, turmeric, pepper, cinnamon and salt. Cook, stirring, until simmering at the edges. Off heat, stir in the gelatin, then cover and let stand for 10 minutes. Place the yogurt in a medium bowl. Strain the cream mixture into the yogurt, then whisk. Divide among 6 rame-kins, then refrigerate uncovered until cold and set, about 3 hours.

Optional garnish: Chopped roasted pistachios

Citrus and Spice Strawberry Compote

Start to finish: 20 minutes
Servings: 4 to 6

This compote is only lightly sweetened so the focus is on the surprisingly delicious combination of fruity, floral strawberries and the spicy, savory chili powder (or garam masala) and cracked black pepper. Grated citrus zest ties together the flavors. We briefly cook then mash only a portion of the berries, then pour them while still hot over the remaining berries. The residual heat softens the fresh fruit ever so slightly. Serve over ice cream or yogurt.

1 pound strawberries, hulled and quartered

2 tablespoons white sugar, divided

Grated zest of 1 lime OR 1 lemon OR ½ medium orange

1 teaspoon chili powder OR garam masala

¼ teaspoon coarsely ground black pepper

Pinch of kosher salt

In a medium bowl, toss two-thirds of the berries with 1 tablespoon of sugar and the zest; set aside. In a small saucepan, toast the chili powder, stirring, until fragrant; add the remaining berries, the remaining 1 tablespoon sugar, the pepper, salt and ¼ cup water. Simmer, stirring, for 5 minutes, then mash the berries to break them down. Cook, stirring, until jammy. Immediately pour over the berries in the bowl and stir. Let stand for 10 minutes.

Swedish "Sticky" Chocolate Cake

Start to finish: 45 minutes
(20 minutes active), plus cooling
Servings: 10 to 12

This gooey-centered chocolate cake, a popular sweet in Sweden, is called kladdkaka, which translates as "sticky cake." With only six ingredients (not counting the salt) and an easy dump-and-stir mixing method, what's not to love? For our version, we brown the butter to add a subtle nuttiness, and we use brown sugar for its molasses notes. The cake can be served warm or at room temperature. Top slices with whipped cream, ice cream or gelato.

1½ sticks (12 tablespoons) salted butter, cut into 12 pieces

½ cup (40 grams) unsweetened cocoa powder, plus more to serve

1¼ cups (250 grams) packed brown sugar

4 large eggs

½ teaspoon kosher salt

¾ cup (98 grams) all-purpose flour

½ cup (75 grams) chocolate chips

Heat the oven to 325°F. Mist a 9-inch springform pan with cooking spray and line the bottom with kitchen parchment. In a medium saucepan, cook the butter, stirring, until the milk solids at the bottom are browned. Whisk in the cocoa and sugar; transfer to a medium bowl and cool. One at a time, whisk in the eggs, followed by the salt. Whisk in the flour, then stir in the chocolate chips. Spread evenly in the prepared pan. Bake until the edges spring back when lightly pressed, 30 to 35 minutes. Cool in the pan for 30 minutes, then remove the pan sides. Serve dusted with cocoa.

Blueberry Crumble with Oats and Tahini

Start to finish: 45 minutes
Servings: 4 to 6

For this crumble, we add tahini to boost flavor in a buttery oat mixture that bakes on top of juicy blueberries. Be sure to use quick-cooking oats; old-fashioned oats won't soften quite enough. Ripe fresh berries are best but frozen work, too. Look for frozen "wild" blueberries—they're tiny, but pack big flavor. If frozen regular berries are a must, add a few minutes to the baking time but don't thaw them before use. This crumble is especially delicious warm, with a scoop of ice cream melting on top.

2 pints fresh blueberries OR 4 cups frozen blueberries, preferably wild (see note)

2 cups (160 grams) quick-cooking oats, divided

¾ cup (164 grams) packed brown sugar, divided

8 tablespoons salted butter, cut into 8 pieces, room temperature

¼ cup (64 grams) tahini

1½ teaspoons ground cinnamon

½ teaspoon kosher salt

Heat the oven to 350°F. In a medium bowl, toss the blueberries with ¼ cup (20 grams) of the oats and ¼ cup (54 grams) of the sugar; transfer to a 9-inch pie plate. Wipe out the bowl, then add the remaining 1¾ cups (140 grams) oats, the remaining ½ cup (107 grams) sugar, the butter, tahini, cinnamon and salt. Mix until evenly moistened, then use your hands to squeeze the mixture into rough olive-sized clumps and scatter them over the berries. Bake until the edges are bubbling and the crumble is golden, 30 to 35 minutes. Serve warm or at room temperature.

Optional garnish: Toasted sesame seeds

315

Rice Pudding

Italian Arborio rice isn't just for risotto. The starchy grains also are ideal for making rich, creamy rice pudding that lends itself to myriad flavorings. Simmering the rice in water before adding dairy shortens the cooking time (simmered in dairy from the get-go, the grains take longer to tenderize). The pudding is delicious warm, at room temperature or cold, but keep in mind that its consistency becomes thicker and firmer as it cools.

Left to right: Rice Pudding with Star Anise and Cinnamon, Earl Grey Rice Pudding with Blueberries, Coconut-Mango Rice Pudding with Dark Rum, Rice Pudding with Bourbon, Orange and Cardamom

Rice Pudding with Star Anise and Cinnamon

Start to finish: 45 minutes
Servings: 6

Star anise and cinnamon perfume this rice pudding with warm, sweet notes of spice. We recommend the optional chopped chocolate garnish—the dark, roasty notes of bittersweet or semisweet chocolate are an amazing flavor match for the spices.

½ cup Arborio rice

½ teaspoon kosher salt

2 cups half-and-half

⅓ cup white sugar

2 whole star anise

1 cinnamon stick

2 teaspoons vanilla extract

In a large saucepan, stir together the rice, salt and 2 cups water. Boil, then reduce to low, cover and cook for 20 minutes. Stir in the half-and-half, sugar, star anise and cinnamon. Return to a simmer and cook, uncovered and stirring occasionally, until the rice is tender and the mixture is creamy and thick, about 15 minutes. Off heat, stir in the vanilla, then remove and discard the star anise and cinnamon. Serve warm, at room temperature or chilled.

Optional garnish: Chopped bittersweet or semi-sweet chocolate **OR** ground cinnamon

Rice Pudding with Bourbon, Orange and Cardamom

Start to finish: 45 minutes
Servings: 6

Bourbon and orange are a classic combination (think a bourbon old fashioned cocktail), but here we add lightly floral, subtly citrusy cardamom to spice up the flavor of this pudding. Be sure to use heavy cream, not half-and-half; the cream's higher fat content is necessary to prevent the dairy from "breaking" when the bourbon and orange juice are added.

½ cup Arborio rice

½ teaspoon kosher salt

2 cups heavy cream

⅓ cup white sugar

¼ cup bourbon

Grated zest and juice from 1 orange

¾ teaspoon ground cardamom

In a large saucepan, stir together the rice, salt and 2 cups water. Boil, then reduce to low, cover and cook for 20 minutes. Stir in the cream, sugar, bourbon, orange zest and juice, and cardamom. Return to a simmer and cook, uncovered and stirring occasionally, until the rice is tender and the mixture is creamy and thick, about 15 minutes. Serve warm, at room temperature or chilled.

Optional garnish: Chopped roasted pistachios

Coconut-Mango Rice Pudding with Dark Rum

Start to finish: 45 minutes
Servings: 6

Flavored with nutmeg and dark rum, this mango-studded rice pudding features the flavors of the Caribbean. Make sure to use full-fat, not light, coconut milk and shake the can well before opening so the fat that rises to the top mixes into the liquid.

½ cup Arborio rice

½ teaspoon kosher salt

14-ounce can coconut milk

1 ripe mango, peeled, pitted and cut into ½-inch chunks

⅓ cup white sugar

¼ cup dark rum

¼ teaspoon grated nutmeg

In a large saucepan, stir together the rice, salt and 2 cups water. Boil, then reduce to low, cover and cook for 20 minutes. Stir in the coconut milk, mango, sugar, rum, nutmeg and an additional ¼ cup water. Return to a simmer and cook, uncovered and stirring occasionally, until the rice is tender and the mixture is creamy and thick, about 15 minutes. Serve warm, at room temperature or chilled.

Optional garnish: Toasted shredded coconut OR grated lime zest OR both

Earl Grey Rice Pudding with Blueberries

Start to finish: 45 minutes
Servings: 6

The tannins and citrusy, flowery notes of Earl Grey tea are a nice match for sweet, fruity blueberries. In the off-season, frozen blueberries work well; use them straight from the freezer (don't thaw them) to minimize the degree to which they tint the pudding.

½ cup Arborio rice

½ teaspoon kosher salt

2 cups half-and-half

⅓ cup white sugar

2 Earl Grey tea bags

2 teaspoons vanilla extract

1 cup fresh blueberries OR frozen blueberries

In a large saucepan, stir together the rice, salt and 2 cups water. Boil, then reduce to low, cover and cook for 20 minutes. Stir in the half-and-half and sugar. Return to a simmer, then add the tea bags (wrap the strings around the pan's handle for easy removal, but make sure any tags will not ignite) and cook, uncovered and stirring occasionally, until the rice is tender and the mixture is creamy and thick, about 15 minutes. Remove from the heat and discard tea bags, then stir in the vanilla and blueberries. Serve warm, at room temperature or chilled.

Optional garnish: Grated lemon zest

DESSERTS

319

Charred Pineapple with Spiced Honey and Coconut Ice Cream

Start to finish: 15 minutes
Servings: 4

Charring fresh pineapple under a broiler brings out roasted, caramel notes while also rendering the fruit tender and succulent. For ease, we use store-brought peeled and cored pineapple so the only prep that's needed is cutting it into rings before broiling. A drizzle of spicy honey over the warm fruit and chilly ice cream (we especially like coconut ice cream, but vanilla is great, too) makes for a sublime combination.

1 store-bought peeled and cored whole pineapple, cut into 8 rings (each about ½ inch thick)

¼ cup honey

1 tablespoon finely grated fresh ginger

½ teaspoon grated nutmeg

½ teaspoon red pepper flakes

Coconut ice cream OR vanilla ice cream, to serve

Heat the broiler with a rack about 4 inches from the element. Line a broiler-safe rimmed baking sheet with foil and place the pineapple rings in a single layer on it. Broil until deeply browned, 8 to 10 minutes, rotating halfway through. Meanwhile, in a small bowl, mix the honey, ginger, nutmeg and pepper flakes. When the pineapple is done, transfer to individual plates. Top with ice cream, then drizzle with the honey.

Optional garnish: Finely chopped crystallized ginger OR fresh mint OR both

Eton Mess with Cherries and Chocolate

Start to finish: 30 minutes
Servings: 4

Eton mess, a dessert of crushed baked meringue, whipped cream and berries, is said to have originated at England's Eton College. For this version, we use store-bought meringue cookies, toast them under the broiler and layer them with whipped cream studded with cherries and chopped chocolate. Frozen cherries make this dessert a breeze to put together; we chop then soften the fruit by microwaving the pieces with sugar and sherry vinegar, which balances the sweetness of the meringues.

2 cups frozen pitted sweet cherries, thawed and chopped

⅓ cup white sugar

3 tablespoons sherry vinegar

4 ounces vanilla OR cocoa meringue cookies, lightly crushed (about 2 cups)

1 cup cold heavy cream

3 ounces bittersweet chocolate, finely chopped

In a small microwave-safe bowl, mix the cherries, sugar and vinegar. Microwave for 5 minutes, then strain, reserving the liquid; cool completely. Heat the broiler with a rack about 4 inches from the element. Spread the meringues on a broiler-safe rimmed baking sheet and broil until browned, 30 to 60 seconds. In a medium bowl, whip the cream to soft peaks. Add the reserved cherry liquid and two-thirds of the chocolate, then beat to stiff peaks. Spread half the meringues and half the cherries in a serving bowl. Top with the whipped cream, then the remaining cherries, meringues and chocolate.

Salt and Pepper Butterscotch Pudding

Start to finish: 20 minutes, plus chilling
Servings: 6

This recipe gives an old standby a big flavor lift. Salt accentuates the buttery caramel flavor of the butterscotch, black pepper adds savory depth and complexity, and ground ginger offers notes of warm spice. For individual desserts, portion the just-cooked pudding into jelly jars or small bowls, then refrigerate.

6 tablespoons salted butter, cut into 6 pieces

1¼ cups packed dark brown sugar

4 large egg yolks

⅓ cup cornstarch

3 cups whole milk

1½ teaspoons ground ginger

½ teaspoon kosher salt

½ teaspoon ground black pepper, plus more to serve

In a large saucepan over medium-high, cook the butter and sugar, stirring, until vigorously bubbling, then continue to cook for 1 minute. Off heat, add ½ cup water and stir until the caramel dissolves. In a medium bowl, whisk the yolks, cornstarch, milk, ginger, salt and pepper, then whisk it into the caramel in the pan. Bring to a simmer over medium, whisking constantly, and cook until thickened, 1 to 2 minutes. Transfer to a bowl, press kitchen parchment directly against the surface and refrigerate until cold. Serve sprinkled with additional pepper.

Optional garnish: Lightly sweetened whipped cream OR chopped crystalized ginger

Coconut-Almond Macaroons with Cherry Preserves

Start to finish: 25 minutes
Makes about 12 cookies

Cloyingly sweet, one-dimensional coconut macaroons get a makeover with this simple recipe. We add sliced almonds for texture, fruit preserves for color and tangy notes, and aniseed for licorice-like fragrance and flavor. The cookies are best eaten the day they're made, but extras will keep in an airtight container at room temperature for up to two days.

1½ cups (120 grams) shredded unsweetened coconut

2 large egg whites

¼ cup (54 grams) white sugar

1 teaspoon aniseed

¼ teaspoon kosher salt

2 tablespoons (40 grams) cherry preserves OR apricot preserves OR orange marmalade

¼ cup (28 grams) sliced almonds

Heat the oven to 400°F; line a baking sheet with kitchen parchment. In a food processor, process the coconut until finely ground. Add the egg whites, sugar, aniseed and salt. Pulse until evenly moistened, about 5 pulses. Add the preserves and almonds, then pulse until just incorporated. Using a small ice cream scoop or 2 spoons, drop heaping 1-tablespoon mounds of the dough onto the prepared baking sheet. Bake until golden, about 10 minutes. Cool on the baking sheet for 10 minutes, then transfer to a wire rack and cool completely.

Freeform Tarts

Frozen puff pastry makes it possible to bake an easy
but elegant freeform tart at a moment's notice.
We roll the thawed pastry into a 10-by-14-inch rectangle
before topping it and baking, and we score a 1-inch
frame around the outside of the pastry so it puffs up
around the filling. By using fruits and ingredients
with complementary flavors, we keep these simple
desserts fresh and bright.

Raspberry-Mascarpone Freeform Tart, Chocolate and Spiced Pear
Freeform Tart, Mango-Coconut Freeform Tart, Cherry-almond Butter
Freeform Tart

Raspberry-Mascarpone Freeform Tart

Start to finish: 45 minutes (25 minutes active)
Servings: 6

Fresh, juicy raspberries find a perfect match in creamy, lightly sweetened mascarpone cheese. You can use cream cheese in place of the mascarpone, but make sure it's at room temperature so it combines easily with the egg and sugar.

1 sheet frozen puff pastry, thawed and rolled into a 10-by-14-inch rectangle

2 pints raspberries

4 tablespoons white sugar, divided

¾ cup (170 grams) mascarpone cheese OR room-temperature cream cheese

1 large egg

½ teaspoon vanilla extract OR almond extract

Pinch of kosher salt

Heat the oven to 425°F with a rack in the upper-middle position. Line a rimmed baking sheet with kitchen parchment; place the pastry on top. In a bowl, toss the raspberries and 2 tablespoons sugar. In another bowl, whisk the mascarpone, egg, vanilla, salt and remaining 2 tablespoons sugar. With a paring knife, score a 1-inch frame around the edge of the pastry, then poke holes in the pastry with a fork, avoiding the border. Spread the mascarpone mixture inside the border; scatter the raspberries on top. Bake until the pastry is golden brown, 20 to 25 minutes. Serve warm or at room temperature.

Optional garnish: Powdered sugar

Cherry-Almond Butter Freeform Tart

Start to finish: 45 minutes (25 minutes active)
Servings: 6

With frozen cherries, you can bake this tart any time of the year. We make a simple filling of almond butter mixed with egg, sugar and almond extract to marry the juicy cherries and flaky pastry. Serve with whipped cream spiked with kirsch or amaretto or with ice cream or gelato.

1 sheet frozen puff pastry, thawed and rolled into a 10-by-14-inch rectangle

2 cups (280 grams) sweet cherries, pitted and halved OR frozen pitted sweet cherries, thawed, patted dry and halved

4 tablespoons white sugar, divided

⅓ cup (80 grams) almond butter

1 large egg

½ teaspoon almond extract

Pinch of kosher salt

Heat the oven to 425°F with a rack in the upper-middle position. Line a rimmed baking sheet with kitchen parchment; place the pastry on top. In a bowl, toss the cherries and 2 tablespoons sugar. In another bowl, whisk the almond butter, egg, almond extract, salt and remaining 2 tablespoons sugar. Using a paring knife, score a 1-inch frame around the edge of the pastry, then poke holes in the pastry with a fork, avoiding the border. Spread the almond butter mixture inside the border; scatter the cherries on top. Bake until the pastry is golden, 20 to 25 minutes. Serve warm or at room temperature.

Optional garnish: Honey, for drizzling OR toasted sliced almonds OR both

Mango-Coconut Freeform Tart

Start to finish: 45 minutes (25 minutes active)
Servings: 6

Make sure to use coconut cream—not cream of coconut, which is sweetened (and typically used in cocktails)—for this tropical dessert. Coconut, lime or pineapple ice cream or sorbet would be a perfect pairing.

1 sheet frozen puff pastry, thawed and rolled into a 10-by-14-inch rectangle

¼ cup coconut cream

3 tablespoons (40 grams) packed brown sugar

2 teaspoons grated lime zest, plus ½ lime

¼ teaspoon kosher salt

2 small or 1 large ripe mango, peeled, pitted and thinly sliced

Wide-flake coconut OR shredded unsweetened coconut, to serve

Heat the oven to 425°F with a rack in the upper-middle position. Line a rimmed baking sheet with kitchen parchment; place the pastry on top. In a small bowl, mix the coconut cream, sugar, lime zest and salt. Using a paring knife, score a 1-inch frame around the edge of the pastry, then poke holes in the pastry with a fork, avoiding the border. Spread the coconut mixture inside the border, then shingle the mango slices on top. Bake until the pastry is golden, 20 to 25 minutes. Squeeze the lime half over the mango, then sprinkle with coconut. Serve warm or at room temperature.

Optional garnish: Chopped fresh mint

Chocolate and Spiced Pear Freeform Tart

Start to finish: 45 minutes (25 minutes active)
Servings: 6

Chinese five-spice powder adds intrigue to the classic pairing of pears and chocolate. We prefer Bosc pears for their firm texture. Don't peel the pears—the russet-toned skins contrast nicely against the creamy-white interiors of the fruit. If you like, serve with vanilla ice cream or gelato drizzled with chocolate sauce.

1 sheet frozen puff pastry, thawed and rolled into a 10-by-14-inch rectangle

2 ripe but firm Bosc pears, not peeled, halved, cored and thinly sliced lengthwise

3 tablespoons honey

2 tablespoons salted butter, melted

1 teaspoon Chinese five-spice powder

½ teaspoon kosher salt

⅓ cup (55 grams) chocolate chips

Heat the oven to 425°F with a rack in the upper-middle position. Line a rimmed baking sheet with kitchen parchment; place the pastry on top. With a paring knife, score a 1-inch frame around the edge of the pastry, then pork holes in the pastry with a fork, avoiding the border. In a bowl, toss the pears with the honey, butter, five-spice and salt. Sprinkle the chocolate onto the pastry, avoiding the border, then shingle the pear slices on top. Bake until the pastry is golden, 20 to 25 minutes. Serve warm or at room temperature.

DESSERTS

327

Miso-Spiced Rum Bananas Foster

Start to finish: 20 minutes
Servings: 4

We've given bananas Foster, an American classic, a big flavor update. Honey sweetens while adding floral nuances and miso balances with a delicious savoriness. We use spiced rum as a one-ingredient way to infuse the buttery sauce with flavor and aroma. An optional dusting of Chinese five-spice powder lends intriguing spiciness that complements the rum.

3 tablespoons salted butter, cut into 3 pieces

3 tablespoons honey

1 tablespoon white miso

2 bananas, peeled, halved lengthwise then crosswise

½ cup spiced rum

Vanilla ice cream, to serve

In a Dutch oven over medium, melt the butter. Stir in the honey and miso. Add the bananas and cook, stirring carefully so as not to bruise the bananas, until the sauce is slightly darker in color, about 2 minutes. Off heat, pour in the rum. Return to medium and cook, stirring carefully, until the alcohol no longer smells raw, about 2 minutes. Divide the bananas and sauce among 4 serving bowls, then top with ice cream.

Optional garnish: Chinese five-spice powder

Semifreddo with Mandarin Oranges and Biscuits

Start to finish: 20 minutes, plus freezing
Servings: 8

Serradura, a dessert that originated in Portugal and is popular in Macau, is made by layering whipped cream sweetened with condensed milk and pulverized Marie biscuits (serradura translates as "sawdust"). It inspired this frozen sweet that looks impressive but is a breeze to make. We keep the biscuits mostly whole and layer them in a pan with fruit-studded cream; after freezing, the "pudding" is cut into slices that reveal a mosaic-like design. For serving, you can invert the semifreddo onto a platter or slice it directly in the pan; if too firm to cut, let it soften for a few minutes at room temperature.

1 cup cold heavy cream

⅓ cup sweetened condensed milk

23½-ounce container mandarin orange segments packed in juice, drained and roughly chopped (2 cups)

2 tablespoons Grand Marnier OR amaretto OR bourbon

½ teaspoon vanilla extract

Pinch of kosher salt

5- to 7-ounce package Marie biscuits

Line a 9-by-5-inch loaf pan with plastic wrap, leaving a 3-inch overhang on each long side. In a large bowl with an electric mixer, beat the cream and condensed milk to stiff peaks. Fold in the oranges, Grand Marnier, vanilla and salt. Place a layer of the cookies in the bottom of the pan, breaking them to fit, then spread with a third of the cream mixture. Repeat the layering 2 more times. Press the plastic-wrap overhang directly against the surface, then freeze for at least 2 hours or up to 1 week. To serve, cut into slices.

Index

Acknowledgments

Milk Street is a real place with, oddly enough, real people. It's a small crew, but I want to thank everyone who has made this book a reality. In particular, I want to acknowledge J.M. Hirsch, our tireless editorial director, Matthew Card, food editor, Michelle Locke, books editor, Dawn Yanagihara, recipe editor, and Shaula Clark, managing editor, for leading the charge on conceiving, developing and editing all of this. Also, Jennifer Baldino Cox, our art director, and the entire design team who deftly captured the look, feel and energy of Cookish recipes. Special thanks to Brianna Coleman, art director of photography, Connie Miller, photographer, Christine Tobin, stylist, and Gary Tooth, designer.

Our team of production cooks and recipe developers kept the bar high, throwing out recipes that did not make the cut and improving those that did. Our team includes Wes Martin, Diane Unger, Rebecca Richmond, Calvin Cox, Julia Rackow, Rose Hattabaugh, Elizabeth Mindreau and Bianca Borges. Special thanks to Courtney Hill for getting the project on solid footing from the outset.

Deborah Broide, Milk Street director of media relations, has done a spectacular job of sharing with the world all we do at Milk Street.

We also have a couple of folks to thank who work outside of 177 Milk Street. Michael Szczerban, editor, and everyone at Little, Brown and Company have been superb and inspired partners in this project. Yes, top-notch book editors still exist! And my long-standing book agent, David Black, has been instrumental in bringing this project to life both with his knowledge of publishing and bourbon. Thank you, David!

Finally, a sincere thank you to my business partner and wife, Melissa, who manages our media department, from television to radio. Melissa has nurtured the Milk Street brand from the beginning so that we ended up where we thought we were going in the first place! Thanks.

And, last but not least, to all of you who have supported the Milk Street project. Everyone has a seat at the Milk Street table, so pull up a chair and dig in!

Christopher Kimball

About the Author

Christopher Kimball is founder of Christopher Kimball's Milk Street, a food media company dedicated to learning and sharing bold, easy cooking from around the world. It produces the bimonthly *Christopher Kimball's Milk Street Magazine*, *Christopher Kimball's Milk Street Radio*, a weekly public radio show and podcast heard on more than 220 stations nation-wide, and the public television show *Christopher Kimball's Milk Street*. He founded *Cook's Magazine* in 1980 and served as publisher and editorial director through 1989. He re-launched it as *Cook's Illustrated* in 1993. Through 2016, Kimball was host and executive producer of *America's Test Kitchen* and *Cook's Country*. He also hosted *America's Test Kitchen* radio on public radio. Kimball is the author of several books, including *Fannie's Last Supper*.

Christopher Kimball's Milk Street is located at 177 Milk Street in downtown Boston and is home to our editorial offices and cooking school. It also is where we record *Christopher Kimball's Milk Street* television and radio shows. *Christopher Kimball's Milk Street* is dedicated to changing how we cook by searching the world for bold, simple recipes and techniques. Adapted and tested for home cooks everywhere, these lessons are the backbone of what we call the new home cooking. For more information, go to www.177milkstreet.com.